MURDERS IN THE SWAMPLAND

MURDERS IN THE SWAMPLAND

Swampland Murders

Patty Shipp

To order additional copies of this book, contact:
Xlibris Corporation
1-888-7-XLIBRIS
www.Xlibris.com
Orders@Xlibris.com

CONTENTS

Dedicated to men and women in law enforcement and newspaper reporters and editors everywhere, especially those who uncovered murders that occurred in Central Florida's swampland–

Also remembering the many victims of these horrific crimes

Thanks to my former editor, family
And many friends
Who encouraged my writing

INTRODUCTION:

Covering crime was new to me when I moved to Florida's west coast and started working for *The Daily Sun-Journal*.

For a couple years prior to giving up the north for the Sunshine State, I wrote for a newspaper in Kankakee, Illinois. Before that, I was a co-editor/co-publisher of a literary magazine, wrote feature stories and a newspaper column about children, and had stories and poetry published here and there. That was it. Zip. A far cry from crime.

I had been living in Florida for three weeks when I returned to my apartment after a photography job interview and noticed the light blinking on my telephone answering machine. That is when I got the most rewarding call of my career as a journalist.

The recorded voice was that of Ken Melton, a man I didn't know but one who would become my boss and friend. Ken was editor of the *Daily Sun-Journal* and needed to replace his crime reporter who was leaving for a bigger newspaper in another county. A copy of my resume had crossed Ken's desk. Needless to say, I returned the call immediately.

I reported to Ken the following morning, was hired and remained with the *Daily Sun-Journal* for the next three-and-a-half years, until the newspaper went to a weekly and along with more than half the staff, I got the ax. Ken's eyes were teary when he said, "We're family here." On that sad day in 1991, the *Daily Sun-Journal* had started to fold—a process that would take a year to complete.

The memories of working at the *Daily Sun-Journal* are lasting. Daily briefings in Sergeant "B" Frank Bierwiler's office were nearly always fascinating. Sergeant B and some of the five reporters from the local media would usually come out with jokes or funny remarks that would bring humor to the morning. We sat in Sergeant B's office and read sheriff reports, sometimes with a chuckle, repeating aloud and commenting about off-the-wall incidents, like somebody picking mushrooms out of cow manure with the intention of boiling them and drinking the juice to get high. But there were many reports far from the light side.

While a lot of incidents reported as criminal seemed somewhat ridiculous, the amount of hard crime in the small county was inconceivable. Recently, some of the former *Daily Sun-Journal* staff gathered on Ken's patio to talk about the old days. He said that when he first relocated to the *Daily Sun-Journal* from a newspaper in the north, he was told Brooksville was a "lousy news town," a place where nothing ever happened. In the early-to-mid 1980s the county's population stayed pretty much at 20,000. "You used to really have to concentrate to find this place," Ken said, jokingly, of the area some 55 or so miles north of Tampa.

"Then bodies were being dug up in Billy Mansfield's back yard. I thought, 'My God!' Come to find out, Billy would take these girls home, rape them, kill them, and bury them in his mother's back yard. They (family) talked about hearing people screaming back there. Of course, nobody ever did anything. They'd say, 'Oh, that's just Billy.' It's amazing to me how his family didn't turn him in. I don't think there was any question whether they knew what was going on. It was like they thought: 'He's just killing somebody in the back yard—don't worry about it.' Mansfield was kind-of scary, like Charles Manson."

Ken recalled a jailbreak when Mansfield was locked up in the "old jail" in downtown Brooksville. Mansfield thought guards had arranged the jailbreak and were waiting for him to try to escape so they could kill him. A "bunch" of prisoners left the jail, but not Mansfield. "He stayed right in the cell. He actually thought the ordeal was a plot so somebody could shoot him if he left."

In an unrelated incident a few years later, four men showed up at a house for various reasons at different times and were murdered.

One man, later convicted of the crime, ran off to a far-away island in the South Pacific. A couple years later, detectives followed his mother when she went to visit her son. "Now why would a killer have his mother fly in for a visit, as if he weren't being hunted anymore?"

Putting murder aside, some wild happenings in the county covered everything from a horse drinking too much wine to a man attempting to drown his wife in the waterbed because he didn't like her new hairdo. And there was the time, during one of the jailbreaks at the new jail, when a couple prisoners actually kicked a hole in the jail wall and escaped through it. Laughing, Ken said, "Didn't they consider when they were building the jail that there might be people locked in who want out?"

Ken recalled hilarious happenings occurred in the old days, too. Deputies in cruisers were chasing a car and the driver got away. When cops found him a little later, after he had smashed up his car, he was beside a garbage bin on the parking lot at a convenience store having sex with a woman he had just met. "It is the funniest story I've ever heard and it happened here."

The man got away from officers again. "I think the cops must have been laughing so hard that night they couldn't even catch the guy. Now what are the odds a man would meet a woman who would do that," he said, laughing.

"They told me Brooksville was a lousy news town. Then they started digging up bodies in Billy Mansfield's yard and another guy got beat to death with a rock–then all hell broke loose. Brooksville was no longer a sleepy little town."

In this book, I am sharing with you some of the criminal acts that have occurred in Central Florida's once far-removed swampland adjacent to the Gulf of Mexico. The "swamp" collection also includes extensive accounts of lawmen and their search for clues in one of the most horrific cases in Tampa Bay history after a boater's sighting led to the discovery of the bodies of a mother and her two teenage daughters weighted with concrete blocks and floating in the bay.

As well as covering most of these murders for the *Daily Sun-Journal*, I wrote accounts of the cases for the various true-crime magazines over a 10-year period. In some stories, the names of witnesses and defendants' families have been changed; some have not. Several cases in this collection occurred before and after my tenure with the newspaper. But they are of crimes that still haunt folks who remember. Be forewarned, some details herewith are gruesome.

I used literary license in writing these stories. Some quotes are assumed, as nobody really knows what was said during the crimes. Many quotes were taken directly from court records, including police reports, depositions, confessions, and trials. The happenings and moods are as close to truth as I could detect while studying the cases.

Patty Shipp

STORY 1:

The Story Of Billy Mansfield

And

Secrets Hidden In The Green Bus

The child

The mist thickened between the river current and the white sun, as if it were hiding a secret in the haze, a secret the river would never share. It was so peculiar, so quiet.

The boy, visiting the Michigan backlands with his family from Florida, was only about seven years old when he took the old fishing boat out. Earlier, he had kicked about on a faded blue raft, splashing water on the toddler so she giggled.

As the afternoon sun lowered behind fog clouds, the boat disappeared into the haze. The child stood behind the boy and held tightly to his shirttail to keep her balance.

The boy started back to shore about dusk, his thin body moving from side to side as he manipulated the boat with the long ore. At the dock, he picked up a rope, threw it in a semi-circle and looped a post. He lifted the toddler from the bottom, his misty-blue eyes gazing at folks congregated on the riverbank. The family picnic was breaking up.

"What's wrong with the baby?" The faint voice was that of a woman.

"She drowned. I found her floating in the river."

A police investigation determined the child had drowned accidentally.

Teenage girls disappear after being seen with Billy Elaine

Halfway between the coastal swamps and Brooksville, the KOA campground was quite filled as the arrival of 1976 drew near. For the most part, out-of-state visitors to this wilderness area liked to squat in the sunshine until the end of winter. Others came for the holidays. Campers often made new friends at the site's recreation hall.

One evening, while cutting through the recreation center on her way to the shower house, Joy stopped to talk with her friend, Elaine Zigler. The two, at age 15, looked a lot alike. They were both pretty, petite, and had neck-length blond hair. The "Johnny Carson Show" was on television. Carson told a joke and the girls giggled.

Elaine glanced often at her watch, then toward the door. She lit a Marlboro cigarette and made remarks about her family. She was unhappy with the man her mother had recently married. "I'm getting ready to leave home, to go south," she said, and sucked in the smoke. "I'm sick and tired of living with my step-father." She looked around, then whispered: "You want to do a joint?"

Joy shook her head. "I better not."

A tall bearded guy with straggly black hair hanging just below his ears entered the hall. "There's Billy," Elaine said, excitedly. Nearing them, he reached into his blue-jeans pocket and pulled out a package of Winston cigarettes and a lighter.

Soon Elaine and Billy were making plans to leave. "Want to go to a party with us?" Billy asked, his icy-blue eyes seeming to stare right through Joy. "I don't think I can. My daddy is strict on me. I'll ask, though."

As Joy had figured he would, her father said: "Absolutely not. You're too young to go off to a party. And you're not going anywhere with a stranger."

The next morning Joy awoke to voices. Elaine's mother was in her camper and questioning her dad. Joy rubbed her eyes and rolled over, but that didn't keep the woman from coming to her.

"Joy, where's Elaine?" Mrs. Zigler asked, nearing her bunk. This woman was upset. Elaine must have really left home as she had said she would.

"I don't know," Joy said, finally. "She left the recreation hall last night with a guy. They were going to a party somewhere." Joy tried to remember what had been said. She tried to answer all Mrs. Zigler's questions, but she really didn't know where Elaine was now.

It was in late December that Jeanne watched her older brother, Billy, drive up to the Mansfield family's trailer house in Weeki Wachee Acres, an area surrounded by forest and marshlands. He and a girl got out of his black pickup truck and disappeared into the woods at the back of the house. Soon Billy returned to the yard and unleashed his attack German shepherd.

Then Jeanne heard screaming.

After about 30 minutes or so, Billy led the dog back to the house. The girl wasn't with him.

"What was going on back there? Why all the screaming?" Jeanne asked.

"Partying. Just partying," Billy said.

Phyllis, Billy's wife of three years, was visiting her parents in Michigan when Billy called her to come home. He had already made her plane reservation. It was a few days after the New Year 1976 had arrived.

Back home at the Mansfield place, Phyllis noticed how interested Billy was in an article published in the *Daily Sun-Journal*. "Why you reading that?" she asked. "Why you interested in this missing girl? You want to collect the reward?"

"Forget it, Phyllis!"

"I can go to the law for information. It must be that somebody wants her pretty bad if they're offering money to get her back."

"You're not going to the law, Phyllis. I killed that girl. She wouldn't do what I wanted her to, so I killed her."

So that was it. Phyllis had always considered Billy hard to please sexually. She remembered a time when he was unhappy with her and looped a rope around her neck. He had nearly choked her to death. She was helpless to do anything to free herself. Finally, he stopped. After that, she tried harder to please him.

Susan

Two of Billy's brothers, Whisky and Jeb, pulled up in front of a country store just a short way from the Mansfield place. They got out of the van and Whisky started talking to a man standing near the opened entrance.

Jeb, eager to get inside, didn't pay too much attention to the conversation but his eyes lingered for a moment on the pretty girl poised beside the stranger. She was about 17 years old, medium height, and had long brown hair. She had a dazzling body, too, that fit nicely into her tight blue jeans and white tank top.

When Jeb came out of the store, the man was gone. However, the girl was still there rubbing her toes against the side of an old tattered suitcase. She handed a $20 bill to Whisky and got into the van. She said her name was Susan.

Susan lived in the old green bus at the Mansfield property for several days. She was quite friendly with the male flow of traffic that came calling.

Upon returning from a brief stay in Tampa, Billy immediately wanted to know about the girl who had come to live at the Mansfield place. When Jeb told him about Susan, he hurried to the green bus. Later that evening, Jeb decided to walk over to see Susan, too. He tried to open the door, but couldn't. Then he knocked.

"What you want?" Whisky asked, cracking the door just enough to whisper through.

"Let me in."

"You can't come in. We're busy," Whisky hissed. "Go on back to the house." Jeb tried to push open the door but his older brother held it too tightly. "Why the heck can't I come in?" he drawled. There was laughing in the bus. Jeb stretched his neck forward to peek through the small opening, then his eyes focused on a bizarre scene. Several guys hovered over Billy and Susan. The two were lying on the floor and covered with a thin spread. Billy was on top. They were having sex, but the girl wasn't moving. It appeared Billy was humping a dead girl.

Jeb missed Susan after that night. He asked several times what had happened to her. Nobody at the Mansfield place seemed to have an answer.

Two teen girls

New Port Richey, some 30 or so miles south of Weeki Wachee, was a sophisticated town where a fellow could get away from the wilderness, take in a movie and do a little barhopping. One afternoon, just outside the quaint town, Billy swerved his car to the right before bringing it to rest on the grassy bank alongside the highway.

"Hop in," he said as he inched forward just a little. Two teen girls giggled and slid onto the back seat.

Twenty minutes later, as Billy pulled up in the Mansfields' front yard, Jeb ran from the mobile home to meet him. "Who you got, Billy?"

"Go to the house, Jeb. Get some covers for the girls," Billy said, as the trio headed toward the green bus.

Jeb got blankets and hurried to the bus. Once there, he was met at the door. He wanted to go in where Billy and two other guys were laughing and joking with the girls. But his mother's calling stopped him. Since the Mansfield daddy, Billy Mansfield Sr., had gone to prison a few years before for molesting children, mama Mansfield had depended on Jeb to do chores.

After taking out the trash, Jeb got in the shower and let the cool water roll down his back. He glared out the bathroom window through the moonlight at Billy stalking toward the bus. He had a shotgun, its butt sticking from underneath a blanket. Billy stopped and adjusted the covering so the entire gun was hidden.

As Jeb lay in bed that night, he wondered what Billy was doing right then. He must have gone out into the woods shooting. He probably took the girls with him.

The next morning, before going to school, Jeb went to the green bus. But—no surprise to him—the girls were gone. He never saw them again.

Tracy and Billy together

For 17-year-old Tracy, school was more a place to find friends than to learn. During the winter of 1980, she met Jeanne and commenced hanging out at the Mansfield place. She had never seen anything like it. There were guys just loitering around for no apparent reason. Day and night, the place was always buzzing. Right away, she started dating three of the Mansfield brothers all at the same time, including Billy.

In March, Tracy stopped her romantic involvement with two of the brothers to give all of herself to Billy. The couple found a little trailer 20 or so miles from the Mansfield place and moved in together.

Tracy stood at the window one afternoon and watched as Billy walked toward the house. It appeared there was blood on his shirt. She watched as he took it off and dropped it on the ground. Tracy saw there were cut marks on his back. He must have gotten hurt somehow, she thought.

That evening, Billy stuck the shirt in the truck when they went to visit the Mansfields. Before going inside his parents' trailer, he washed the soiled garment out in the dog's bowl, turning the water to blood. Tracy didn't mention the shirt or the scratches to

Billy, and he didn't bother to explain anything, either. Lately, they just couldn't communicate at all.

On the ride back home, Tracy thought about how rocky things had become between Billy and her and how much she wanted out of their relationship. A few days later, their ill affair worsened. Billy beat her up after reading a letter she had received from a male friend. She cried and told Billy she was leaving him. She could no longer deal with him getting drunk and hitting her. He cursed, and stomped so hard from the room the whole trailer shook. Then he stood in the yard yelling obscenities so loudly she figured the whole country could hear him: "I said you're not going anywhere, cunt."

Billy was meaner than a rattlesnake when he drank. And now he was drunk. She was afraid of him this way, knowing that at any moment he could open the door and choke the life out of her. The only good thing about his drinking was that his thinking got bad. If she could hold out long enough, if she could keep him from killing her long enough, his thoughts might take a turn.

She waited like a prisoner. Finally, her sister's friend, George, came into the trailer.

"I'm in here, George. I'm locked in the bedroom."

George picked up Tracy's bags. As he did, Billy came in from another room. "What the hell do you want, George?"

"I'm taking Tracy to her sister's house in New Port Richey."

"Like hell you are," Billy yelled. Before either knew what was happening, Billy grabbed a hammer and started swinging.

Tracy ducked. "You're crazy, Billy. What you doing? You trying to kill somebody?"

Billy swung the hammer again and again. Tracy kept ducking. She and George scurried out while Billy's mind apparently was on the weapon.

Once safe at her sister's home in New Port Richey, Tracy called her parents in New York. They sent her an airplane ticket; five days later she arrived in Albany.

Tracy had only been in New York a few weeks when she received an airplane ticket from Billy. The two had talked on the phone and she had agreed to return to Florida. He said he loved her more than anything. He needed her. He wanted to start over. He had rented an apartment in Tampa, 55 or so miles south of Brooksville, which he knew she would like. They would have fun living in the city. He would never hit her again. They would be happy.

Tracy looked from the plane window. Beneath the puffs of snow-white clouds lay green landscapes dotted with patches of water. She was back in Florida. Soon she would be with Billy. Billy would keep his promises to her. She felt it in her heart.

She leaned on his arm during the 15-minute ride from the Tampa International Airport, then up the back steps to the little upstairs apartment Billy had rented. This was their new home and she loved it already.

During the first couple days, Tracy noticed that Billy seemed a bit different than he had before she went north. He was calmer. He dressed differently. Billy, who usually wore flannel shirts in the winter and T-shirts in the summer, had a closet full of silk shirts and was carrying $20 and $100 bills. He must have had at least $1,500 on him.

She just had to ask: "Billy, where did you get all that money?"

"I got a job. A good one."

Life was a dream. Billy was nice to her and they had all the money they wanted. It was too good to last. And it didn't. Three days after Tracy had arrived in Tampa they packed up everything in the apartment. Billy had even brought his 12-guage shotgun and large hunting knife from Weeki Wachee and packed them, too. They were leaving Florida and going to live in California. Billy's brother, Wayne and his wife, Penny, and their three kids, who lived a little ways north of Billy's apartment, packed up to go, too.

It was a long way to the Pacific Coast. But the traveling was easy. Whenever they would get tired, they would pull off the road and sleep in their vans. Finally, after five days, they reached California. In Santa Cruz, Wayne and Penny rented a small camper trailer and Billy and Tracy rented a tent to live in at a KOA camp.

Things didn't go too well for Tracy and Billy in California, though. They nagged and argued with each other all the time. Pretty soon Billy was knocking her around again.

One night, Billy brought a friend to the tent with him. Tracy sat on a blanket on the ground. She didn't say anything while the two men undressed. "We're all going to have sex," Billy informed her.

"I don't want to, Billy"

Before she even knew what was happening, Billy had knocked her down and was sitting on her chest with his hands tightening around her throat. Afterwards, Tracy wondered if maybe she had passed out or gone into a seizure. She had seizures every once in a while. She wished she were away from Billy. He was always drunk and mad at her for no reason. She wished she had stayed with her parents in New York, but it was too late to think about that now.

Tracy felt she was in danger living with Billy, that he would kill her if he so took the notion. In the past, Billy had talked of killing girls.

A day or so later, Penny had finished cooking supper for Wayne and their kids. She went into the bathroom. When she came out, Billy and Wayne were in deep conversation, with Billy telling Wayne about a girl named Sally he had killed in Tampa. He had picked Sally up in a bar, raped her, and then killed her and dumped her body alongside a dirt road north of the city.

"What were you and Billy talking about? What was Billy saying about killing that girl?" Penny asked after Billy left their trailer.

"Nothing," Wayne said. "Don't worry about it. It was nothing."

The next day, Penny warned Tracy: "You better get out of here. You're in danger living here with Billy. It's no good, with him beating you, and you having seizures and all. Tracy, he's mighty apt to kill you. Him being drunk every single night."

"I'm not worried about Billy. He hits me, but he loves me. He wouldn't kill me. I know Billy."

"Well, you better be worried about Billy. He killed a girl in Tampa. Sally was her name. He killed her then he dumped her off on a dirt road. That's why we're running. I heard Billy telling Wayne about that girl when he was in our trailer last night. Billy said he raped her, and then he killed her. I heard him myself."

Actually, Tracy did know Billy. There were many times when she had thought she was taking her last breath. But she wouldn't admit that now. Penny was worried too much already.

But when Penny suggested she place a telephone call to Tracy's mother to ask for money for an airplane ticket to New York, Tracy didn't object.

"She needs help. She's got to get away from Billy. She has to get away before he kills her like he killed Sally," Penny said to Tracy's mom. Tracy's parents took Penny for her word. An airplane ticket would be waiting at the airport.

Tracy's friend, Richard, came over that day while Billy was gone. He gave her money and drove her to the motel.

Tracy figured she would be safe in the motel that night. Richard would pick her up the next morning and take her to the airport.

But, Billy found Tracy. "You're coming home, now," he said, on his arrival at the motel room. He grabbed her suitcase with one hand and yanked her arm with the other. "Where do you think you're running off to?"

That night, back in their tent, Tracy cried: "I just want to go see my parents. They sent me a ticket. I won't be gone long."

The next morning Billy agreed to drive Tracy to the airport. But the route he took was remote. He was surely driving the long way around, traveling down all the back roads. Suddenly he drove into an area marked "no trespassing." It was a country club, with a golf course and wooded areas. Tracy thought if she saw somebody nearby, she would jump from the car. She might get hurt a little, but it would probably save her life.

"He's going to kill me," she thought. Trembling with fright, she remembered a time shortly after arriving in Santa Cruz when Billy's hands had left bruises on her neck after he had strangled her. Just before death, he had turned her lose, leaving her gasping and coughing for breath. Billy never said why he was mad that night.

Now, here she was with this confessed murderer riding around in an out-of-the-way place. If Billy were to kill her here and toss her over a cliff, her body might never be found. Even if it were, authorities might never identify it. She didn't have a record; her fingerprints were not in any police files.

She shivered. "If you're going to kill me, Billy, just go ahead and do it."

Billy stared at her. "I don't know what you're talking about."

Billy made a few turns. Finally, Tracy caught her breath and relaxed. It looked as if they were headed in the right direction at last. By the time they reached the airport, though, Tracy's flight had long departed.

"The plane's gone. We'll cash the ticket in and get the money," Billy said.

"No, we're not going to do that, Billy."

Tracy was at the airport now and she was alive. She promised herself she would never go anyplace with Billy again.

Murder in California

Renee Saling tucked her jean bottoms into her brown knee-high boots. Standing straight, she eyed herself in the mirror and slipped a vest over the blue India-made blouse her stepsister had picked up at a local import store. Grabbing her multi-colored purse, she hurried outside.

On this December 6th night in 1980, Renee was ready to barhop. She knew she drank too much, often getting drunk to the point of total inebriation, but–oh well. You only live once.

Renee walked straight to the Whisky Hill Bar. She shot-the-bull with the bartender and tried unsuccessfully to talk him into cashing a check for her. Then she made small talk with his daughter, who was a little older than her, and asked to borrow her identification so she could get into some other bars. She wouldn't let her use it, though.

Renee made the rounds, talking with different customers and hanging on to men. She asked if anyone in the bar had seen Raymond, her husband. Yes, he had been there earlier in the evening. In a little while, with a fountain of alcohol flushing her brain, Renee left the Whisky Hill Bar, not even remembering to take her purse.

Renee had an aching to visit the Wooden Nickel, another of her choice hangouts. There would be lots of action there by now. The Wooden Nickel was a bit too far from the Whisky Hill Bar to walk, so Renee decided to hitch a ride. She hung around outside the nearby Kentucky Fried Chicken until it closed and Jose, the associate manager, appeared outside. Then, in the darkness, she approached him.

Jose agreed to drop her off at the Wooden Nickel. He could try to discourage her from drinking more, but he knew Renee and he knew to lecture her would do no good. She would get to the bar somehow. If he didn't give her a ride, she would hitch one with somebody else. And perhaps that person would not treat her right. Renee rode with him to drop off a couple restaurant employees at their homes, and then he drove her to the Wooden Nickel.

In the bar room, Renee wobbled straight to a group of Mexican men. She hugged and they danced with them.

The bar manager knew Renee, having seen her and her husband both in the pub often. Raymond usually barhopped after work. Renee would frequently come stumbling in drunk and fighting-mad looking for Ray. Now, as in times past, the manager could smell problems brewing. It would definitely be best if Renee would go home, or at least someplace other than the Wooden Nickel. He tried to remain calm as he escorted her out the door.

Billy, who was partying with friends at the bar, took notice of the goings-on. He slid from his stool and hurried through the loud bar room. Passing by the huge, bald bouncer, Billy grabbed the drunken woman's shoulder.

Two girls Billy had tried to put the make on earlier scrutinized the couple as they moved by the window. "It's only eleven and he has already scored," one said.

In about 45 minutes, Billy re-entered the bar room. His hair was a mess and sweat bubbled from his forehead. He ordered another Seagram 7 and water. "You'll have to get it from the bar," the waitress said, an angry tone in her voice. "You didn't pay for the last drink you ordered."

Billy looked though the crowd to fine June, whom he had talked with earlier that evening. He had invited her to spend the weekend with him.

"What's it going to be?" he asked, upon locating the young woman.

"I'm going to stay here with my friends," she snapped.

Billy glared at her disgustedly and left the barroom.

He returned at about 1:30 a.m. Jack, with whom he worked at the Mushroom Factory, was perched at the bar. "I got a chick out in the car," Billy said. He handed Jack his car keys. "You can take a look but don't let her out. I want somebody to take home tonight."

Jack went to the parking lot and got into the older model Toronado. He tried to talk with Renee. However, she was too wasted to know what was going on. He considered having sex with her but then decided sex with someone so drunk wouldn't be worth the effort.

"You awake?" he asked.

"I'm cold," she mumbled.

Then Billy walked up.

At about noon the next day, Santa Cruz County Sheriff Deputy Jim Johnson accompanied George and Janet Tucker to an unpopulated area near the county dump where the couple had discovered a body. It appeared the partly clothed woman had been killed and then tossed in the ditch alongside the roadway. A loosely woven cloth cord was looped around her neck so tightly it partially disappeared into the flesh and was fastened with a knot at the back just below her hairline. The young woman's jeans were pulled down to her ankles and her panties to her knees. Her vest and blue blouse were hiked up to her shoulders. Scraps of blue fabric from the ripped blouse were scattered alongside the road several hundred feet north of her body. She wore one tan, high-heel boot. Deputy Johnson glanced around for a second boot.

A couple days later, Jack approached Billy at the Mushroom Factory. "What did you do with that girl? I read in the newspaper about a dead girl being found. It sounds to me like she might be the one you had in your car at the Wooden Nickel. The cops are looking for you. You better jam it."

"Thanks," Billy said, quickly turning and hurrying from the factory. He didn't even bother to punch out.

He called the electric company where his brother worked. "Have Wayne Mansfield call his brother. It's an emergency," Billy said to the receptionist. "There's been an accident in the family."

Billy impatiently waited for a while. Finally, since Wayne hadn't called, he dialed the factory phone number again. This time he talked with one of the owners of the company. "Did Wayne get my message? He didn't call. Tell him it's an emergency," Billy demanded.

Later that day, Wayne informed his boss that he needed to get his paycheck, that his mother had been hit by a semi-truck in Florida and he had to fly home.

Meanwhile, detectives began an investigation on the case involving the death of the woman found in the ditch. Dr. Richard Mason, forensic pathologist, performed an autopsy. Investigators took photographs and samples of urine, bile, and liver and kidney specimen. A gastric contents and A Rh negative blood samples were collected and sent to a lab for testing. Also, a complete rape kit was performed. Autopsy findings indicated the cause of death was strangulation.

Detective Dennis Clark, who had been assigned to the case, received a missing person report from the Watsonville Police. Based on clothing and jewelry descriptions given to Clark by the missing woman's relatives, authorities believed the dead woman was Renee Saling.

Detectives talked with people who had been at a barbecue Renee had attended the day before the murder. They learned she had spoken of plans to party at the Wooden Nickel.

Detectives also learned Renee had gone to the Kentucky Fried Chicken restaurant at the corner of Main Street and Freedom Boulevard about 10:15 Saturday night; a manager had taken her to the Wooden Nickel; and she had left the bar with Billy Mansfield.

June, who had been at the Wooden Nickel the night Billy picked up Renee, told detectives that on Saturday night, Billy had invited her to accompany him to Colorado. When she refused, he got up from her table and moved elsewhere in the bar. She later saw Billy and the young woman walk past the window arm-in-arm.

June later picked Billy's picture from a photo lineup. Authorities had taken the photo when he was arrested in 1980 in Hernando County, Florida, for false imprisonment and felony sexual battery.

Detectives showed June another photo line-up, this time of six white females, and asked if one of them was the woman she had seen leave the bar with Billy. She instantly picked the photo of Renee Saling.

While detectives interviewed June at the sheriff's office, Detective Joe Henard interviewed people at the campground. He showed a picture of Renee to the campground manager. The manager said she had seen the woman on the night of the murder playing the pinball machine with Billy in the game room. She showed detectives the tent Billy had rented. They peeked inside. A mattress was on the dirt floor. Just in front of the tent was a 1967 Dodge van with Florida license.

Detectives left the campground to check more leads. They learned that Billy had punched his timecard at the Mushroom

Factory the day after the murder but had left before noon without punching out. Detectives also learned Wayne Mansfield had left his job at the electric company, saying he had to go immediately to Florida. When detectives returned to the campground, the van was gone.

Detectives obtained a warrant allowing them to search Billy's tent. They found blue threads they believed were from the victim's torn blouse, latent fingerprints belonging to Renee Saling, and samples of soil similar to the soil located at the scene where Renee's body was found.

"Look," a detective said. "One tan high heel boot."

After Billy learned from Jack that cops were on his tail, he and Wayne left Santa Cruz heading for Colorado. Billy was driving the van and Wayne followed in the Toronado. In San Jose, they stopped long enough to paint the van. Not far from town, the Toronado ran out of gas, so they left it parked on the roadside and continued on in the van. Before reaching their destination, however, the Winnemucca, Nevada, police stopped them.

Both Mansfield brothers were arrested and charged with the murder of Renee Saling, with bonds set at $250,000 each. Detectives took possession of the van and upon its being processed, found various pieces of evidence including torn portions of embroidered fabric.

Three months later, criminologist Stephen Cooper completed a physical evidence examination report on tests made on body samples taken from Renee Saling, Wayne Mansfield, Billy Mansfield, Raymond Saling, and others known to have been in direct contact with Renee the night of the murder.

The semen stain on the jeans was consistent with having come from Billy Mansfield and not the other men tested, Cooper noted.

The charge of murder was later dropped on Wayne Mansfield, but the case against Billy was building.

Digging Up Bones

In the spring of 1981, while detectives were putting together a case for the murder of Renee Saling in California, detectives in Florida were doing some real digging. Actual digging. Information had come out during trial proceedings in an unrelated Hernando County case that bodies were buried at the Mansfield home place.

On March 16, 1981, detectives obtained a warrant to search the Mansfield property. Along with the Florida Department of Law Enforcement (FDLE) forensic lab team, sheriff's detectives started probing the ground near a wooden shed in the front yard. The following day, detectives searched at the rear of house directly north of the fenced area.

Detective Tom Blackman carefully stuck his five-foot probing iron into the sandy earth. He felt something down there. He started digging with a shovel, carefully scooping dampened sand from the area and tossing it to the side. When Blackman took a break, Detective John Whitman took over the digging. Barbara Vohlken, from the FDLE, cautiously poked about as Whitman dug. At mid-morning, she halted the digging. "There's a body in there," she said. She warned the team to proceed with extreme caution as they uncovered skeletal remains of a human body. By the end of the following day, with the county medical examiner on the site, remains of another human body had been uncovered.

Three days later, the team started digging on the east side of house within a fenced area. It wasn't long before detectives had found bones of another body barely buried in the ground near the exterior chimney wall.

On the second day of April, Detective Ron Elliott had a county crew worker start digging with a large backhoe outside the fence at the rear of the house. Shortly before noon they unearthed a bunch of trash and what appeared to be a human bone. Use of the backhoe was immediately ceased and detectives started digging with a shovel.

That night, at about 9 o'clock, skeletal remains of a fourth victim had been unearthed.

While FDLE dug for bodies around the Mansfield house, at the same time finding articles of clothing and jewelry, sheriff's detectives climbed onto the roof and checked the chimney. They pulled out pieces of a sleeping bag and an old army type blanket. These items were put into evidence. Dog bones, along with an old stereo in a plastic bag, were uncovered a couple hundred feet west of the house in the trash dump area.

Detective Elliott continued the digging near where the fourth human remains were found. There he located more bones, including part of a pelvic and an upper thighbone, which he figured were pulled loose from the last victim by the backhoe blade. These bones were taken to the FDLE lab in Tampa and put with the others.

Digging continued through May. Finally, under direction of investigators, the digging stopped.

Detectives' findings

As the investigation unfolded, witnesses in the case provided information so bizarre it seemed fiction. How could the burying of human bodies in the Mansfield yard have been done so indifferently? It appeared the back yard being the gravesite for young women was a shared bit of knowledge by quite a few folks in the area swampland. What did people think when they would hear of a girl's body being buried at the Mansfield place? And what were they thinking now? What was going through their minds? After all, it wasn't like a team of detectives went out and uncovered bodies of murdered girls in somebody's back yard everyday.

Sheriff's detectives interviewed numerous people during a short investigation. Lisa, age 17, lived a few miles north of the Mansfield place at the Camp-A-Wyle campgrounds. Lisa said she had dated one of Billy's brothers but the relationship became strained when she got word he was having sex with boys inside the green bus.

The story of Billy and one of his brothers raping a girl, killing her, then burning her trailer with her inside, gave her reason to back away from the romance really quick-like, she said.

"I'm afraid of the Mansfields," Lisa whispered. "I believe that whole family knows about the bodies."

It was just common knowledge that, back in 1973, Billy killed a girl hitchhiker and burned her up in a camper. Then he buried her in the woods west of his family's trailer, a neighbor of Billy's said on a sworn statement.

Maria, who had hung out at the Mansfield place on occasions, informed investigators she had gone to the green bus several times. She had gotten spaced out from smoking pot and had sex with Billy and several other boys all at the same time. The boys often talked about a blue camper, which had been parked in the family's front yard, burning to the ground with a woman inside.

People in and out of the Mansfield place always talked about bodies of young girls being buried on the property, said Patrick, who had hung around with one of the Mansfield brothers about a year prior to the digging. He thought nothing of it, he said. After all, the Mansfields were not your local high-society type. Billy's father, Billy Mansfield Sr., had been convicted of molesting children and was serving time in prison. All the boys who were tight with the Mansfields knew about the bodies, he said, matter-of-factly.

Gordon, a friend of Jeb's, said he often had heard Jeb say some pretty wild things about his older brother. Jeb had told him of having witnessed Billy choking a girl to death then burying her in the backyard.

Linda, who had dated Jeb for two months while visiting in Florida from Michigan, said she was not surprised to hear about bodies being unearthed in the Mansfield back yard. During the whole two months she was in Florida, she had listened to talk among guys about bodies buried under the glass sliding doors in front of the trailer.

A year or so prior to the investigation, Alex, a friend of the Mansfield boys, said he was cutting through the woods by the Mansfield property one evening after dark. There was a white Ford pickup truck parked at the rear part of the property. Billy Mansfield Sr. and a couple of the Mansfield boys were digging a hole. They were using the truck headlights in order to see. Two days later, Alex went back there and saw the bottom of the hole was covered with trash. He recalled one of the Mansfield brothers once saying: "To hide something, you dig a hole, then a tunnel, and put the thing you are hiding in the tunnel. If you put burned ashes over the ground where someone is buried, it will keep the dogs from smelling the body and digging it up."

Whisky told Sharon, in June of 1977, how he had a strong stomach. He said weird incidents that had involved Billy didn't bother him at all. Also, Whisky said, his own past was quite tarnished. Whisky said he had shot a guy but somebody else was serving time in jail for the crime. It was a shooting that had taken place in the swampy area across from a little Church In The Wildwood in May of 1977. She and another girlfriend, who was present when Whisky made the statement, told him they didn't think he would do anything like that. "Whisky said, 'you don't know me as well as you think you do.'"

Jeb disclosed things he had witnessed from his brothers, including the time Billy had unleashed the German shepherd and took it to the woods where he had first gone with a girl. He told of the screams he had heard, and how he had never seen the girl after that. Jeb also told about Susan, how one of his brothers had picked her up, brought her to the bus, then how she disappeared after Billy came home from Tampa. He had seen Billy on top of Susan, who looked dead at the time, he said. He revealed knowledge regarding the two girls Billy had picked up hitchhiking in New Port Richey and how they had disappeared the first night after coming to the green bus.

If detectives had started arresting people for withholding evidence, they probably would have to add a new wing to the jail, authorities said.

When interviewed, Charley, a relative of Billy's, said he had not been involved with the Mansfield family for many years but he could believe any accusations. "I don't trust any of them in any way. Every time I go away on a trip or have to go into the hospital, they rob me blind." While living in Michigan in the late 1960s, the relative said Billy had shown up on the riverbank with his 2-year-old baby sister, who had drowned. Billy's story was that he had gone across the river in a boat and had found the toddler. But he truly believes Billy killed her, he said. Authorities in Grand Rapids said the baby's death was an accidental drowning and no charges were filed.

Billy Mansfield was sentenced to life in prison for the murder of Renee Sailing, in California. He was also sentenced to four concurrent life terms in Florida, which means he will serve a minimum of 25 years for the strangulation death of four women: Sandra Jean Graham, of Tampa; Elaine Zeigler, from the KOA Campground; and two labeled each as Jane Doe.

There were stories of Billy being with other women who also disappeared. There were even stories that he killed other women and that they, too, are buried on the Mansfield property and other locations in the swampland. We know he killed five.

STORY 2:

Gay Encounter

Cost Priest His Life

Grief hung in the choir of black clouds over the city of Brooksville the morning of July 17, 1979. That day, summer rains mixed with tears from heaven flooded the peaceful, God-fearing community.

The secretary for St. John's Episcopal Church walked toward the vicarage. She stopped to read a note left hanging on the door that advised visitors: "Please call tomorrow." Father Jon's name was signed at the bottom. She wondered where the good priest might be. His bronze 1976 Mazda was not parked out front.

Victoria put the key in the lock and turned it.

Click.

All at once . . .

Oh dear Lord!

Her hand rushed to her face. Then she froze. A nude male lay on the floor in the hallway with his hands tied behind his back. A blood-soaked towel covered his head.

She screamed and ran from the house. Out of the blue, it seemed, she found herself surrounded by police, paramedics, and church people. "Oh God, oh God, oh God," she cried. The world was coming apart. Then fear that had possessed her since she had discovered the body became reality. The dead man in the vicarage was the Reverend Jon Hunt. Someone had killed the priest.

Officials inside the house found Hunt had been beaten severely on his head by a heavy object. Two hammers near his body and a broken chair in another room indicated there had been a struggle between the priest and his assailant. A broken claw hammer, on some old copies of the *Daily Sun-Journal*, could have been the murder weapon, a police officer observed.

News that something terrible had happened to Father Jon washed over the town like a storm. By the time paramedics had put the priest's body on the stretcher and loaded it into an ambulance, many church members had gathered in the churchyard. They cried and tried to comfort each other: "Why would anyone want to hurt Father Jon? Why would anyone do such a horrible thing to the good preacher?"

A visibly saddened long-time neighbor said it was very hard for him to believe anyone would kill the cleric. "He was a quiet man. He was friendly, mild mannered, always willing to help. He was one of the nicest fellows you'd ever want to meet."

When questioned more that same day, the neighbor told police he had seen Hunt two days prior outside the vicarage. "I waved to the preacher from my car, but I didn't get out to talk," he said.

While the crowd continued to congregate near the church, a passing car stopped and a young girl leaned her head out the window. "Is Father Jon going to be all-right," she asked. The officer looked at her but did not answer.

The murder of a priest occurring in Brooksville, a peaceful town with a population of about 6,000 people, was a shocker. Brooksville, at the top of a hill and surrounded by many miles of forests and cow pastures, was the only city in the county. Though most of the community's residences were "good-ol'-boys," Central Florida's warm sunny days always knocking at winter's door drew transplants and drifters. The town's draw included its uniqueness, with huge liveoak trees and hammocks separating houses, country stores, churches, and railroad tracks.

Even the 37-year-old Father Jon was a transplant, locating here after his graduation from the Seminary at Seaberry Western

College in Chicago. He had joined the Episcopal Diocese of Southwest Florida in St. Petersburg and was assigned to St. John's Episcopal Church in May of 1971.

From the moment the homicide investigation started, officials found nobody had anything bad to say about the priest. He was definitely a loved man.

Police roped off the entire block around the church vicarage and started investigating the murder. They looked for a motive, the murder weapons, and anything they could that might be used as a clue as to who killed Father Jon. At first, robbery was not suspected. Whoever had killed the priest had not bothered the container of church funds.

Police learned that Hunt had just returned from a month-long vacation. He could have met and befriended a stranger who had then followed him home and killed him. Or, perhaps someone had been watching the church and the vicarage to see when the priest was alone, and then slipped inside and killed him. In any case, the question was why would anyone want to kill this man of God?

Police Chief Ron Novy and other officials spent several hours processing the crime scene because of the large amount of evidence found near the body. A crime scene technician from the Florida Department of Law Enforcement (FDLE) in Tampa was sent to the site. Lawmen wasted no time in transporting 11 bloody fingerprints and two bloody palm prints, along with other evidence, to the Tampa Crime Lab for processing. Other evidence was analyzed including a ball-peen hammer that serologists found contained the same blood type as that of the dead priest.

However, Father Jon's car was the key. If the vehicle could be located, there was a very good possibility cops would find their killer. An all-points bulletin was put out for the bronze 1976 Mazda.

As cops worked day and night on the investigation, church people and friends of the priest mourned his death. A special mass was held at the church the night after the slaying. A second mass was held later that week. On Friday, when the town paid its final respects, the church was packed to standing room only. Speakers were placed outside for the overflow.

After the ceremony, a bishop from St. Petersburg said the rite had been joyous because of the church's belief of the "everlasting" life Hunt had fallen into.

"Father Jon was a very loving, gentle individual," the Bishop said. "Because of the circumstances involved, we are filled with hostility. But a greater voice also cries out within us–the voice of the Lord. Father Jon was the finest example of what our Lord told us to believe."

While the town mourned its loss, rumors began to buzz through the peaceful neighborhood that the dead priest had been involved in homosexuality. Many people had seen a young man with Hunt the weekend prior to his death.

On the other hand, Hunt had often befriended strangers, the homeless or whoever else called on him.

"Right now, we're working on a lot of speculation," Chief Novy said. "We won't know what's fact or rumor until we finish interviewing several people." As the investigation got underway, detectives determined that Hunt had been murdered the morning of July 17, sometime between midnight and 2 a.m.

Hunt's autopsy showed blood had flowed to his hands and was trapped there before he died, thus presenting the reddish-purple coloring. This proved the priest was alive when his hands were tied behind his back. There was also some sperm on the dead preacher's penis.

The week after Father Jon was found dead, a nation-wide manhunt for a young man believed to be driving Hunt's car centered in eastern Kentucky, in an area where small towns were neatly tucked between hillsides. Cops were suddenly playing hide-and-seek with an eluding suspect driving a bronze Mazda.

The Mazda was reportedly seen here and there in Mount Sterling. This was an area where a murder suspect would be hard to find. And whoever had killed Hunt was not someone who would just stand still and wait for authorities to arrest him. The killer was on the run driving a stolen car.

While detectives questioned townspeople in Mount Sterling, they learned a local resident had seen a man driving the described vehicle at a grocery store where she shopped. He had been well dressed and clean-shaven but had appeared quite nervous. A man in that same mountain town claimed he had seen a man hitch-hiking and then a few weeks later, he saw the same man back in town driving a bronze Mazda.

At the time authorities in Kentucky tailed a suspect, Florida cops tracked leads in several other states including Georgia and Oklahoma. Cars fitting the description of the one stolen from Father Jon were popping up all over the south, but it was the tag that would make the difference. Only the suspect would be driving the car with the license plate number matching the one that belonged to the dead priest.

Thirteen days after the brutal slaying, Detective Nelson Patton got a tip that a Mazda fitting the description of the one being hunted was seen at Salt Lick, Kentucky. Upon driving through the area, police spotted the car. And the driver of the Mazda obviously spotted the police.

The Mazda took off like a bat out of hell, detectives said later. The cop made a quick spin, and then floor-boarded the gas pedal. The pursuit had begun. Detectives were led on (what they described as) "a hell of a chase" speeding up and down a 10-mile stretch of roads winding through the hills. At one point, the pursuit whizzed right through a funeral procession at a speed of more than 100-miles-per-hour, cops reported.

The quest finally ended at a roadblock set up by the state police on the interstate near the Owingsville exit. There, Deputy Bobby Bowman walked up to the suspect in the Mazda. The lawbreaker, in his mid-20s, was dressed in a leather vest and hat and ragged jeans. He looked as if he had not slept in days. Bowman ordered him out of the car and told him to raise his hands and spread his feet.

Upon frisking the sleepy-eyed driver, police found a Gulf Oil credit card that had belonged to the Reverend Jon Hunt. This was their man.

The following day, the man identified as William Howell Gilvin, age 26, was arraigned on fugitive warrants from Florida.

Detectives Bob Johnson, of the Brooksville Police, and John Whitman, of the Hernando Sheriff's Office, flew to Sharpsberg to continue their investigation into the murder of the priest. Once in Kentucky, Johnson and Whitman went to hideouts where they believed Gilvin might have laid low for almost two weeks. While the detectives combed the countryside collecting information about Gilvin, crime technicians from the FDLE processed evidence from the Mazda, which had been positively identified as having belonged to the slain vicar.

In early August, almost a week after detectives Whitman and Johnson had flown from Florida to Kentucky, they returned with their murder suspect. They arrived at the Hernando County Jail in Brooksville at about 11 p.m., almost eight hours after Gilvin signed extradition papers in a Kentucky courtroom. Gilvin was held over for trial, without bond, for the beating death of the preacher.

While being fingerprinted and searched, and before being taken to a one-man jail cell, Gilvin talked easily with detectives. He was called Bill, he said, a Christian from Kentucky and a construction worker. He had a tattoo of the letters W.H.G. on his right wrist.

When Gilvin's January trial date arrived, numerous county residents were questioned before a jury was picked. State Attorney Gordon Oldham, Assistant State Attorney Jimmy Brown, and Gilvin's Public Defender Ray Shaw, asked possible jurors their feelings about the case. They asked if they were influenced by pretrial publicity, if they believed in the death penalty, if they could discard things they had heard or read about the case, and if they could base their verdict only on the evidence presented during the trial. Prospective jurors were also asked whether Hunt's alleged homosexuality would affect their decision.

By Friday, January 4, a 12-member jury with two alternates, who would be used in the event any of the 12 jurors could not fulfill their duty, had been sworn in to hear and decide Gilvin's fate. Hernando County Circuit Judge L.R. Huffstetler Jr. would preside.

During opening statements, Shaw contended that Gilvin and the priest had been fighting. Hunt had died from the beating he had received during the fight. The two had gotten intoxicated and the defendant just happened to have a hammer in his hands.

This is how the defense claimed Hunt was killed: Hunt and Gilvin drank two pitchers of martinis, and then Hunt started making sexual plays for the good-looking younger man. The attorney claimed the priest had appeared before the drunken visitor nude and began to kiss him on his head. As things progressed, Gilvin picked up the hammer.

The defense maintained that Hunt had been killed in self-defense, but the prosecution took a different stand. Oldham, who did not claim to know all the details of the killing, said evidence clearly pointed to a brutal, premeditated murder by the defendant. He said the defendant had planned, killed and robbed Hunt. After killing the preacher, Gilvin had hung towels over the vicarage windows, searched through the offices looking for money, stole the priest's credit card, and then left a note hanging on the door with Hunt's forged signature.

The pathologist and associate medical examiner, Dr. William Winter, presented gruesome details of Hunt's murder. Winter testified that when Hunt's hands were bound behind his back, he had been alive.

But the story Gilvin gave was the one his public defender had also pled for him—that of self-defense. According to Gilvin, he was the intended victim of a sex crime. Gilvin said he and Hunt had drunk the martinis the morning of July 16. They were both feeling high, and then Hunt went to the bedroom to rest. Gilvin remained in the television room, watched a news program, and smoked some marijuana. In a little while, the nude priest approached Gilvin in the television room and started pawing and kissing him on the temples of his head.

The two men had discussed having sex prior to that, but Gilvin claims he resisted the preacher's advances and pushed him away. This time, Father Jon came on stronger and the struggle began. The priest ran from the den and into a closet. Not knowing if Hunt was going for a weapon, Gilvin saw the claw hammer and grabbed it.

Armed with the tool, Gilvin moved toward the bedroom to face the man who had made advances toward him. The priest saw him and started swinging and kicking, Gilvin said. As the two men struggled, Gilvin dropped the hammer. Then it was like a tug of war, with both men trying to get possession of the deadly weapon. Gilvin said he grabbed the hammer. Galvin swung, and the hammer hit hard against Hunt's forehead. The pressure of the deadly weapon cut Hunt's skin and blood started to flow.

This did not stop the priest. It only made him more vicious, the defense claimed. Hunt ran to the living room. Gilvin ran after him, pushed him, causing him to fall. The two were still struggling for the hammer. Then Gilvin and Hunt both spotted a ball-peen hammer that Gilvin had used that day to repair window screens.

"We both started for it," Gilvin said. "And I got it. I struck him a couple of times in the head." Then, as the priest "kept mumbling something," Gilvin pulled him across the living room floor to the hall. "We struggled again and I picked up the first hammer and hit him again and he went down. I felt there was no need for more hammer blows."

Gilvin had previously told officers he had hit the pastor in the head several times but that the blows had only hurt him badly. He had seen Father Jon suffering so he got a second hammer and beat him in the head to stop his anguish. But, Gilvin said, when he told that story it had been a lie. He had since found Jesus Christ and now he was telling the truth.

After beating Hunt, Gilvin said he tied his hands with a rope used to tie back the shower curtain. At this time, Hunt was still breathing.

Since the day he killed the priest, Gilvin said he had become a child of God. A local Church of God minister agreed that the accused murderer had been "born again." But in giving his closing statement to the court, assistant State Attorney Jimmy Brown said that Gilvin was not a convincing liar. Brown pointed his finger at Gilvin, who sat straight at the defendant's table.

"The murder of Jon Hunt did not bother Gilvin when he took the hammers and beat the priest to death and it does not bother him now. It doesn't bother him today, and I don't think it ever will."

But Public Defender Shaw said Gilvin was not the same man he was when the priest was slain, that since then Gilvin had found a new outlook on life. Shaw said that at the time of the slaying, Gilvin's mind had not been functioning logically due to the alcohol and marijuana he had consumed the day of the killing.

Shaw reminded the jury that several witnesses had been reluctant in testifying that they knew Hunt was gay. "Mr. Gilvin is not a homosexual," the public defender said. "If he were, we would not be here today."

State's Attorney Gordon Oldham presented the final word. "But we know what the defendant is. He's an ex-con, a forger, a thief, a drifter, and by his own confession, a liar."

The jury spent nine hours the first day going over testimony. They reached a decision after forty minutes of deliberation the following day. They found William Gilvin guilty of first-degree murder for the beating death of the Reverend Jon Hunt.

The adjudicators recommended that Gilvin be sentenced to life in prison instead of death. Judge Huffstetler had other ideas and overturned the jury's recommendation and sentenced Gilvin to die in the Florida electric chair. The judge said that death was the only proper sentence for the convicted murder and that no reasonable mind could differ.

Gilvin's death sentence since has been overturned; he was re-sentenced to spend life in prison.

STORY 3:

Torture Murder

In The Swamp

Hernando County Sheriff's Deputy Carlos Douglas slowed his cruiser as he neared a convenience store just west of Brooksville.

Normally, the young clerk would come to the window and wave to assure him that everything was fine.

But on this wee morning hour, Douglas pulled onto the parking lot and glared at the store. Instantly, his gut feeling told him something was wrong. The store appeared empty. The young clerk's truck was parked near the building but he couldn't see her. The conscientious girl would never go away and leave the store unattended, Douglas thought.

He pulled closer to the building and manipulated the spotlight so it shined inside. Perhaps the girl was in the washroom, he reasoned, or maybe she was stocking beer in the cooler.

His hand riding the gun on his hip, Douglas walked cautiously through the store. He peered around the aisles. "Lee Ann, you there? Lee Ann?" But she didn't answer.

The deputy became more anxious. Usually the pretty woman with light brown hair and a smiling face would answer instantly. He could almost hear her laughing and chatting about country-western singers, or see her behind the counter quietly engrossed in her college studies.

Douglas stepped behind the cash register and looked around. He noticed a multicolored purse and jacket was on the shelf behind the counter. It didn't seem normal that Lee Ann would leave the store willingly without her purse.

Douglas walked from behind the cash register to the microwave oven a few feet away. A hot hamburger on the counter was still steaming and a container of relish beside it. Someone had just left the store.

Douglas hurried from the building and got on his radio with the police dispatcher. "The girl who works the night shift here is missing. She knows what time I make my rounds. It's very suspicious." He paused. "I think she's been kidnapped."

Deputies were dispatched to comb the county in search of 23-year-old Lee Ann Larmon.

Officers went to the girl's residence and awakened her parents. She had not come home, they said. They did not know where she went. They said Lee Ann's former boyfriend might have returned to town.

"Could he have picked her up at the store and taken her someplace to talk?" Douglas asked. Perhaps they were getting back together. Perhaps she left with him in his vehicle. That would explain why her truck was still at the store. But if she had left with him willingly, why wouldn't she have taken her purse?

Lee Ann's parents had heard nothing from her since she had left for work. At that time, everything seemed normal. Lee Ann, wearing jeans and shirt, had slipped her multicolored purse over her shoulder, gotten into her truck, and hurried off to the convenience store. She had said nothing about going anywhere else. Lee Ann would not have left the store to go anywhere, they assured the officers. She took her job seriously and was working her way through Pasco-Hernando Junior College.

Sheriff's lieutenants Jerry Calhoun and Royce Decker were awakened at their homes by telephone calls. "You've got to do an air search," they were informed. Both men quickly dressed and hurried through the fog to the sheriff's airplane hanger at the Brooksville Regional Airport, about five miles south of town.

Through the wee-morning hours, the officers sat impatiently in the helicopter wishing the thick fog that covered the west end of the county would lift. If they tried to take the chopper up in such a white cloud they would not be able to see their hands in front of their faces. They had no choice but to wait and pray that the fog would lift soon.

Deputies in patrol cars circled areas where young people had partied through the midnight hour. In Spring Hill and other areas along Florida's Suncoast, parking lots are popular hangouts for teenagers who stay out late at night and have nothing else to do. Often, some of the county's young people will meet in parking lots and from there go to secluded sinkholes, which have filled with water and become lakes, or to houses where they can drink beer and smoke marijuana without the threat of cops or parents popping in on them. Sheriff's detectives and deputies looked in every direction for something that might lead to Lee Ann's whereabouts.

At the store, detectives noticed newspapers had been delivered in the early-morning hours. Detectives contacted and questioned the newspaper carrier. The young man said that he had been at the store at 2 a.m. that morning. Lee Ann had been on duty. She was fine when he left the store, he said.

Deputies contacted the store manager. Lee Ann had never left the store before, he said.

Detective Jim Blade also was acquainted with Lee Ann. Blade went into the store occasionally and drank coffee while Lee Ann was on duty. He had never seen a problem between her and any of the store customers.

Meanwhile, at Brooksville Regional Airport, the sheriff's helicopter propeller whirled with an impatient hum. As lieutenants Calhoun and Decker waited for the fog to lift they became more and more anxious. As day started to break, the lawmen felt they could wait no longer. Although there was still too much fog to go up safely, they would take the risk.

The chopper was soon hovering over land near the store where Lee Ann had last been seen. It slowly veered over construction areas, housing developments, and shopping centers.

The helicopter moved over the east side of U.S. Highway 19, the main north-to-south corridor on Florida's West Coast.

If Lee Ann had been kidnapped, her abductor might have left her someplace along the highway. She could be trying to return from some isolated place at that very moment. Lieutenant Decker climbed out of the helicopter and positioned himself on the runner. From this angle, he got a better look at the ground. Through the thick mist, both officers kept their eyes combing landscaped and backwoods areas below. Reaching the northern part of the county, Calhoun turned the helicopter in a swoop across the highway and started back south on the west side.

At about 10 a.m., while flying over the long stretch of swamp adjacent to the gulf, deputies in the helicopter spotted a blue Ford pickup truck. With Decker still sitting on the helicopter runner, Calhoun made a sweep over the immediate area. The men were trying to get the vehicle out of a mud hole. A woman stood near a car behind the truck. She looked up at the helicopter and waved.

Calhoun got on the radio and reported the incident. The sheriff's dispatcher sent a patrol car to the scene. Without help, the three could be stranded in the swamp indefinitely.

While patrol deputies searched throughout the country for Lee Ann, others were dispatched to the swamp.

A deputy walked in front of the car to the pickup. "Y'all have a problem here?"

Yes, they acknowledged.

"What were y'all doing out here this time of morning?"

"We've been mud bogging." (Mud bogging, or driving a truck through a swamp for sport, is a popular but often an illegal form of recreation around the Florida wetlands.)

The middle-aged woman identified herself as the mother of the truck owner. The owner of the truck was her son's friend, but she didn't know him well. The two had come to her home earlier that morning to ask for help. They needed equipment to free the truck. The men identified themselves. The one with long, straggly light brown hair, peach-fuzz mustache and goatee, said he was Philip Frantz, of Spring Hill. The other, with shorter, wavy black hair, black piercing eyes, and a thick black goatee, identified himself as Todd Mendyk, from the next county south. Both were 20 years old.

Above the people on the ground, and with Lieutenant Decker still on the helicopter runner, Lieutenant Calhoun made another sweep over the truck. He saw that help for the stranded people below had arrived. Still, Calhoun put the helicopter in hovering mode and scrutinized the surroundings.

Suddenly Calhoun's eyes widened. Below, about 400 feet from the truck, a female form was lying in a cluster of palmetto bushes. "Take a look down there," Calhoun said. Decker's eyes were already focused on the nude girl. Portions of her body were bound with wire and she was curled in a fetal position. Looking closely, the men could see the girl was wearing nothing but socks.

Without hesitation, Lieutenant Calhoun got on the radio. "Don't let those two men out of sight," he ordered. "Keep them there. They might be involved in what has happened out here."

Deputies kept the woman and men talking while other law officers pounded like an army into the swamp.

Moments later, lawmen surrounded the truck. The trio shook their heads at the mention of the female in the bushes. They had been mud bogging. They had seen nothing, they said.

While sheriff's officers started gathering evidence, Jeff Cario, an assistant state attorney, and Jane Phifer, an investigator for the state attorney's office, were sent to view the crime scene and watch while officials gathered evidence.

As they walked alongside the yellow crime-scene tape that stretched across a large area of ground around the stuck truck, Phifer, who had been to many crime scenes, felt a cold chill come over her. She could hear the ghost of the young woman screaming through the swampland, she later said.

Detective Jim Blade was called to the scene. He identified the dead girl as Lee Ann Larmon. He followed the ambulance to Lykes Memorial Hospital morgue in Brooksville where the body was turned over to Dr. John Sass, pathologist and assistant medical examiner for the state's Fifth Judicial Circuit.

The convenience store manager also was called to the morgue to identify the body. He, too, said this was the clerk.

In the swamp where the body had been found, sheriff's Detective Ralph Decker (no relation to Lieutenant Royce Decker), found articles of clothing that had been discarded in the swamp. The garments were sent to the FBI lab in Washington, D.C. to be analyzed; they were later identified as having belonged to Lee Ann.

A knife, found in the mud underneath a truck wheel, also was sent to the FBI. They subsequently determined that it had been the knife used to cut the electrical wire that had bound Lee Ann's neck, wrists and ankles.

Other FBI agents became involved in the case. Raymond Rawalt, an expert mineralogist, compared soil samples taken from the bottoms of the suspects' shoes to dirt samples from various swamp areas. The samples taken from near the scrub oaks and the bushes matched those taken from the bottoms of Todd Mendyk's shoes.

FBI agent Michael Malone determined that hair, which had been vacuumed from Todd Mendyk's truck, had been removed from Lee Ann's head by some act of force.

Philip Frantz and Todd Mendyk were indicted by a grand jury and held in jail until the case went to court in October of 1987. Frantz agreed to exchange a guilty plea for a life sentence, which would put him in jail without possibilities of parole for 25 years, rather than chance being sentenced to death in the Florida electric chair. In order to get this deal, Frantz had to agree to testify against Mendyk, who, detectives said, was the "mastermind" of the crime.

But there would be no plea-bargaining for Mendyk "unless he wants to plea for high voltage," Tom Hogan, the assistant state prosecutor, said to reporters outside the courtroom on the day they struck the deal with Frantz.

Due to enormous publicity about the case, the trial was moved from Brooksville to Tavares, in Lake County, about 60 miles northeast of Brooksville.

On Monday, October 12, 1987, a chained Mendyk was escorted to a black vinyl court chair where his shackled feet were locked to the defendant's table. He made a facial gesture at Hogan and said, "I'll get out and I'll be back to get you. Your court clerk can put that on her record."

During the proceedings that followed, Mendyk sat with a pen in hand, drawing what appeared to be a dagger. He would point the "weapon" at the judge, at witnesses, at jurors, and at cops and reporters in the courtroom.

A hush came over the courtroom when Hogan made his opening statement.

Hogan described the kidnapping, telling how Lee Ann had walked around the counter to get relish for Mendyk, how he then grabbed her around the neck, and how he forced her into his truck and held her on the floor while Philip Frantz drove away.

Detective Decker testified that Mendyk told him that he and Frantz had been riding around looking for a "target" when they went to the convenience store. The two men hung around the parking lot for a while, waiting for a customer to leave the store. It was about 2:40 a.m.

Once inside the store, Mendyk ordered a hamburger. Then he grabbed Lee Ann around the neck, hit her, and forced her to the truck.

Frantz drove the truck into Pasco County while Mendyk tied Lee Ann's wrists together with stereo speaker wire. Mendyk continued to fondle the kidnapped girl as they rode. Lee Ann begged him to leave her alone.

They went to an isolated. Finding the gate to the property locked, they went to the illegal dump ground in the swamp.

With the headlights shining, Mendyk made Lee Ann bend over a sawhorse he had taken from his truck bed and tied her

wrists and ankles to it. Mendyk sexually molested her with a stick
and forced her to perform oral sex. He then dragged her to two
scrub oak trees and using electrical wires, tied her wrists to the
limb of one tree and her feet to the other.

With Lee Ann still alive and tied to the trees, Mendyk and
Frantz decided to go someplace and find a shovel to dig a hole to
bury her–just in case they decided to kill her. At this point, the
two men had not decided whether to kill Lee Ann. Another idea
was to keep her there, tied to the trees, and make her their sex
slave.

Mendyk started to drive the truck out of the swamp. That's
when the wheels bogged deep in the mud. While Frantz worked
to get the truck free, Mendyk went back to the trees. He told Lee
Ann he was trying to decide what to do with her. Should he kill
her or should he make her his sex slave?

"Trust me. I won't tell anyone. Please don't kill me. I'm too
young to die," she pleaded. But the idea of her begging him not to
kill her excited him. After teasing her with his ideas, Mendyk left
her and returned to the truck.

"She's still there," Mendyk said to Frantz. Soon, he returned
to the trees.

"Trust me, trust me. I don't want to die. I'm too young to
die," was her final plea.

Mendyk put a bandanna around her neck and, using his knife
as a tool, tightened it slowly. Hanging there, Lee Ann shook, so
Mendyk wrapped her neck with wire. He cut the ropes that had
secured her to the trees, and took her to the palmetto bushes where
he stabbed her in the throat.

"Anyone will say anything to get out of dying," Mendyk said
when he confessed the crime. Killing the helpless girl gave him an
"incredible high," he assured Decker.

While Mendyk was in the county jail awaiting trial, Detective
Kim Curlew asked him how he felt about killing the young girl.
Mendyk responded that he wasn't sorry. He would do it again if
he could, Curlew testified.

Co-defendant Philip Frantz testified that he did not help kill Lee Ann and that he did not sexually batter her, although he admitted that he stood by and did nothing to stop the horrible crime. According to Frantz, he and Mendyk had been looking for a girl before they stopped at the convenience store on the morning of April 9th. Frantz said that on April 8th, the day before the murder, he was in his room playing his bass guitar when Mendyk showed up uninvited. At about 10:30 that evening, the two decided to go out. Frantz said he drove Mendyk's truck because he didn't trust Mendyk's driving when he was drinking.

They picked up a six-pack of beer, and then went out looking for the house of a female friend in Brooksville. When they couldn't find her, they went to Spring Hill in the hopes of finding a party someplace. They drove by a couple 7-11 stores where kids usually hung out in parking lots. But they didn't find a party. By this time, their beer was gone.

The two men then drove to a friend's house and partied there for about half an hour. When they were ready to leave, their truck wouldn't start so they stole a battery out of a nearby car. Then they went to the convenience store to get something to eat.

As they got out of the truck, Todd suggested they "grab this babe," Frantz testified.

Inside the store, they went to the cooler and looked at sandwiches. "Todd got a hamburger and put it in the microwave. I was talking about wishing we had money to get beer. About that time, a man came into the store and looked me directly in the eyes."

Todd asked the girl for onions. She didn't have any. Then he asked for relish. When she got the relish, he stepped behind her and grabbed her around the neck.

Mendyk then directed Frantz to drive to an area in Pasco County.

Public Defender Alan Fanter asked Frantz if he knew what was happening at the time. Frantz replied, "I had a good idea. We were kidnapping the girl. We were going to do something. She wanted to know if we were going to kill her. Todd said, 'no, just be a good girl.'"

After the killing, Mendyk appeared to be the "normal Todd," Frantz testified. Frantz said he never went back to look at the body. But together, he and Mendyk threw the victim's clothes in the swamp and started walking to find the closest phone.

Evidence showed one set of footprints going to the trees where Lee Ann had been tied belonged to shoes worn by Frantz. Shoes worn by Mendyk had left several sets of tracks between the stuck truck and the trees. Evidence also showed prints belonging only to Mendyk's shoes going to the palmettos where the body was found. This evidence showed that Frantz was pretty-much telling the truth about what had happened in that swamp.

Upon delivering his closing statement to the jury, Prosecutor Hogan walked rapidly across the courtroom. With an angry look on his face, he pointed to Todd Mendyk, who sat comfortably in the vinyl chair with his feet still shackled to the legal table. "This the last face Lee Ann Larmon ever saw," he said with a raised voice. "This is the face Lee Ann Larmon saw while she begged for her life. While she pleaded that she was too young to die!

"Three hours of terror for Lee Ann Larmon. Why?" Hogan asked. Then he answered his own question. "So Todd Mendyk could practice his domination. His lust."

It took only about 30 minutes for the jury of three women and nine men to return to the courtroom with their verdict. While Judge L.R. Huffstetler read the verdict over to himself, the courtroom was full of anticipation. Huffstetler handed the written verdict to the court clerk to read aloud. While she read, four bailiffs moved closer to where Mendyk sat shackled. Mendyk laughed lightly and whispered something to his public defender. The bailiffs never took their stare off Mendyk.

Mendyk was found guilty as charged of first-degree murder, two counts of sexual battery, and for the kidnapping of Lee Ann Larmon. The same jury recommended unanimously that he be sentenced to death in Florida's electric chair. Judge Huffstetler abided by the jury's wishes and said that Mendyk must die in the Florida electric chair for his actions. The judge called the crime "heinous, atrocious, cruel, cold, calculated, and premeditated."

Philip Frantz was sentenced to life in prison without any possibility of parole for 25 years.

From: A Writer's Notebook Covering the Todd Mendyk trial

I had worked the crime beat for the *Daily Sun-Journal* for only a few months when the murder case against Todd Mendyk and Philip Frantz was ready for trial.

I drove to the daily hearings held in the Lake County Courthouse in Tavares, where the trial was moved due to publicity in Brooksville.

Since my copy had to be in by noon, in order for the *Daily Sun-Journal* to be printed and on the streets by 2 p.m., I would scribble out my story in longhand, and then call it in to the type sitter at my office from a pay phone.

I think I was present every minute of the Mendyk trial. As he sat at the defendant's table, I watched him draw a dagger on a yellow tablet. Every now and then he would change the position of the note pad so the blade pointed to a different person in the courtroom.

The next murder that I covered was quite different; but it was one I watched develop from the time detectives learned of the killing to the last day of trial. The story tells how a woman pushed authorities into capturing her husband's killers.

STORY 4:

A Christmas Rabbit Hunt

Became a Night of Murder

On Christmas morning 1997, Carolyn got up early to prepare for a family day reunion with Drew.

Carolyn and Drew Snyder had been separated for several months. Lately, however, things were going great between them. They might even try living together again. A common interest was their eight-year-old daughter, Kayla.

Perhaps it was the time of year that acted as a force pulling the two together. The joy of Christmas was in the air.

The family had made plans to be together for the holidays. So naturally, Kayla was excited. "Can I call daddy?" she asked, as she pulled presents from under the tree.

Carolyn assured the child it would be okay to call her father. Kayla dialed the phone and listened to the ringing. "Daddy isn't answering."

"Wait a little while and we'll try again. Maybe he turned the phone off so he can sleep in."

Kayla was too excited to wait more than a couple minutes before dialing again. There was no answer. She waited a while longer, then dialed the number yet another time. No answer.

Carolyn tried not to let her disappointment show but it was difficult.

Yesterday, on Christmas Eve, Carolyn and Drew had spent the evening together and had talked seriously about their future.

They also had talked about some trouble Drew had gotten into with a couple other guys.

Drew was scheduled to go to court for burglary in January. He would plead no-contest and take whatever punishment the judge handed over. He had learned an expensive lesson and would never do anything to screw up his life again, he sworn to Carolyn.

"I'll make it up to you happy. I'll change," he promised. "I'll be a better man."

While Carolyn sat on the sofa, Drew's head resting on her lap and her fingertips rubbing gently over his forehead, she felt a fever. He was sick. "I'm going home, Drew," she said. "You get some rest. I'll call you in the morning."

On her way to the door, Carolyn turned back to Drew. "Kayla is so excited about Christmas. She knows you're coming over and going to Dad's house with us. I'm happy too, Drew." Already Drew was falling asleep. But, after all, it was 2 o'clock in the morning.

This morning, after Kayla tried several times to reach Drew, Carolyn attempted herself. Not once. Not twice. But over and over and over again.

Finally, she gave up. She left a note on her front door and she and Kayla went to her father's house. Even without Drew, Christmas Day was filled with the excitement of a ham dinner with the trimmings, lots of family and friends together, and giving and unwrapping gifts. Carolyn and Kayla ended up staying the night.

The following day, Carolyn tried again to phone Drew. Still, there was no answer.

Just after the New Year had arrived, she went to the Hernando County Sheriff's Office to file a missing person's report. Drew had vanished from his home on Christmas Day without a trace. He had not called. He had not sent a letter. Even after the way he had promised to make things right for Kayla and her. Something was wrong and Carolyn knew it.

Deputy Ronald T. Rags took Carolyn's report. Perhaps Drew left town to avoid going to court, the deputy said.

"No. He would have made arrangements for somebody to take care of his dogs. Drew had been pretty sure he would go to jail. He wasn't trying to avoid it. He had even lined up somebody to look after his property. He didn't run off," she assured the deputy.

Rags listen, taking notes now and then. Carolyn explained how Drew had promised to spend Christmas Day with her. They had planned to have dinner with one of Drew's best friends, Bruce Demo, on December 26th; then the whole group was to go from there to a party at Rick Shere's house. Drew wouldn't have made all those plans and then left town without saying a word to anybody. She knew him better than that, she said.

For him to just disappear didn't make sense. She had contacted everybody should could think of to see if they knew of his whereabouts. Nobody had seen him. She had even talked with Rick and Bruce's girlfriends. The women said their men had been with them all through the holidays; they had not seen hide-nor-hair of Drew for weeks.

Deputy Rags asked what kind of friends Drew had. What were Bruce and Rick like? Carolyn recalled the men both treated their women rough, but that was none of her business. Drew wasn't like either of his friends. Drew was gentle and caring.

In recalling as much as she could about Christmas Eve, Carolyn remembered that Drew had spent some time at Bruce's house earlier in the day. "Brewster," as Bruce Demo was called, "was putting bikes together for his girlfriend's kids." Afterwards, Drew spent a couple hours at her home. He then left her to go to some other friends' houses to wish them a merry Christmas.

On Christmas Eve night, Drew waited at his apartment until Carolyn arrived at about 11 o'clock. "I was late getting there because my parents were having a party. I went to it first," she told the deputy. Carolyn recalled that some of Drew's friends had attended the party at her parents' home.

"How do you and Drew get along?" Deputy Rags asked. "Could he have gotten mad at you and left town?"

"No," she said. "We would argue but I can tell you right now that I'm the one who usually started it. I've even hit him a couple of times trying to get him to hit me back. But he wouldn't do it. And he would drink beer, yes, but you'd never see him drunk. He just didn't get drunk."

Deputy Rags suggested that perhaps Drew had gone away with friends, perhaps on a hunting or fishing trip to North Florida or Georgia. "Does Drew have hunting buddies? Perhaps they know Drew's whereabouts."

"Drew has a good friend in Bruce," Carolyn said. "If he were going away he would tell Brewster. But that didn't happen. Rick is always around, too. But I don't really have any confidence in Rick Shere. However, Drew gets along well with both men. Whenever they need something fixed on their cars or trucks, they go to Drew for help. He gives them anything they need, if he has it. That's the way he is."

Getting back to Christmas Eve night, Carolyn recalled that Rick's girlfriend Cindy had been at her parents' Christmas party. Then on Christmas night, Bruce Demo came there. Brewster had broken down and cried because Drew had not shown up and nobody could find him. He was crying and said, "Carolyn, I'm really sorry things are bad for you on Christmas."

Bruce Demo's sympathy made her feel even more sorry for herself. Then Bruce had put his arm around her and hugged her. This had made her feel a lot better.

Three days after Christmas, Carolyn had begun to wonder if Drew had gotten deathly ill and perhaps died in his apartment. But, checking the matter out, she had found everything was as it had been on Christmas Eve.

With Drew being 31 years old and having a police record, a missing person's report was not appropriate, Rags said. If Drew didn't appear for his January court hearing, a warrant would be issued for his arrest.

If Drew had wanted to run off to avoid prosecution, it would have made sense to pick a day other than Christmas to do it, Rags noted. He had the idea that Drew might be in jail somewhere. He could have gone out partying on Christmas Eve night after Carolyn left his apartment and gotten arrested for one reason or another.

During the next few days, Rags checked jail records in surrounding counties, then throughout Central Florida. Nobody using the name Drew Snyder had been booked.

While Deputy Rags did his work, Carolyn continued her own investigation. Five days after her first trip to Drew's apartment, she returned. On her first trip there, she had found everything intact. But on her return, his clothes were gone. She looked though the closet and found all his favorite things still there, including his Harley Davidson shirts. If Drew had come back for his clothes, he would have taken his motorcycle shirts. She noticed a picture of Drew and herself on the dresser. And his army picture was there. If he had left town for good, he would have taken the pictures. Even his cherished army jacket had been left.

Also, his truck was still parked out front. Carolyn opened the truck door. His keys were lying there on the seat. Keys to everything: his apartment, his toolbox with more than $1,000 worth of tools. Normally, when Drew was not driving the truck, he kept his keys hooked to a chain on his belt.

Carolyn talked with Annie, who lived in a stilt house next door to Drew. "There was a blue car over at Drew's the other day with two or three people inside," Annie said. "They ran into the house and took a bunch of stuff out. They put it in the trunk."

Annie had noticed the car because it had been parked so close to her house. After the car left, Annie went to Drew's door. It was unlocked so she went inside. Everything was a mess.

"Have you seen Drew anyplace?" Carolyn asked.

"No. Nobody has seen him. He hasn't been home," Annie said.

This was so weird. Where in the world had Drew gone on Christmas Day that would cause him not to return? How could he have just vanished?

Carolyn went home and called Deputy Rags. "Something is not right, you know."

"I'm checking all the jails in Florida," Rags said. Drew Snyder's court date is coming up soon. If he fled to avoid prosecution he might possibly get second thoughts and return to avoid more trouble with the law.

After that second trip to Drew's house, Carolyn came down with scarlet fever. The illness tightened the reins on her investigating efforts for a few days.

While she was sick, Bruce Demo's girlfriend, Sharon, called. She was crying. She was worried about Bruce's friendship with Rick. She was afraid Bruce was being influenced by Rick to do things he wouldn't normally do.

"Rick called Christmas Eve night," Sharon said. He got Brewster out of bed. Brewster left with him. He said Rick was going to do something stupid. During that conversation, Sharon told Carolyn to stop thinking about Drew because Drew was gone and he wasn't coming back.

Soon, during Carolyn's interrogating, Sharon broke into sobs. "They went out Christmas Eve night." When Bruce got home it was daylight. He went straight to the shower. He stayed in the bathroom about an hour getting sick and crying. They did something to Drew."

The following morning, while in a state of hysteria, Carolyn called Deputy Rags. "I've got to talk to you right away. In person."

Arrangements were made for Rags to meet Carolyn at her parents' home. The deputy was there within a half-an-hour after receiving Carolyn's phone call. "They've killed Drew," Carolyn said, crying. "They've killed him."

"Who?" Rags asked.

"His friends," she cried. "Bruce and Rick."

Carolyn's assumption triggered more involvement into the matter by sheriff's deputies. Detectives James Blade, Alan Arich and Lieutenant Michael Hensley started contacting people who knew Drew. Blade, Arich and Hensley went to talk with Sharon.

They asked her to come with them to the sheriff's office to make a statement regarding whatever she might know about the disappearance of Drew Snyder.

It looked like Drew had been with Bruce and Rick on Christmas morning after Carolyn had left his apartment. Detective Arich obtained a warrant to search Rick's 1966 Chevrolet.

For several days, detectives kept a close watch on friends and acquaintances of Drew Snyder's. Major Gary "G.Z." Smith, commander of operations for the sheriff's office, obtained information that Bruce Demo was working on a construction job in Dade City. Arich, the lead investigator in the case, and Blade drove to the location, about 10 miles south of Ridge Manor, in Pasco County. According to his employer, Bruce Demo had come to work that morning, but had left with his girlfriend, Sharon.

Detectives went to Sharon's house in Dade City and Bruce came walking out the front door, a can of beer in his hand. He seemed agitated. "If you're back here looking for Drew, I already told Deputy Rags I don't know where he is. I don't know what happened to Drew," he said, and then took a swallow of beer.

Detective Arich asked Bruce to accompany him and Detective Blade to the sheriff's office in Brooksville. Bruce agreed to do that. Once at the sheriff's office, Bruce was read his rights and questioned about the disappearance of Drew Snyder. Detectives Arich and Blade told Bruce they thought Drew might have been murdered.

"I don't know anything about any murder," he said quickly.

"I believe you're lying," Arich said.

It didn't take long for Bruce Demo to crack. "Okay. Drew's dead. Rick Shere forced me into it. I went out with Rick Christmas Eve night. He was mad because he thought Drew was going to squeal on him about some burglaries Rick committed. Drew knew about the burglaries."

Bruce's story was that Rick had called him on the phone then came to his house. They drank a few beers. Bruce thought he had calmed Rick down, so he agreed to go with him to pick up Drew so the trio could have a holiday night out rabbit hunting and target shooting at mailboxes, he said.

After they had ridden into the backwoods in the country north of Ridge Manor, they got out of the car to urinate. "While Drew was peeing, Rick shot him," Bruce said.

He admitted he and Rick had buried Drew Snyder in the forest. He agreed to lead detectives to the spot.

Major G.Z. Smith teamed up with detectives to escort Bruce to the wilderness. They searched for a couple hours in the thick Florida hammock area where people rarely venture. As darkness fell, finding the gravesite seemed hopeless. Detectives decided to take Bruce back to the sheriff's office until the following day when they could again search for the grave.

Early the following morning, police officers were on the lookout for Rick Shere. Officers located his 1966 Chevrolet at the MidState Bank parking lot, across the street from the Hernando County Court House. Detective Blade went to the location and stood by the car until Detective Arich obtained a search warrant.

Evidence technician Tim Whitfield arrived at the bank parking lot and sealed the Chevrolet doors with tape and the vehicle was transported to the sheriff's impound. Whitfield went to work looking for anything that appeared suspicious. He sprayed a chemical onto contact paper, and then he placed the contact paper onto the area believed to contain the gunpowder. (The spray chemical sends off a color reaction when it comes into contact with gunpowder.) Using this method, Whitfield discovered gunshot powder in various areas of the vehicle, including the headliner, door panels, and passenger side of the rear seat area, on top of and behind the drivers seat, and on the carpeting.

While Whitfield was busy processing the Chevrolet, Blade went to the courthouse. Rick was there. He was scheduled that day to appear in felony court on burglary charges. Blade informed Rick he was a suspect in the disappearance and possible death of Drew Snyder. Blade escorted Rick to the sheriff's office for questioning.

Arich advised him of his rights and Arich and Blade conducted an interviewed.

Rick denied any knowledge of the disappearance of Drew. "I believe Drew left town so he wouldn't have to go to jail," Rick said.

Arich questioned Rick about his 1966 Chevrolet. "What happened to the back seat?" he asked.

"I'm a construction worker. It's easier to carry tools and supplies without a back seat.

"Where's the seat now?" Arich asked.

"I got rid of it at the junk yard," Rick answered.

"I'm tired of answering the same questions over and over. I want to go home," Rick said after about an hour of interrogation. But Arich didn't allow Rick to leave. Instead, he took the suspect, who was out of jail on a bond, to the county building. Rick's original bond on the burglary charges was pulled. Cops locked him up.

With Bruce having already admitted being a party to killing Drew Snyder, detectives went to the jail to further question Rick. "Bruce has admitted to the killing," Arich said. "He indicated you're the bad guy. You did the shooting. You forced him into the killing. It would be in your best interest to cooperate."

"I been thinking about calling you guys," Rick said. "The jailer took your business cards from me. I didn't know your phone number. I didn't have any way to contact you." Rick said Bruce had been the one who killed Drew. "I want to cooperate," he said, crying. He agreed to show detectives where Drew's body was buried.

The following day, Saturday, January 16, Major Smith teamed up with a group of deputies and escorted Bruce, cuffed and in ankle chains, back to the area where they had been the previous morning to look for the grave. Smith was in the process of putting together a search plan. Deputies would comb the area on the ground and from the air. At the same time, Arich and Blade were on their way to the wilderness with Rick.

Prior to their arrival, Smith and his team walked with Bruce through the thick woods. Suddenly Bruce hesitated. "This is where the car was parked," he said. "This is where the back of the car was." He pointed at some bloodstains on the ground. "This is where we dragged him through the woods."

Suddenly Bruce quickened his pace. Reaching a hilly area, he stopped. "This is where we laid the body. That area over there," he pointed to a spot of disturbed earth, "that's where the body is buried."

Several officers sealed off the area. Others stayed at the gravesite, and still others escorted Bruce to the place where he said the actual shooting had occurred.

He pointed out the area where the car had been parked and places he, Rick and Drew had been on the wee hours of Christmas. Bruce explained just how the 10 shots were fired into Drew's body.

Russell Knodle, crime scene technician, who also was dispatched to the scene, had no idea how to get to the wilderness spot. He waited on State Road 50 until a patrol car arrived to lead him in. A caravan of lost newspaper and radio reporters also followed the patrol car down the dirt roads. In this wilderness, old boards nailed to trees with spray-painted arrows pointing in various directions and with notations of either "in" or "out," served as road signs.

Once at the site, Knodle got together with Tim Whitfield and Gary Kimble, who were already processing the scene. Kimble and Whitfield had found bloodstains on a path leading from a dirt road. Knodle collected the blood samples. A phenolphthalein test done in water in the sheriff's crime lab showed the samples were actually blood.

Detectives transported Bruce to Rick's home. Bruce showed them where the back seat to Rick's Chevrolet had been removed and burned.

During the excavation of Drew's body, Knodle, Whitfield and Kimble carefully dug so not to disturb any evidence.

Doctor John Sass, medical examiner for Hernando County, remained at the gravesite in order to "document everything while remains were being removed from the pit," he noted in his report.

After an hour of careful digging, Knodle, Whitfield, and Kimble came to a body buried underneath 30 inches of sand. They removed the skin from the deteriorating hands to obtain fingerprints.

That afternoon, Carolyn Snyder's father identified Drew's body by a tattoo on the right arm.

The following day, Whitfield and Kimble went to Rick's residence to examine the area where the Chevrolet seat had been burned. They collected parts of the charred item to be used as evidence in the case. Then they went to the sheriff's impound and sprayed the Chevrolet interior with the chemical luminal, a substance used to locate blood. A number of areas reacted positive. In addition, technicians found burned gunshot powder in the passenger area of the car. Bloodstains on car interior fabric were collected and sent to the Federal Bureau of Investigation in Washington D.C. for testing.

Gary Kimble photographed the vehicle, capturing tiny spots of substance, which were confirmed as human blood when tested in the sheriff's crime lab. Kimble also collected .22-caliber shell casings from inside the automobile.

Taped interviews between detectives and Bruce and Rick, of which each blamed the other for the killing, were added to the collection of evidence.

Rick claimed he had stopped the car to urinate, put his rifle on top of the vehicle, and then Bruce grabbed it and pumped six bullets into Drew. Rick said he then pulled Drew from the back seat of his car and Bruce used a handgun to shoot Drew twice in the head and once in the heart. These final shots are what killed Drew, Rick said.

Bruce's story was just the opposite. Bruce said Rick fired seven shots into Drew with the rifle. Bruce admitted he then shot Drew with the handgun, finishing him off, to put him out of his misery.

But both men were guilty of murdering Drew Snyder, according to Assistant State Attorney Anthony Tatti. The trio had gone out in the wee morning hours Christmas Day. Drew Snyder had thought they were going rabbit hunting but the purpose of the rabbit hunt was to do away with Drew Snyder, Tatti proclaimed. They were going to do away with Drew Snyder because they thought he was going to squeal to the law on them for some burglaries they had committed, Tatti said.

During closing statements in Shere's trial, Tatti stood before the jury with a .22-caliber pump rifle in his hand. He pointed the barrel upward toward the ceiling. In the quietness, he pumped the gun and pulled the trigger: pump, click, pump, click. He did this six times—the number of times the gun had been pumped and the trigger pulled on Christmas morning when its bullets ripped into Drew Snyder.

Tatti didn't buy the theory presented by the defense that Rick Shere had nothing to do with the shooting, that Bruce Demo had done it all. "One phone call got all this started, Tatti said in his closing statement. "Demo had called to invite Shere to Christmas dinner. Demo got angry because Rick Shere made him angry. Rick went to Demo's house to pick him up so the two of them could pick up Drew Snyder, take him out and kill him. They went out shooting rabbits, then when Drew Snyder turned his back to relieve himself, that man," Tatti said, pointing at Rick Shere, who sat at the defendant's table sniffing tears, "that man, who brought this rifle, opened fire."

With both hands, Tatti clutched the rifle. "Shere and Demo are in the murder together. They cannot be separated. He is a killer and the tools of his trade were a .22-caliber rifle, a .22-caliber handgun and a shovel to bury the body. It makes no difference who fired the bullets, he is responsible for every bullet in Snyder."

During his sentencing hearing, after the jury had found him guilty for first-degree murder, Shere took the witness stand to say he had become a born-again Christian since being confined to jail.

He said he prays every morning and every night. He said he prays for Drew Snyder, that he would be saved, so he could enter through the pearly gates of Heaven, too.

Brad King, state attorney for the Fifth Judicial Circuit, asked Rick if he prayed over Drew Snyder's grave after he buried him.

"He was buried in a beautiful place. I said a prayer over him," Rick replied.

The jury recommended Rick die for his part in the crime. Following these recommendations, Circuit Judge Raymond T. McNeal sentenced Rick Shere to death in the electric chair. In passing sentence, McNeal noted the aggravating circumstances in the case far out weighed the mitigating circumstances and that the only appropriate sentence was death. McNeal noted the crime had been committed to hinder "a governmental function or the enforcement of law" and that the crime was "especially evil, wicked, atrocious or cruel," and that the murder was committed in a "cold, calculated and premeditated manner."

Rick showed little emotion and no surprise at being sentenced to death. He was escorted from the courtroom in cuffs and shackles, and then led to an unmarked white car parked alongside the courthouse under a palm tree. As the car pulled away, Rick puffed a cigarette.

A different jury tried Bruce Demo. Taking the stand in his own defense, Demo testified that on the night of the slaying, the trio had stopped to urinate alongside the road and Rick had opened fire on Snyder, shooting him six times. Bruce said that Rick then forced him to shoot Drew. Bruce said he fired at least four bullets into Drew, hitting him in the head and in the heart.

Bruce Demo's defense laid the blame on Rick, claiming Bruce had no reason to kill Drew, and advised the jury to use common sense in the matter.

But Tatti said Demo was trying to wash Drew Snyder's blood from his hands. "You can't wash the blood off," he said. "Drew Snyder's blood won't come off Bruce Demo's hands and it won't come off his soul."

The jury that decided Bruce Demo's fate went easier on him than the previous jury had done for Rick Shere. Demo was found guilty of second-degree murder, which saved him from Florida's electric chair. Still, Judge John Futch sentenced him to spend the rest of his life in prison.

From: A Writer's Notebook
A sister's search for brother

The Ocala Hilton is so different than the Hernando County courtroom. Music of the Great Masters emerges from a piano and sounds through the hotel lobby, through the huge mezzanine of mirrors and glass. Shoe heels click on the shiny tiled floor and wine glasses clink at a distant bar.

Outside, the air is cool with smells of December. The sun, finding its way through groups of white clouds, hovers over sunseekers around the spacious pool.

Beyond the patio, Spanish moss hangs from liveoak trees that separate the Hilton from an Ocala horse farm.

Little air moves inside the courtroom back in Hernando County. The bit of ventilation there is just happens to be as thick as dirt, especially during a murder trial.

Especially if a man on trial is one who helped kill your brother. Donna sat through two such trials. She sat toward the back of the courtroom and listened while assistant state attorneys prosecuted the killers.

I watched Donna during these trials. I watched her head bowed over the needlepoint work lying on her lap. I watched her long dark hair fall over her hands as she buried her face in them to hide emotions.

As I watched Donna, I saw myself, though I didn't attend the trial of the men who murdered my brother. But I saw myself just the same. I saw the agony I had known. The pain clearly showed on her trembling hands, on the fright masking her face, and in the hurt tearing her eyes.

I wanted to talk with her as a person who understood, not as a reporter. I wanted to tell her that I, too, had experienced this.

On a courtroom break, I followed Donna to the washroom. I said, "I know how you feel. My brother was murdered."

In early May, after both trials were over, I handed one of my reporter cards to Donna. I said, "I'd like to write a story about you. I'd like to let people know how you feel. Not now. But whenever you're ready. If you're ever ready."

Donna called me at the *Daily Sun-Journal* a few months later. We decided to split the drive between her horse ranch in North Florida and the newspaper office. After lunch at the Hilton, we talked about the murder and the trials.

Both defendants were convicted of murder. But who knows if either will serve their sentences? The legal system often fails victims, she noted.

One of the two men who killed my brother was sentenced to 30-to-life in Kansas. I would hate to know he would ever be set free. The second murderer never went to trial; he didn't live long enough to get arrested. He was found dead on a sidewalk in New York City, so I was told.

STORY 5:

Shootout

In Sumter County

Sheriff's Deputy Ronald Dockham was on routine patrol the night of April 14, 1989. The events that occurred on that date, in a very short while, will live in his memory as long as he has breath. In a rural area in Central Florida, Dockham was involved in a bloody shootout that left him crippled, another man wounded and another dead.

Dockham's shift ran from 6 p.m. to 3 a.m. His job was to patrol the thinly populated area of Interstate-75 near Bushnell, just over the Hernando line in Sumter County. One of the places he wanted to keep an eye on was Gidden's Auto Parts and Service Station on State Road 48, just off the interstate. The owners recently had been burglarized.

However, all had been quiet on this spring night.

As Dockham sipped a cup of coffee at the local McDonald's, a couple in their early twenties and driving an older model Monte Carlo, entered the quiet county where even small towns are few. Jeff was at the wheel. Traci sat on the passenger side. She had one fist full of stolen jewelry and the other holding a marijuana cigarette. She sucked on the dope and joked about a loaded revolver underneath her seat.

The two had known each other for two weeks and were heading from Sarasota, 60 or so miles south of Tampa, to his home near

Atlanta, Georgia. Traci was beautiful and sexy. She was just over
five-foot and slim with dark bouncy hair.

For the past four days, Traci had been drinking booze quite
heavily. She had smoked a bag of marijuana and had done several
lines of cocaine. Jeff was no saint either. He was good-looking and
a smooth talker but a previous run-in with the law had left his past
scarred.

He had served time in a Georgia prison for burglary and
aggravated assault after he had attempted to rape a woman in her
home in 1986. He had tried to escape after that incident, but had
been run down by police dogs in a field. Jeff was sentenced to 10
years in prison for the crime. After serving only eight months, he
was released. Rather than remain in Georgia according to his parole
directions, he left the state for Florida.

Suddenly the Monte Carlo slowed, its tires seeming to thump
like driving over bad road, but the road was good. Jeff pulled to
the side of the interstate and got out. He put the "doughnut"
spare on. This would take them a little ways further, but they
would need a real tire soon. He drove to the next exit that displayed
service signs and swerved down the exit ramp.

At about 11:15 p.m., Deputy Dockham walked from
McDonald's and got into the patrol car. He relaxed, positioned
himself in the seat and pulled onto the parking lot at the ABC
Liquor Lounge. It was a good place to park the cruiser and keep an
eye on traffic while he listened to the police radio and did his
paper work. Also, from here he had a good view of Giddens Auto
Parts.

But this night as Dockham pulled onto the parking lot he
noticed a strange car at Giddens. There should be no one there.
The station was closed and the lights off. Dockham cautiously
maneuvered the cruiser from the ABC parking lot to the auto parts
business across the street. He pulled the cruiser up behind an
older model Monte Carlo.

The man was changing a tire. Another car at the auto parts
business was propped up on a jack and had a tire off.

"You got a problem here?" Dockham asked, as he casually walked in the dark night toward the man.

"Yeah, I got a flat."

"Is that your tire you're putting on?" the cop asked.

The man looked up. "Nope," he answered, soberly.

"No? It's not yours?"

"No. It's not mine. I'm stealing it."

"Well now, I think you just better hold everything here. Let me see your driver's license."

Dockham kept his eyes on the man as he walked to the Monte Carlo. He noticed a woman sitting on the passenger seat. It appeared the two might have exchanged words, but Dockham was not sure. The man walked back to the officer and handed him the license.

"You take a seat in the patrol car," Dockham said, opening the back door.

The man did as Dockham ordered.

Dockham radioed to the sheriff's dispatcher. "I got a couple here at Giddens Auto. Caught 'em red-handed stealing a tire," he said. He asked that the department contact the storeowners.

After Dockham had radioed in he left the man sitting in the back of the patrol car and strolled over to the Monte Carlo. The woman appeared annoyed with the situation.

"I've had it with the thieves just coming in here and taking what they want," Bartley Giddens said as he and his son, 38-year-old Raymond Giddens, pulled into the parking area and stopped between the patrol cruiser and his auto parts business. Bartley left the keys in the Oldsmobile and he and Raymond got out and approached the deputy.

"I caught 'em red-handed," Dockham said. "Guess they had a flat down the road a piece and just drove on in here to take care of it."

Dockham neared the patrol car. He looked at the man sitting there. He didn't seem at all worried. "Looks like you're in a heap of trouble. Them folks don't take too well to thieves. Somebody just stole a tire from 'em a few weeks back. I'm going to have to lock you in here until they decide what they want to do."

The young woman had gotten out of the car. Her dark hair hugged her shoulders as she stood beside the Monte Carlo.

"Do y'all want to call somebody?" Dockham asked.

"No sir," she answered.

Dockham left her standing there and walked back toward Bartley and Raymond Giddens. But the woman didn't wait to see what might come of her fate. She reached into the Monte Carlo and pulled a 45-caliber automatic revolver from under the front seat. She had watched television and she knew how to hold the gun. She knew how to pull the trigger.

She held the gun to her side and slowly walked past the men. As she passed they all stood up, then she turned back toward them. She brought the gun straight out in front of her, holding it steady with both hands, suddenly taking the appearance of a trained gunman.

Dockham knew she intended to kill them all. The deputy moved toward the Giddens, making himself the target of any gunfire, should she shoot. "Don't do it, lady," he said. "Give me the gun."

"Oh no," she said quickly. "I have to do what I have to do." She moved closer to the men.

Bartley and Raymond Giddens stood close to each other. "Please lady, don't shoot," Raymond Giddens said. "Think about what you're doing. We can work something out. Please, just put the gun down."

"You don't want to shoot anybody. Please put the gun down," Bartley Giddens reinforced.

"Oh, no," she said. "I'm sorry. I hate to do this to you guys but this thing is ready to go," she said, and commenced firing.

Dockham didn't realize he was hit at first. The girl had pulled the trigger and he had fallen. But as he fell his quick reflex was to draw his gun. He fired back almost instantly. Dockham didn't know if he hit anything or not. He barely saw the woman run behind the cruiser. Then he lost sight of her, but he knew she was back there somewhere behind the blinding headlights toting a loaded gun.

At some point, Traci unlocked the patrol car and let Jeff out. The exchange of bullets from both sides blasted like fireworks in the darkness. Lying on the dirt parking lot alongside the garage, Dockham's stomach burned like on fire. He propped himself up with his left hand and kept firing. Sparks from a distant gun discharged toward him and dark-moving objects looked like smoke shadows in hell.

The officer could see the muzzle of the automatic flash, but from his position on the ground, he could not tell who was pulling the trigger. Then he saw both suspects' shadows moving about behind the police car. The shots kept coming.

The man jumped into the driver's seat of Bartley Giddens' Olds and started pulling away. The woman ran alongside, trying to catch onto the car door. The car slowed. "Get in," he yelled. "Quick. Get in the car!"

She grabbed onto the back door. "Hurry up and get in," he yelled again. As she jumped into the back seat behind him, she felt a bullet strike her leg. "I'm hit!" she screamed. "I'm hit!"

"Shut up. Just shut up," he cried, his voice pure fright as glass from the windows crashed all around him.

Dockham keep firing, his bullets shattering glass as the car sped away. He didn't know for sure if he hit either of the suspects but he though he might have hit the woman.

Dockham realized just how bad the shootout was once the Olds was out of sight. He was shot in the stomach. Raymond Giddens lay on the ground, possibly dying. And Bartley Giddens was hit in the leg.

Detective Travis Farmer, a 14-year-veteran at the Sumter County Sheriff's Office, was spending a relaxing evening at home when he heard the screaming sirens pass. He immediately called the sheriff's office and was informed that Deputy Dockham had been shot. By the time Farmer arrived at the scene, Dockham was being placed in an ambulance.

A few minutes later, the detective was informed by radio that the suspects had traveled north on Interstate-75. Farmer wheeled from Giddens Auto Parts and headed to the highway.

Evidence in the Monte Carlo alleged the two suspects as Jeffrey Raymond McGuire, age 23, and Traci Grosvenor, 26. An all-points bulletin was put out for the suspects. Authorities were to take every necessary precaution, as the suspects were considered armed and dangerous. They had already killed a man.

Though the officers were not far behind Jeff and Traci as they fled in the Olds, the couple managed to elude them, with the Olds speeding north on the interstate. They had gone only a few miles when they saw a sign announcing a Texaco station ahead. The Olds whizzed down the interstate ramp and pulled between two semi trucks parked at the station. "You okay, Traci?" Jeff asked, his voice still shaky and scared as he got out and opened the back door. "I got you," he said, lifting her out. "Just stay here. I'll be right back. I'll get some help."

A couple at the station agreed to drive them to Leesburg, in Lake County, in exchange for some of the stolen gold jewelry. Jeff hurried back to the Olds. He scooped Traci up into his arms and carried her to an older model Cougar. He put her in the back seat and crawled in beside her. Then the long, green Cougar wheeled from the Texaco and headed north up the interstate.

Lawmen were not far behind. Detective Farmer received information that the Olds used by the suspects to escape had been spotted at a Texaco station at an exit off the interstate just north of where the shootout had occurred.

Upon arriving at the Texaco station, the detective located the Olds. He noticed its windows had been shot out. Farmer cautiously walked to the car. Upon checking inside he found a .45-automatic pistol with the slide back in a locked position lying on the floor near the driver's seat.

A team of investigators arrived and dusted the vehicle for prints and collected projectiles from inside. Other detectives asked questions. They would get their suspects. There wasn't a doubt.

"Yes," a man in the service station said to officers. "A white guy came in here and asked me for a ride. Told me his girlfriend got shot. I told him I couldn't take him anyplace 'cause I was busy working. Then, about five minutes later, he was talking to a black guy."

"Exactly what did the man say?"

"He said, 'somebody shot my girlfriend.' He was almost crying. Then this black guy drove them away in a green nineteen-seventy-eight Cougar."

Travis Farmer's cousin, Lieutenant William Farmer, was contacted at home shortly before 1 a.m. He hastened to join other authorities already working on the crime scene investigation.

The lieutenant photographed the area where the shootout had occurred. He also measured distances between shell casings left by the .45-automatic pistol that had been fired by the suspects. With his previous expert training, Farmer could detect the exact spot from where each bullet had been fired.

The following day, detectives located Kool Luke Jones, a man local folks said owned a 1978 Cougar. Jones didn't want to talk at first, but after learning about the shooting, he opened up to officers, admitting that he and his wife had driven the fleeing couple to Leesburg.

"We stopped at the Texaco to get something for my old lady's headache," Jones said. "This man told me and my old lady he was jacking up his car to fix a tire and it fell on his old lady's foot. He asked me to give them a ride to Leesburg. He said he didn't have any money, so he gave me a diamond ring to take him up there. He said he wanted me to give him a ride to the hospital."

But rather than to the hospital, Jones said he had taken Jeff and Traci to a motel. Jones' wife, Tish, went to the motel office and rented the room.

For her services, Jeff gave her a gold chain. "This is worth several hundred," he said, affectionately handing the woman the necklace.

Jeff then lifted Traci from the back seat of the Cougar. Propping her beside the car, he reached for Tish's hand, lifted it to his lips, and kissed it. "Thank you ma'am," he said.

The following morning, authorities located the motel in Leesburg and went straight to the registration office. The motel clerk said that at around midnight a black lady had registered in room 24.

Detectives gave orders to evacuate rooms 23 and 25, but not 24. Officers took cover at the rear of the motel and outside room 24. Then a Lake County deputy made a telephone call to the room. "The police are here. Unlock the door," the officer said when Jeff answered.

Jeff unlocked the door and quickly fell in a spread-eagle position on the floor.

Traci helplessly lay on the bed, her injured foot propped up on a pillow. She pulled the blanket over her head as detectives rushed into the room. Following the cop's orders, she slowly pulled the blanket from her body. As she did this, officers saw blood had seeped through the wrapping on her lower leg. She obviously needed help. "We better take her to the hospital," a lawman said.

At the hospital, a security officer stayed with Traci. Upon her release from the hospital, she was arrested.

Both suspects claimed to be innocent of shooting Deputy Dockham and Bartley and Raymond Giddens.

Jeff claimed he was locked in the patrol car during the entire shootout. Traci claimed she had shot no one, that she had unlocked the patrol car, and that Jeff had gotten out and she had given him the gun. He had done all the shooting, she said.

Both Deputy Dockham and Bartley Giddens saw Traci with the gun. Dockham knows she shot him. From that point, he was down and blinded by the car lights. He could not say who did the rest of the shooting.

Giddens swore: "The girl did the shooting. She shot Ray. She saw me trying to help Ray and she shot me."

So convincing a jury that Jeff McGuire did any of the shooting took some sophisticated testimony from investigators. Also, Traci Grosvenor made an agreement with the State Attorney's Office to plead "no contest" to first-degree murder in exchange for two concurrent life terms in prison rather than to face Florida's electric chair. She was one of the 60 people, including investigators, to testify against Jeff.

The Sumter County case was moved to Hernando County due to pre-trial publicity. Jeff McGuire pleaded not guilty in court. His attorney, Mark Shelnutt was confident he could save McGuire. After all, Shelnutt contended, Jeff was locked in the back of the patrol car during the shootout.

"If I hadn't tried to steal that tire, none of this would have happened," Jeff said. "I tried to steal the tire and the man came up."

But McGuire said, "I didn't shoot nobody. I didn't have anything to do with what that girl did. I did not shoot that gun."

Lieutenant Farmer showed the court via a chart the spot from where bullets were fired to land in certain areas. The State Attorney's Office summoned Doctor Janet Pillow, a pathologist, who testified as to where three bullets entered Giddens' body. Investigators contended casings from the murder weapon were fired from over the roof of the patrol car.

"Traci Grosvenor, at five-feet, is too short to have done that," Assistant State Attorney Anthony Tatti said.

The jury found McGuire guilty. And after hearing a plea from McGuire's mother and sister on abuse McGuire had suffered as a child, the jury recommended the judge sentence McGuire to life in prison rather than to the electric chair.

On July 25, 1990, at the Hernando County Courthouse, Judge John Booth, of the Fifth Judicial Circuit in the State of Florida, sentenced Jeffrey Raymond McGuire to spend the rest of his life in prison for the consequences of the shootout at the Giddens garage.

No Crying Allowed

During A Murder Trial

I wonder
how can she sit there,
silently holding a white handkerchief

to her mouth,
to her nose.

The woman on the witness stand
holds up a small bottle.
This is his blood.
She is a pathologist. Just more than
a year ago she performed the autopsy
on the man after he was shot
to death.

A young man on trial for murder
claims he is innocent of the crime.
The defendant's mother
hunches on a bench behind him,
her eyes embrace her son.
She worries and weeps.

"I would ask you
not to write anything bad about him,"
she pleaded to reporters during recess.

I hold my pad, my pen:
I must tell the story.
I take notes.

From the doctor's hand, *the dead man
eyes the jury*; he watches
as she points to holes pictured in a photograph:
"Bullets ripped his body here."

And in this courtroom,
the dead man's widow
is not allowed to cry;

such might cause a mistrial–
so says the bailiff.

That tiny white cloth must hold the tears.
The widow clutches the handkerchief,
to her lips,
to her face,
as she watches.
Her man–
His blood is in the bottle.

STORY 6:

He Killed The

Pretty Young Women

Detectives in Hillsborough and Pasco counties spent four years searching for clues and following leads they hoped would point toward the killer of three young women in 1986. Noting the similarities between the three homicide cases, authorities suspected they were dealing with a serial killer. All three women had been abducted; all three had been brutally stabbed and beaten to death; and all three bodies had been dumped in isolated areas.

The killings started with 25-year-old Natalie Blanche Holley. The last time friends had seen her alive was during her working hours at a fast-food restaurant in Tampa where she was employed as a manager. The following day, a passerby spotted her body lying in an orange grove.

Ten months after that January day in 1986, 17-year-old Stephanie Ann Collins stopped by the drug store where she worked part-time to ask her boss if she could work more hours. Stephanie wanted to earn extra money for Christmas. She then headed off to band practice for an upcoming school concert. But she never got there.

One month after Stephanie disappeared, a county road crew found her body partly clothed and covered by a light green hospital sheet. The girl had been left in a ditch off a country road just north of Tampa.

On the same December day when Stephanie's body was found, another young woman was reported missing. Teri Lynn Matthews had left the home of friends in Tampa at about 2 a.m. Detectives believed the 26-year-old stopped at the post office in Land O' Lakes, halfway between her home and Tampa, about 40 minutes later. Postal employees reporting for work on the morning of December 5th found Teri's unlocked car on the parking lot with the lights still on.

Later that day, two men driving to a store near Gowers Corners, a small community about five miles north of the post office where the young woman's car was found, noticed a flock of large birds swarming. Taking a closer look, the men saw buzzards were flocking over a human body. The carcass was partly wrapped in a light green hospital sheet. This was Teri Matthews.

With sentiment deep in the Tampa Bay area, local residents and business people offered rewards for information leading to the capture and conviction of the monster responsible for the slayings.

Michael P. Malone, fiber analysis for the Federal Bureau of Investigation (FBI), was working on several murder cases when he was brought into the Holly, Collins, and Matthews murder cases. He studied evidence brought to Washington D.C. by investigators Kenneth Hagan and Bob Jarred of the Pasco County Sheriff's Office.

"We were able to link three of the cases through fibers," Malone said, later, noting that the related fibers were from wool.

One type of fiber found on Teri Matthews' body matched fibers found on Natalie Holley; another found on Terri matched fibers found on Stephanie Collins. Both Matthews and Collins had been found partly wrapped in light-green hospital sheets bearing the stamp of St. Joseph Hospital, in Tampa.

Malone noted the sheet that had wrapped Teri Matthews' body contained several impressions that could have been made by either a tire or shoe.

According to Agent John F. Paulsick, the FBI lab also determined the tire track impressions at the site where Teri's body was found had the same physical characteristics and design as a tire used on large trucks.

Despite developments showing similarities in the cases, federal and local officials had found no meaningful leads in identifying the apparent serial killer until on July 12, 1990, when the investigation blew wide open. An anonymous telephone call placed to the Indiana Crime Stoppers, a radio program conducted by the Police Department in Fort Wayne, Indiana, stated that he might know something about the murder of a fast-food restaurant manager in Tampa, Florida.

Fort Wayne officials notified Florida lawmen about the tip. Tampa cops were dispatched immediately to Indiana to see if they could learn more about the apparent suspect in Natalie Holley's death.

The man named by the Crime Stopper tipster was 28-year-old Oscar Ray Bolin Jr., who was then being held in an Ohio prison for kidnapping and raping a 21-year-old woman there in 1987. Bolin, who had been working as a long-distance truck-driver, had raped the woman repeatedly in the sleeping compartment of a tractor-trailer truck, then wrapped her head in a smock, led her to a field, and told her to run for her life. Bolin had then fired a revolver at her while she ran through the field. Witnesses told authorities they had heard what sounded like a gun misfiring at the time the incident occurred, according to a statement by Detective Marlene Long of Ohio's Lake Township Police Department.

Cops learned Bolin had been in the Tampa area when Holley was murdered. In the early 1980s, after getting in some trouble with the law in Greenville, Ohio, Bolin, originally from Portland, Indiana, headed to Tampa and remained there until at least April 1987, when he was arrested for threatening a motorist with a shotgun during an argument over a traffic incident. His next arrest was in Ohio in December 1987, cops learned.

Now that lawmen had a suspect, investigators looked in new directions. While in Indiana, Florida detectives checked into Bolin's background and interviewed his relatives, acquaintances, and friends. Detectives checked out Bolin's addresses in the Tampa area and ran checks on vehicles he had owned.

The vehicle check led investigators to a 1984 Grand Prix that Bolin had owned around the time of the Holley murder. Now the car was in Pennsylvania, and although it had gone through two owners, investigators hauled the car in to be processed for blood traces and other evidence. Surprisingly, detectives found what they were looking for. Although they did not disclose what the evidence was, they told reporters back home in Florida that it tied Bolin directly to the Holley murder.

By the end of July 1990, investigators had collected a mass of evidence that pointed to Oscar Ray Bolin Jr. as the man who had killed the three young women—possibly others.

About two weeks after detectives had returned to Florida from Indiana, they had enough evidence against Bolin to extradite him from the Ohio prison back to Florida on murder charges for the slayings of Holley and Collins. He was later indicted for the murder of Matthews, also.

While being held over for trial in the Hillsborough County jail, in 1990, Bolin and an accomplice started making bizarre plans for his escape. In a surreptitiously recorded conversation between Bolin and a woman who visited him in jail, police learned that Bolin was plotting to kidnap the wives of several detectives and hold them for ransom. Bolin asked his woman jail-visitor to find a map showing the jail and surrounding area so they could pinpoint a place to hide their hostages until the ransom could be collected. When the conspiracy case went to trail, Bolin and his friend were found guilty of plotting a kidnapping.

In another incident, police recorded a conversation between Bolin and the woman, in which Bolin asked her to bring him some poison that he could take to commit suicide if his jailbreak plan didn't work out. "If you can't help me and there's no way to get out, I want you to find something that's very lethal and put it on a stamp and send it to me. Don't leave me here to die."

Meanwhile, detectives located Bolin's ex-wife, Maggie, in Indiana. In the course of their interview, the ex-wife told detectives that she had been in and out of St. Joseph's Hospital several times during 1986. Bolin had visited her there often. St. Joseph's Hospital was where the light-green sheets that had wrapped the bodies of Collins and Matthews had come, detectives recalled.

Detectives learned that on the night of January 24, 1986, Bolin took his then-wife Maggie with him to a fast food restaurant in Tampa. He parked in the area where he could see the goings-on inside. One of Bolin's relatives had worked at the restaurant in the past, so he knew some of the employees.

Bolin explained to Maggie that he was checking the place out to see if it might be an easy target to rob. After a while, Bolin drove Maggie home. He then left alone. Later, he told Maggie what he had done that night.

Bolin had driven back to the parking lot at the fast-food restaurant. Natalie Holley was locking up. He shined the car lights on the pretty girl as she got into her car. Natalie walked over to Bolin's Grand Prix.

"You scared me," she said, after she recognized him as someone she had seen at the restaurant before.

He suddenly pulled a gun and ordered her into his vehicle.

A sheriff's cruiser pulled up at about 2 a.m.

"What's the problem here?" the officer asked.

Bolin told the officer that one of the cars had broken down.

"You okay, ma'am?" the officer asked.

Bolin discreetly pushed the gun against Holly's ribs and mumbled a threat. Holley looked at the officer. "Everything's fine," she said.

When the officer left, Bolin put on a pair of surgical gloves and took out a knife. He began to stab Holley in the chest and throat. She wouldn't die. So he stabbed her again and again. He had a gun but didn't use it because it would make too much noise, he later explained to Maggie.

Finally Natalie Holley was dead.

Bolin returned to the apartment where Maggie was sleeping and woke her. "Get dressed," Bolin said. "I have something to show you."

Maggie looked at her husband. "What's going on?"

He turned the light on and she tried to focus on him. Looking at his feet, she saw blood on his new sneakers.

Bolin had a woman's purse in his hands. He turned it upside down and dumped the contents on the foot of the bed.

"That's not my purse," Maggie said.

"I know it's not yours," Bolin said. "It belongs to the manager at the restaurant."

At Bolin's request, Maggie went with him to dump the body. They left Holly's body in an orange grove. Bolin used a towel to wipe blood from inside the car. He then picked up a tree limb and used it to erase tracks made by the car tires.

Once Bolin and Maggie had left the rural area and were driving on Interstate-275 in Tampa, Bolin threw his bloody shoes and the victim's purse out the car window.

On the night of November 5th, 1986, not quite 10 months after the murder of Holley, Bolin met Maggie at a café in Tampa. As Maggie started to get out of the car, Bolin stopped her.

"There's something you should know before you go inside," he said, casually. "There's a dead body in the trailer. She got in the middle of a spoiled kidnapping. She could identify me. She had to die."

Maggie watched while Bolin carried a wrapped body to his pickup truck. She was dazed; she really didn't know what to do. She didn't know what was going on. This was the second woman her husband claimed he had killed. He had said the first slaying was the result of a robbery; now he was saying he had killed a second woman because she had been in the way of a kidnapping attempt.

Maggie was frightened that she might become involved in the two murders. She felt that she had no choice other than to do as Bolin ordered. She rode with him to a rural area where he threw the woman's body in a ditch alongside a country road.

On December 5ᵗʰ, 1986, a month after Maggie had gone with Bolin to dump that second body, Stephanie Collins's body was found.

Bolin was in Maggie's room where she was hospitalized when the news come over the television. "That's her," Bolin said. "That's the girl in the travel-trailer. That's her."

That same day, authorities were looking for Teri Lynn Matthews. The young woman's car had been discovered at the Land O' Lakes Post Office.

That morning, prior to visiting Maggie at the hospital, Bolin was killing Terri.

Bolin took Teri, whom he had kidnapped from outside the post office, to a mobile home located on the same property where he kept his travel-trailer. Upon reaching the mobile home, he woke up Benny, who had been left in Bolin's care while the youth's parents were away. Bolin told Benny to put on his clothes and come outside. Benny did as he was told. It was too dark to see well, but Benny could hear a strange whining or moaning sound. He didn't know where it was coming from, but his first thought was that someone had run over his dog. As he walked in the darkness toward the noise, he suddenly saw two feet sticking from under a light-colored sheet lying ghost-like on the ground.

Benny stood there speechless as Bolin straddled the sheet-covered body and began spraying it with a water hose. Apparently, Bolin was trying to drown the person inside. Benny watched in horror as Bolin picked up a wooden tool from the nearby wrecker-truck he had driven home from work. Realizing what was about to happen, Benny turned his head, but he couldn't help but hear the thumping of the tool against the sheet. When the thumping finally stopped, so did the whining.

"There was a drug deal in Land O' Lakes," Bolin told the youth. "A woman got shot. I didn't know what to do with her. Help me load her on the wrecker."

Not knowing what else to do, Benny obeyed. He grabbed the woman's feet. He could feel her nylon stockings. When the body was loaded onto the wrecker, Bolin asked Benny if he wanted to help get rid of it. Benny said no.

That morning, while Benny was waiting for the schoolbus, he told a friend what had happened. After school, Benny showed the friend the grass where the person wrapped in the sheet had lain. It was covered with blood.

After Bolin had dumped off the body, he drove the wrecker back to the towing company where he worked in Tampa. Bolin's boss noticed Bolin's unshaved, shabby appearance. He appeared "pumped up" or "high" about something, she later told detectives. Then the television news flashed a bulletin. The announcer told about two bodies being found. The news seemed to excite Bolin, she explained.

"Hey, come see the TV. Come see what's on," Bolin shouted to fellow employees.

A few weeks later, detectives learned, Bolin and Maggie were out riding around and stopped at a wooded area in central Pasco County. Bolin pointed toward the woods and said, "That's where the Matthews girl was found."

After about five years of investigation, detectives and state prosecutors had gathered enough evidence to prove that Oscar Ray Bolin had killed the three women.

Bolin went to trial in July 1991 for the murder of Natalie Holley. "The evidence in this case will show you Oscar Ray Bolin is a methodical, cold-blooded killer," Bill James, a state's attorney, said to the jury.

Taking the stand, Bolin told the jury that he had not killed Natalie Holley. He said a man who looked like him had borrowed his car and had killed the restaurant manager.

But the prosecution called such a man the creation of Bolin's imagination. The jury agreed with the prosecution and convicted Bolin of the first-degree murder of Natalie Holley. Later that month, a different Hillsborough County jury convicted Bolin of the first-degree murder of Stephanie Collins. He was sentenced to death in the electric chair for both murders.

More than a year after the two Hillsborough County convictions, Bolin stood trial in Pasco County for the murder of Teri Lynn Matthews. In October 1992, the details of the violent way Bolin had beaten the young woman to death were unveiled. As it was with Bolin's two Hillsborough County trials, a Pasco County jury convicted Bolin of first-degree murder for the Matthews slaying.

During the trials, defense attorneys claimed Bolin's childhood had been abusive and that he suffered from brain damage.

Bolin had murdered Teri Matthews, the jury determined. Assistant State's Attorney Mike Halkitis asked the jury to recommend that Bolin die in the electric chair for the slaying. He called the killing "shockingly evil and extremely wicked.

"The defendant burns a violent flame," Halkitis said. "A flame that you folks should recommend extinguished."

As with the previous two murder convictions, Bolin was sentenced to die for killing Matthews.

After the final sentencing on October 30th, 1992, Bolin was taken to Death Row at the Florida State Prison in Starke. But the Florida Supreme Court overturned Bolin's convictions and death sentences in the murder cases because Bolin's former wife had testified against him.

In all three retrials, Bolin was found guilty and sentenced to death. During these procedures, Bolin met a woman who worked for the Public Defender's Office. The woman left her well-to-do husband and children for the Death Row inmate. The two were married over the telephone.

In addition to waiting his appointment with death, Bolin was sentenced to serve 25-to-75 years in prison for the rape of the Ohio woman.

Oscar Ray Bolin is suspected of committing multiple murders in 26 states across the country while he worked as a cross-country truckdriver following the murders of the three young women in Florida and the rape of the Ohio woman.

STORY 7:

Murder

To Be Popular

Newspapers had begun to pile up on Douglas Wright's lawn. This made absolutely no sense. The 78-year-old retiree, a widower who lived alone, always kept his yard clean and neatly trimmed. Wright was a tidy person, the kind of man who did everything on schedule, whether it be bringing in the mail or taking out the garbage, golfing daily at the nearby Seven Hills Country Club, or picking up the newspapers. His movements had always followed a definite plan.

It just didn't seem right that newspapers would be accumulating outside his neatly kept home on the curving Spring Hill Drive.

In this west-central part of the state, where retired people are many, the fall weather is somewhat muggy with remnants of summer heat, but the nights are usually cool enough to make running the air-conditioner unnecessary. Most of the homes in the 25-year-old community have attached screened rooms with sliding glass-doors usually left open so the fresh air, filled with songs of birds and chirping of crickets, becomes as much a part of the interior atmosphere as the soft humming of ceiling fans.

On Wednesday, November 15, 1989, Douglas Wright's closest neighbors, Frank and Tina Goodson, were wondering why they had not seen Wright for several days. Had he gone out of town without telling them, without asking them to look after his property or pick up the daily newspapers?

"He never mentioned anything about going away to me," Tina said to Frank. So she suggested they walk over to check on him.

The wind, unusually strong for Florida that day, whipped Tina's dress against her thighs as she and Frank reached Wright's house.

"Wait here, I'll check inside," Tina said, leaving Frank standing in the backyard.

She opened the unlocked door and entered through the screened room. The breeze made the curtains flutter across the open sliding doors. Pushing them aside, she stepped into the dining room.

A sudden wave of nausea went through Tina. She caught hold of a chair and tried to avert her eyes from the horrible sight on the kitchen tile, but the gory image had already impressed itself in her mind.

On the floor Douglas Wright, her neighbor and friend, lay face up and legs crossed in a pool of blood. His pockets were turned inside out, as if someone had rolled him over and emptied them.

Tina caught her breath, turned, and hurried outside. "Frank, you don't want to go in there!" she cried. "Call nine-one-one and let them take care of everything."

The 911 call brought a team of investigators, led by Detective Jim Blade, to the home. First they sealed off the property with yellow crime scene tape. During their careful inspection of the premises, they took note of every little thing that possibly offered a clue that would lead to the killer. Fingerprints were lifted from the screen door where it had obviously been tampered with.

A sheriff's photographer took pictures. Forensic experts arrived to determine what trauma Wright had undergone during the killing and to record the blood-spatter evidence.

Detectives conducted a thorough search of the victim's house. From the condition and position of the body, lying on the floor with the legs crossed in a rolled-over position, detectives theorized that robbery had been the killer's motive. One thing puzzled the cops, however: there was $250 in Wright's wallet and some loose change on a table in the master bedroom. Yet the old man's pockets had been turned inside out.

Checking into the victim's recent movements, investigators learned Wright had missed his usual golf outing on Thursday morning. And with his light-blue Thunderbird gone, everybody in the neighborhood had assumed he had gone on a vacation. Shortly after news of Wright's murder hit the streets and law enforcement officers posted notices announcing they were looking for the victim's 1988 Thunderbird, a lead came in. A woman called the sheriff's office and said she might know something about the automobile that was reported missing.

Detective Blade went to interview the woman. She told him she had heard about some teenagers who had been riding around in a car that fit the description. While Blade was interviewing the woman, her grandson, Patrick Keebler, listened closely to what was being said. The teenager said he had seen the car detectives were looking for.

"Yes, I've seen the car," Patrick said. "I even rode in it. I didn't have any idea it was mixed up with a murder until I read it in the newspaper." Patrick said his friend Max Seyfried had stolen the car.

"Will you show me where this Max that you say stole the car lives?"

Patrick nodded.

Blade obtained permission from Patrick's grandmother to take the teenager with him to look for Max.

Detective Blade drove Patrick around the area, following his directions, but the teenager couldn't find the way to Max's residence. Blade decided to start back toward Patrick's home. Then Patrick nervously asked Blade to stop so he could make a telephone call. Blade watched Patrick at the pay phone. The investigator's feeling grew that something wasn't quite right about the youth's story. He just couldn't buy everything he'd heard so far.

Then out of the clear blue sky, Patrick said, "I did it."

By the time they got back to Patrick's home, Blade knew he would have to take Patrick in for more intense questioning. He advised the boy of his rights and placed him under arrest.

Blade arranged for authorization and took into evidence some of the clothing and shoes that belonged to Patrick. The articles were later sent to the Florida Department of Law Enforcement (FDLE) lab in Tampa. An examination by lab experts established that a pair of trousers in the package contained a patch of blood that matched Douglas Wright's blood type.

While Detective Blade concentrated on collecting evidence against Patrick, other investigators were interviewing neighbors and searching the neighborhood for the knife that had been used to kill Wright. Deputy R. Robinson questioned a woman who lived across the street from Wright's house. She told him she had found a knife in her front yard. She had not touched it. She had wrapped it in a paper towel and placed it in her garage.

Robinson carefully put the knife into a paper bag and hand delivered it to the Florida Department of Law Enforcement (FDLE). Lab tests determined the knife, too, contained blood that matched Wright's blood type.

During the following days, weeks, and months, detectives and prosecutors uncovered damning evidence against Patrick. Meanwhile, as the state continued to collect evidence, defense attorneys were hiring social workers to talk with Patrick and draw forth details about his childhood—disturbing details, which they no doubt hoped to use eventually to gain sympathy from a jury.

Upon making inquires at the high school he attend, investigators learned Patrick had been an almost anonymous face in the crowd. Most of the other students didn't even know his name. He'd wanted to impress the girls but apparently none paid any attention to him.

The investigation showed that Patrick often walked down Spring Hill Drive. Residents on this busy street had nice cars, cars that weighed heavily on his mind. If only he had a nice car to drive around for a while. If only his mother had a new car he could drive, just to take kids for a joyride. Perhaps then schoolmates would like him, he must have thought according to information gathered by cops.

According to what investigators learned, Patrick stopped at the corner one day and looked at a blue 1988 Ford Thunderbird parked in the driveway. If only that were his mother's car . . .

For the following four days, according to the scenario developed by investigators, Patrick's mind stayed on the blue car. He went back to the address again and watched to see who owned it. He saw the driver get into the car with a bag of golf clubs. The man was old.

On Wednesday morning, November 15, before Douglas Wright was murdered, Patrick went to a hangout near Springstead High School where LSD could be bought. Someone had marijuana. A joint was passed around. Everybody got high.

That evening, apparently, Patrick could wait no longer. He had to show his friends he was somebody important. He had to take them all for a ride in that old man's T-bird.

The evidence later established that Patrick waited until it was dark. Then he made his move. The T-bird was there but no keys in it. So Patrick slipped into the house through the screened room and stood behind drapes that covered the sliding glass doors. Mr. Wright was watching television in the living room. Patrick saw a knife lying on the kitchen counter. Keeping out of Wright's sight, he reached for it. Patrick held his breath for fear he would be heard, if not seen. He had to have the car keys but he didn't see them anywhere.

Wright got up from the sofa and started toward the kitchen. Patrick slipped back outside and waited for a while. The screen was fastened when he was ready to reenter the house. He used the knife to slit the vinyl on the screen door and reached through to unhook the latch. He slipped into the house, again walking through the screened-room area and positioning himself behind the curtains.

Now the old man was sitting at the table, a deck of playing cards spread out before him in a game of solitaire.

Patrick emerged from his hiding place and crept up behind the old man. Suddenly he stabbed Wright in the neck. As Wright turned quickly, Patrick stabbed him on the other side of his neck.

Wright fell from his chair face down on the floor. Patrick rolled him over and quickly went through his pockets. He grabbed the keys and a few dollars and ran from the house. He got into the Thunderbird, slid the key into the ignition, backed out of the driveway, and sped away. Later, Patrick found the victim's golf clubs in the trunk of the car. He traded them for some LSD.

Then the joyrides began. Patrick got all the attention he wanted from everyone, even from the girls who never before gave him the time of day. He told his newly found friends the car belonged to his mother and he was breaking it in for her. He picked up Max at the high school. Max shared his acid.

The next day, Patrick and Max drove back and forth from the bowling alley to "The Tree," a teenage hangout near the high school. Then Patrick told Max the car didn't really belong to his mother, that he had stolen it from a Winn Dixie parking lot when a man got out and left the engine running. The fact that the car was stolen didn't matter at all to Max.

For three days, Patrick and his friends were high on pot and acid. They drove to every hangout in Spring Hill, picking up girls and having more fun than anyone could imagine. All of this was possible because Patrick had the Thunderbird.

On the third day of the joyrides, Max started to wonder if the police might be looking for the stolen car. "We better ditch it," Max said, and Patrick agreed. So, with another car following the Thunderbird, the pair drove to an out-of-the-way wooded area to ditch the car. On the way, they went by Douglas Wright's house and saw it was cordoned off with the yellow crime-scene tape. Patrol cars were everywhere.

One of the guys in the Thunderbird said, "Oh, my God. Somebody got murdered!" But Patrick said nothing. He just laughed and drove on, sideswiping several trees and then ramming head-on into a parked truck, thus bringing the car to a jolting stop. Laughing, the teenagers scrambled out of the T-bird and got into the other vehicle.

Patrick spent about nine months in jail before his trial began. During that time he must have been praying that he would not be convicted of first-degree murder, a conviction that could send him to "Old Sparky," as the state's electric chair is often called.

A friend of Patrick's called him while he was in jail awaiting trial. "Hey, man, why did you do it? I mean, you had no reason."

"I don't know, man. I was just tripping out and it happened."

By the time Patrick went to trial in October of 1990, almost a year after the slaying, he was 18 years old. His public defenders, Alan Fanter and Gennie Buckingham, had arranged for Patrick to get his straggly hair cut. Fanter had even gone to the Junior Service League's used-clothing store and bought a couple pair of trousers and shirts for Patrick to wear at his trial.

Assistant State's Attorney Anthony Tatti didn't consider Patrick's age. While preparing his case, Tatti gave every indication that he would ask for the death sentence if Patrick were found guilty of first-degree murder for killing Douglas Wright. "I don't' feel sorry for the little creep!" Tatti declared outside the courtroom prior to the opening of the trial.

Once the 12-member jury was selected, Circuit Judge Jack Springstead read off the charges against Patrick: first-degree murder, burglary of a dwelling with battery, robbery with a deadly weapon, and grand theft.

In his opening statement, Tatti said he would prove the defendant planned the crime for four days before the killing actually occurred. He would prove that Patrick entered Wright's home through an unlocked back door while Wright was watching television. Then, Tatti declared, he would show how Patrick went into Wright's kitchen and took a knife from the cabinet.

Wright, who was hard of hearing, got up from the television and started to the kitchen, Tatti said in outlining the case. Patrick went back out. Patrick reentered the house and stayed behind the curtains at the sliding glass doors until Wright sat down at the table and started playing cards. Then, the prosecutor said, the defendant stabbed the old man in the neck. When Wright started to turn, the defendant stabbed him in the other side of the throat.

The evidence will show, the prosecutor continued, that Patrick Keebler went out and threw the knife across Spring Hill Drive into a neighbor's yard. He then went back into the residence, pushed over Wright's chair, turned his pockets inside out, and took his keys.

The public defenders maintained that the state couldn't prove that Patrick had premeditated the killing. Evidence would show the client was on "acid" at the time the crime was committed and that Max Seyfried, age 16 at the time of the murder, had bragged to friends about "knocking the old man down."

The jury didn't buy Fanter's insinuations that someone other than Patrick had killed Wright and that Patrick was taking the rap to look important to his friends. After hearing all the evidence presented during the trial, the jury found Patrick guilty of the premeditated, first-degree murder of Douglas Wright.

Judge Jack Springstead sentenced Patrick to life in prison, with no chance of parole for 75 years.

From: A Writer's Notebook

Seeing 17-year-old Patrick Keebler in court made me wonder so much about him. What was going on in his head? Why would this young man commit such a senseless crime? Cops alleged Patrick had killed just to drive the old man's car.

Of course, doctors hired by the public defender said the kid did it as a result of an unhappy childhood.

During the trial, I sat in the courtroom, my note pad and pen in my hand and camera handy. I watched Patrick, seated at the defendant's table. He appeared more a kid than a man. I saw Patrick giggle and turn often to make funny faces at a girl sitting on a front courtroom seat (I guess a young relative). I reached to my side for my camera and proceeded to focus on the young defendant.

As I snapped a photograph of Patrick, the people sitting behind me in the courtroom drew my attention. "Will you please give him a chance? Don't crucify him!" a woman said.

Aside from pissing off a Klue Klux Klan leader, called a "granddaddy," in the past, I had experienced no real problems with people I had run into on the crime beat. And actually, I had written about some real crazies. But on the day testimonies began in the Patrick Keebler case, his family members took an immediate dislike to my profession and to me.

I said nothing.

Then the man with her said, "Who is she?"

"She's a reporter!"

It was as if the woman suddenly had lit a fire under him. "There's not going to be any pictures taken in this courtroom," he exclaimed, nearly shouting. "There's not going to be any pictures taken in this damn courtroom! And there's not going to be any stories put in the paper either!"

He had gotten up and was standing right over me—yelling.

"What's your name?" I asked, calmly.

I don't really need to repeat the four-letter words he used first. Then he said, "I mean it. There's not going to be any pictures taken in this courtroom."

About that time the bailiff ushered him out and informed the people who had been sitting with the man that they would have to calm down or they would have to leave, too.

At the next court break, Judge Jack Springstead called the reporters and photographers there covering the trial to his office: WWJB Radio, the *St. Petersburg Times, Tampa Tribune,* and our *Daily Sun-Journal.* He said he had heard of a problem with one of the reporters and members of the defendant's family. "Nobody," he said, "nobody runs my court except me." He made it clear we could take all the photographs we wanted.

Some of Patrick's family members stared at me for several hours after that incident.

As the trial ended and I wrote my stories, I thought about the old man at home minding his own business, and the 17-year-old showing up out of nowhere and killing him. And it was just to drive his car. I also though about how Patrick had screwed up his own life—seventy-five years in prison is a long time.

But then, you never know what might happen on down the road. Murderers often are set free. Is that a scary thought?

STORY 8:

A Gunman's Intent

She's As Good As Dead

Who's who in the plot to kill Joann Sanders

John Barrett's Chevrolet Blazer slowed as he neared the only traffic signal in Floral City. Then as the light turned green, he gripped the steering wheel and accelerated. If anybody had ever screwed up, he had done that today. He had screwed up on a job he was hired to do. His bosses at the car lot had promised him money to kill Joann Sanders.

This August 3 day in 1990 should never have come.

He was watching television, it seemed, as his actions played back in his mind's eye.

The show began the previous year, when he stopped to look at a car at the International Auto Sales in Melrose. He soon made the car lot his hangout and landed a job as the shop's part-time mechanic.

Loose talk between John and the business owners, Dorsey Sanders III and Scott Burnside, ended with John deciding to be their hit man. The plan was that he kill Dorsey's mother to prevent her getting a large divorce settlement from Dorsey's father, Doc Sanders.

John was 24-years-old, stout, with a head of thick sandy-colored hair hanging over his tanned face. He usually wore short-sleeved shirts, thus allowing folks to see the Mighty Mouse tattoo on his right upper arm.

John liked mechanic work and the extra money gave him more to spend on Paula and their five kids.

Paula, too, spent a lot of time at the dealership. It was a pretty good place to meet new friends. She and Scott's teenage wife, Tonya, soon became chummy.

Hanging out at the car lot was convenient for the Barretts. Their trailer was just around a long swerving curve about a half-mile away. They could drink beer and then drive the short distance home without too much worry of getting ticketed for driving under the influence.

At the time, Paula was employed as a clerk at the Suwannee Swifty convenience store in Melrose. John called her there often about little things, but the telephone call in the summer of 1990 was to tell her of the murder-for-hire offer. "That sounds like drunk talk," she had said.

After that day, the plan to kill Joann was the main topic of conversation among folks hanging out at the car lot and with the shed gang at Doc Sander's 350-acre Big Ben Ranch. If John didn't grab this opportunity someone else would, they all joked. Joann Sanders was a good as dead.

The movie played over and over in John's head as he got closer to Melrose. If the story had ended as planned; if the players had been true to script; if he had acted out his part—if only he had not screwed up—he and Paula would be rich tomorrow.

Conspiracy

The plan to kill Joann Sanders took shape so easily, like a hurricane building speed in the Gulf of Mexico, with John taking a plunge right into the eye. He was the focus of the deal, the important one. He was selected to pull the murder off. With Paula's support, he could do it.

John and the guys talked about the murder plan often, whether selling at the car lot, fixing vehicles at the ranch shed, or drinking beer and socializing under the oaks. They'd joke about how much money there was on Joann's head. After all, $20,000 was nothing to sneeze at. They were all smart enough to know that. Different ones would say things like: "You know, people talk about having that kind of money, but to really have it . . . When you're talking twenty-thousand dollars, you're talking big bucks."

The conspiracy to kill Joann was developing more everyday. The plot was thickening like a thriller movie. Parts were awarded without tryouts. It was like the writing, producing and directing just happened, with no slaving over the script. No one seemed at all concerned that a real live woman would be executed, or that the story was fact instead of fiction. No one seemed to care that Joann was targeted to die. In fact, her death would be the climax.

John, Paula, Scott, and Dorsey became tighter as the plot deepened. Paula quit her job at the Suwanne Swifty and went to work at the car lot. She was only there a week when Scott sent her to the neighboring community of Keystone Heights to purchase a 9-millimeter pistol and a box of ammunition.

Paula laughed, making light of the assignment. "I don't know how to buy a gun. What if I get the wrong thing?"

"You won't."

When Scott talked the ends of his reddish mustache hugged the corners of his mouth and his eyes twinkled. He was cute. All the women thought so. And he was smart. Scott was a leader; they all knew that.

Paula drove her Firebird to Keystone Heights, parked, and went into the Gun and Pawnshop as Scott had instructed. A big-framed woman with a blond ponytail was behind the counter. Paula walked toward her. "I want to buy a nine-millimeter pistol," she said.

"You want it for protection?"

"Oh, it's not for me. It's for my husband's birthday."

The woman unlocked the glass showcase where three such guns were kept and removed one. The gun she placed on the counter was a 9-millimeter semi-automatic. "I think this is what you want."

"I need a box of ammunition, too. If this ain't the right kind of gun, can my husband bring it back?"

"Sure. As long as he returns it within the next few days."

Paula wrote out a check for $162 to cover the price of the gun and ammunition. Buying the gun had been easy.

But the revolver Paula bought didn't suit John Barrett. Later that day he exchanged it for a 19-inch, black weapon with a 15-round magazine. The barrel had grooves so a flash adapter could be added. He handed the clerk the cash difference, showed his Florida driver's license, and filled in the necessary form that would be turned over to the Federal Government.

In late June, the shed group gathered. They laughed and joked while they drank beer and talked about killing Joann Sanders. Paula had left her kids in her car behind the shed, so they were no trouble.

The shed was hot but there was work to be done this day. John, Scott, and Dorsey fooled around with the new gun. They packed steel wool into a piece of pipe with holes in it, their way of constructing a silencer.

Dorsey took the gun. He screwed on the self-manufactured silencer and held the pistol in front of him, pointed toward an oak tree, and pulled the trigger. There was a phuff-ff of a noise, like a BB-gun might make. Ah, it worked well!

John took the gun from Dorsey and fired twice: bang! bang! The silencer had screwed up. Sonovabitch!

"What's the matter, John, can't you make it work," somebody joked. They laughed and swigged their beer.

Joann, Jerry and a new place to live

Joanne Sanders and Jerry Lee Clark socialized often, drinking at local clubs all along the central gulf coast, going to friends' houses and entertaining some themselves. They were good-looking, Joann being short with dark brown eyes and platinum hair, and Jerry Lee the ruggedly handsome cowboy-type.

In their early 50s, the couple had been together for about four years. They lived part time in a trailer near the Weeki Wachee River, and part time in a little house they were remodeling just south of Floral City. The house was small, but once it was remodeled it would be a right nice place to live. Roger Wilson, their long-time friend, had agreed to help with the refurbishing. Roger was a good carpenter and a heck of a lot of fun to have around. Besides, he was trustworthy and worked for $50 a week, a place to sleep, and all the beer he wanted.

As days past, being at the Floral City house became a fun thing for Joann, Jerry Lee, and Roger. They started hanging out at Mac's Place, a pub across the narrow highway

Equipped, ready and able to kill the curious woman

That summer, John Barrett made several trips to the little house. This was one way to work out the kinks in his plan to kill Joann Sanders. And Paula's brother-in-law, John Withers, it appeared, was John Barrett's right hand man.

In July, John Barrett and John Withers made two trips, only a week apart. The first was just for the ride, with nothing coming of it. The second was different.

At dusk, John Barrett and John Withers headed toward the swampland. John Barrett was driving a white and maroon Mercury Cougar that he had borrowed from Dorsey Sanders. Withers sat on the passenger side. A short distance from Melrose, they noticed a police car following them had lights flashing. Barrett pulled over.

"You know you got a tail light out?" the police officer asked, and wrote out a warning ticket. "Better get it fixed. It's dangerous. If anybody runs into you, your insurance may not be any good."

They drove on to Ocala, got lost, and then meandered their way out of town. Soon they were on Highway 41 heading south. Though John Withers was tired from working all day, he found the ride fun. The two talked, drank beer, and laughed about lots of stuff, even about the murder plan.

Often, John Barrett would look over at John Withers and make jokes. Withers would laugh, too, and glance at John. John Barrett explained that after he killed Joann they could take anything from the house they wanted. "I'm told she wears good jewelry," he noted.

"Damn it! Those cars aren't supposed to be there," John Barrett declared, as the little house came into view. He drove by, and then made a U-turn.

The two men got out of the car and walked across the grassy lawn. At the front door, John Barrett pulled his hat down so it hugged his forehead tightly and shaded his eyes. He glared from under the brim. Jerry Lee Clark opened the door. Joann Sanders was sleeping on the couch.

"I've got some car trouble down the road," John Barrett lied. "Can I get some water off you?"

Jerry Lee gave John Barrett a couple water jugs and walked with him and John Withers to the water faucet, chatting while John filled the jugs. "If that's not enough, come on back for more," he said.

"He must be the old lady's boyfriend," John Barrett said, opening the car hood and pouring the water so it spilled on the ground underneath the engine, yet making it appear he was filling the radiator.

Then he slipped into the driver's seat and reached underneath. He pulled out a derringer and the 9-millimeter assault revolver. "Look, the men are outside now. She's in the house. We should do it now," John Barrett said.

It was then that John Withers realized the game was over for him. He couldn't be a party to murder.

"You're crazy," he said, abruptly. "I can't do it. I can't do murder."

"Look here you chicken-shit. It's all set. You'll get six thousand dollars for your part. All you got to do is help me. I'll do the killing. All you got to do is drive the car."

"I can't do it," Withers said again. "I just can't. I won't be a part of murder."

During the drive home, Barrett cursed because Withers had not gone along with the murder plan while they had the opportunity. During the next few days, if Barrett's tongue had been a whip, Withers would have been cut to shreds. He was a looser, an intruder among the people at the car lot, those he had considered his friends.

The next time John Barrett went to Floral City alone. Jerry Lee and Joann were standing in the doorway when they saw a car drive up out front.

"Who's he?" Joann asked.

"I don't know," Jerry Lee answered.

The man got out with a six-pack of Bud Dry beer. "I was just in the neighborhood. Wanted you to know how much I appreciated the water," he said, as he walked toward the house.

"What's he talking about?" Joann asked.

"Oh, I remember who he is," Jerry Lee said. "He came a few days ago. He had car trouble."

John pulled out a Bud Dry and offered it to Jerry Lee as he neared the front steps.

"No, thanks. I've go my own beer," Jerry Lee said, lifting his hand to show his can of Bud Light.

John popped open a Bud Dry and took a long swig. He hung around, just talking and drinking, for about half an hour.

"Hey, look buddy, I have something I've got to get done," Jerry Lee said, finally. John left, but soon returned.

"I just wanted to know if you found my keys," he said.

"No. Sure haven't." Jerry Lee answered. They began to look around. "Sure you lost them here?"

"Who's out there?" Roger Wilson asked, peeking from the front door.

"He's the guy y'all gave water to the other day," Joann said. She set down at the table and started shuffling through a stack of bills, receipts, and other papers.

A few days later, John prepared to again make the 100-mile trip to Floral City. He was damn tired of all the running back and forth. This time would be the last—he must do the woman in. He slipped into a pair of black docker pants, a sleeveless denim shirt, and tennis shoes. He packed up his pistol and his big knife.

He got into the 1977 white-and-green Chevrolet Blazer, a vehicle that would be his as part of his pay-off after Joann was dead. He was sitting on top of the world with so much wealth awaiting him.

Reaching Floral City, John stopped at the town's traffic light then wheeled quickly into the Shell station. He pulled his hat down, Billy-Jack style, and went inside. He picked up a 12-pack of Bud Dry beer and slapped money onto the counter. The store smelled good, like food. He was suddenly hungry. He took his beer and walked back to the deli.

"This chicken costs too much," he said, his voice loud, drawing the attention of a couple shoppers.

The clerk gave him a dirty look.

That same day, Paula and Tonya went to a health club near Gainesville, about 20 miles west. John was still gone when Paula returned to her trailer. She flicked on the television.

Murder while she danced was none of her business

Tonya thought about it all day—what she had heard that morning at the Barretts' trailer—what John and Paula had talked about. Even while she worked out, their voices jumped about inside her brain as if her head were an exercise floor.

"You need to go down there and do it," Paula had said.

This was not the first time Tonya had heard John Barrett talk about killing Joann. Tonya had heard him discuss the matter several times with Scott. "She is greedy," they had said. They thought it terrible the court had ordered Doc Sanders to pay Joann $200,000. He was even supposed to give her deeds to several properties, including his animal hospital in Gainesville, they had said.

But now it appeared John would really kill Joann. After all, he had taken off to her house with that big gun. None of it was her business, though. She wouldn't even have known that the day for the murder had come if she had not gone to the Barretts' trailer to ask Paula to go with her to the health club. She liked to workout. But with all the working-out that day, she couldn't erase what she had heard and the fact somebody might be dying while she danced.

The shabby stranger comes calling

Joann Sanders arose from bed early on Friday morning, August 3. She, Jerry Lee, and Roger had loads of things to do. Before leaving for their trailer, Jerry Lee planned to get a couple coats of varnish down on the hardwood floors so it could settle over the weekend.

Joann drove to Brooksville for paint. On her way home, she stopped at her parents' place and dropped off biscuits she had purchased in town. Her mother was sick and unable to cook. After visiting for a couple or so minutes, Joann got in her El Dorado Cadillac and drove the half-a-mile home. She whirled from the highway and stopped near the house. Jerry Lee met her outside, opened the car door, and reached for the paint cans.

Inside the house, she was startled by that same shabby stranger who had been there a few days before, the one who had brought the Bud Dry beer that neither Jerry Lee nor Roger would drink, the one who had claimed to have car trouble. The man gazed at her from under a hat that partly covered his eyes. He grinned, and Joann couldn't help noticing his rotten front teeth. She wondered where was his car. It wasn't parked out front.

"What brings you back this way?" she asked, finally.

He hesitated. In a moment he chuckled and said, "I'm seeing this nasty old girl down the road."

Joann could not help but speculate as to who might have sent this man. Strangers suddenly hanging around for no reason raised suspicions in her mind. She had suspected someone was spying on

her in the past. At that time, she had told Doc Sanders that she
would run over the "sonovabitch" if he didn't call him off. Joann
tried not to glare as she studied the man's face.

She listened as John told stories about himself. He was an
"army brat," and he liked tae kwon do. While they talked, John
would stop in the middle of a sentence, apparently to think, before
he spoke or answered questions.

He made himself more at home every minute. He tried to fit
in with Jerry Lee and Roger, making conversation while they marked
and cut boards. As Roger pulled the long tape measure along the
wall, John grabbed hold of the end to help.

Occasionally, the men would sit and drink a beer. Joann
thought John was almost like a child, walking back and forth behind
Jerry Lee and Roger until he found something he could do, like he
was trying to please them.

The telephone rang often, taking Joann's thoughts from the
stranger to her sick mother. While she talked on the telephone,
she watched him move about. For a moment her eyes stared absently
at a huge knife tucked in his shirt. Also, she noticed a bundle
inside his shirt that kept sliding out of place. John would turn
often, like he was sneaking to adjust the knife and the bundle.

The telephone's ring again broke Joann's concentration. She
picked up the receiver. "Mama's worse," her dad said.

"I'll be right there, Daddy." Joann turned to Jerry Lee. "I'm
going to check on Mama. I'll be back soon as I can."

"Don't worry about anything here. If I can get the truck running,
I'll take a load of trash to the dump. I want to get these floors sanded
and varnished. You go on. Let me know how your mama is."

Joann hurried from the house. Even though her thoughts
focused on her mother, curiosity about the stranger nagged at her
mind. She started her Cadillac and slowly pulled from the yard. A
green-and-white Chevrolet Blazer, parked northward-bound
alongside the highway close to the trees, seemed to beam at her.
Obviously, the stranger had parked there so she wouldn't see the
kind of vehicle he drove.

Joann whipped across the highway and pulled in behind the Blazer. Looking quickly for something to write on, she grabbed a pizza parlor flier from the dashboard and dug into her purse for a pen. She pulled closer to the Blazer, but the rusted license plate was bent over so she couldn't read it clearly. She got out of her car, twisted the tag back, and quickly printed the numbers.

This Blazer being parked here was confusing, but right now she had to think about her mother. Back in the car, she hastily shifted to reverse and pressed the gas pedal. The car hesitated, and then rolled into a ditch. No problem, the Cadillac was a front-wheel drive. But as she started to press on the gas pedal, a voice inside her head said, "NO!" She looked again at the Blazer, her eyes moving straight to a temporary tag in the window. She quickly wrote that number alongside the other, and on the corner of the flier, she wrote the name, "John." Tomorrow, or whenever she got around to it, she would find a way to have the name and tags checked to find out if John had indeed been sent to spy on her.

Joann pulled from the Blazer, making a U-turn in the highway, and drove the short distance south to her parents' home. Once inside, her fears were confirmed. Her mother needed medical attention right away. She dialed 911 for help.

She followed the ambulance as it sped from her parents' home north toward Inverness. As she reached her house, she wheeled into the driveway to tell the men what was happening. She noticed that Jerry Lee's truck was gone. He must have gone to the dump. She ran to the front door. "Roger," she yelled. "Tell Jerry Lee I'm taking mama to the hospital."

Somebody, she thought maybe it was Roger, yelled something back to her that sounded like "woo-wait." But Joann had already fled down the front steps and was hurrying toward her car. She stopped, turned, and started back inside. Then somebody said, "That's all right. Catch ya later." She didn't think about what was said. She couldn't wonder about anything right then. She slid into the Cadillac and stepped down on the gas pedal until she caught up with the screaming ambulance.

Joann and her sister stayed at the Citrus County Memorial Hospital in Inverness until about 9 o'clock that evening, then stopped at a restaurant. While she waited for her food order, she found a telephone and dialed her home phone. There was no answer.

They must be over at Mac's Place, she thought. After finishing her snack, she got into her Cadillac. The night was so still. She listened to the soft hum of the car engine and let her thoughts wander as she drove south on Highway 41. In a couple of weeks the remodeling job on the house would be finished. She and Jerry Lee might even lease Mac's Place and run it themselves. They could still go to the river and camp and fish whenever they wanted to. The future looked good for the two of them.

He was the star of the show playing in his head

John Barrett stood in the woods and watched Jerry Lee pull away in an old truck loaded with rubbish. He adjusted the heavy knife close to his side, and then let his hand rest on the revolved bulging from his denim shirt. Jerry Lee was out of the way. Now he would wait for Joann to return. If Joann would hurry on back, he could kill her and be long gone by the time her boyfriend returned from the landfill. John clutched the bag of Bud Dry as he crossed the sunny pasture. Once inside the house, he hid behind the couch.

There was a sudden noise out front. Must be her. She was back. The door opened. Someone entered. But those were not the footsteps of the woman. He peered over the sofa. It was the bearded man, Roger.

John listened to Roger's shuffling about in the kitchen. He was mixing paint. Then Roger moved to the breakfast nook.

Squatting quietly behind the couch, John brought the gun from underneath his shirt and screwed the homemade silencer onto the barrel, adding about a foot to the length.

John got up quietly. Roger was on his knees then. John watched him dip a roller into a pan of paint, bring it out carefully, then push it up the wall. John pointed the pistol at the back of Roger's head.

There was no loud bang, just a mollifying "puff-ff".
He pulled the trigger again, but the gun wouldn't fire. The
silencer had screwed it up. But Roger was dead. John watched his
head slide down the wall leaving a valley in the fresh paint until
his face smashed against the floor.

John made himself at home. He pulled a Bud Dry from the
plastic grocery bag and popped open the spout. He drank it down,
then popped open another.

John walked about. Minutes passed. An hour. Two hours. He
rubbed his head. It had been more than two hours since he had
killed Roger and Joann still had not returned.

A truck pulling up out front drew John from reverie. He moved
to the window and peered out. Jerry Lee was back. Someone was
with him. Jerry Lee was carrying a sander.

John held the gun toward the door and as the two men entered,
he pointed it at them and picked up a drywall hammer; it was
blunt on one side and a hatchet on the other.

"What is this?" Jerry Lee demanded.

"Just both of you put your hands up." He waved the gun
toward the bedroom. "Get in there."

"What do you want? Take anything you want," Jerry Lee said.
"Take it and leave. You don't need to do anything to us." His voice
faded as his gaze dropped to his friend Roger, who lay face down
on the floor with the paint roller poking from under his chest.
"My God, man. What's happened here?"

"Shut up! Just get on in there!" John ordered, again waving the
gun toward the bedroom.

"What do you want?" Jerry Lee asked. He opened his wallet
and held out credit cards. "Take it all."

John waved the gun again. "Just do what I told you!"

Once in the bedroom John made the men lie on the floor.
Then he started beating them on their heads with the hammer
and the gun while bits of steel wool flew from the silencer and
floated about the room.

John didn't know how many times he hit the men before he dared stop. They were not likely to wake up, but just to make sure, he took the knife from his waistband and sliced their throats.

He stumbled into the living room, dropped onto an easy chair, and popped open another Bud Dry. Somebody was coming toward the front door. Joann–it was about time she got back. She had been gone for hours.

But it wasn't Joann. A man called, "whoo," and entered the house without knocking. "Where you at? I saw the truck pull in and I . . ."

"Come on in," John said, pointing the gun at a hunchback man. "Get in the bedroom."

"What's the deal?"

John recognized the man. He had seen him wandering about the yard next door.

"There's no deal. Just go," John ordered. He held the inoperable weapon on this man just as he had held it on the other two. When the man got to the doorway where the stairs led down into the breakfast nook, his gaze fell on Roger's body. Then he turned and swung at John.

John drew the drywall hammer back, brought it down to crash on the hunchback's scull–once, twice, again and again–until the man couldn't fight anymore. Then John grabbed his knife, held the man's head so he couldn't move, and slit his throat.

John popped open another Bud Dry and sat down on the couch. He was tired. Everything happening here was like a television show and his head was the stage. There was one more act to come, the climax act when he finally got his hands on Joann Sanders.

Everybody in the house is dead

Joann pulled close to the white stucco house and parked. Shutting off the headlights, she saw the truck and van were both there. She walked to the front door, her mind at ease knowing that her sick mother was being cared for. She tried to turn the doorknob.

It was locked. That was odd. They never locked up unless they were going to the river. Obviously, the men were not there.

She fumbled through her purse, found her key, and worked it around in the lock until the door opened.

The house was dark except for a dim light streaming from the bathroom. Nobody ever left the bathroom light on because the window screen was torn and the light drew bugs. Walking carefully through the dark living room, Joann noticed a pillow lying on the floor. She picked it up, tossed it toward a table, and started on toward the bedroom to turn on a lamp.

Suddenly she stopped. Roger was lying on the floor in the breakfast nook. What an unusual position, she thought. He must have gotten drunk early in the evening. She wouldn't mess with him. Jerry Lee would have to see to it Roger got on the couch.

She moved on toward the bedroom. Someone on the floor in front of the television startled her. Why on earth would anybody be lying there? She reached for the lamp, but stumbled. Looking down, she realized she had tripped over Jerry Lee's feet. What had happened here? She flicked on the lamp then bent to wake Jerry Lee.

Her breath stopped in her chest. Jerry Lee's head was there in a pool of blood. She reached for his hand, and then quickly dropped it. Jerry Lee was dead.

At 10:45 p.m., Edward Stucky, a communication officer, was taking 911 calls at the Citrus County Sheriff's Office when Joann called to report there were dead men in her home. Her voice choked with confusion and fear. "I just got home and I think there are three dead men in the house. They're all over the place. There's blood everywhere."

Stucky tried to calm her, telling her to relax and asked if she knew the names of the men she thought were dead.

One was Jerry Lee Clark. One was their friend Roger Wilson. She didn't know who the third man was, she said.

Joann gave directions to her house, telling Stucky it was directly across Highway 41 from Mac's Place, and that her Cadillac El Dorado was parked on the front lawn.

Check the condition of the men, Stucky coached, "but come right back to me."

"I think they're all dead. I don't know who the third one is."

"I know you're all shook-up, but I've got to have your help, okay. There's someone on the way. Are they all white males?"

Joann's breathing was heavy, making it difficult to speak.

"Does it look like there was a struggle? Fighting among themselves?"

"No. Not really. They're all bellied down. There are three of them."

"A deputy should be there any minute, ma'am. I want you to go out and talk to him."

Cops swarm the little stucco house in Floral City

Within a few minutes after Joann had dialed 911, deputies and the SWAT team covered the countryside south of Floral City. Detectives Marvin Padgett and Jerry Thompson, along with Deputy Don Lestinsky, were the first officers to enter the white stucco house where the dead men lay. The sight was the worst of nightmares. Three male bodies lay slaughtered on the floor. Two were face down in the main area of the master bedroom. Blood soaked into the carpet around their heads. Another was on his knees, face to the floor, in the breakfast nook. Credit cards lay spread over the floor, and blood spatters covered objects and walls everywhere.

Joann was hysterical, yet coherent, when Detective Padgett spoke with her outside the house shortly before midnight. "I know it is hard for you, but I need to ask you a couple questions." Padgett said, his voice soft.

"I left the house," Joann choked out the words, "to take mama to the hospital. When I came back...," she couldn't finish the sentence.

"Who was here when you left?"

"Jerry Lee. Roger. Another man. A stranger." She hesitated, trying to reason in her mind. "I think Doctor Sanders sent him to spy on me. His name, I think it was...," she paused, "His name was John. I think Doctor Sanders sent him. I wrote down his tag number."

"You wrote it down, where? Do you have it?"

"In my car. On the seat in my car."

"The Cadillac?"

"Yes."

"Where are the keys?"

"In the house, I guess. I don't know. I dropped them in the house some place."

While Padgett tried to calm Joann, Deputy Lestinsky went into the house to look for the Cadillac keys. Once inside, he stopped suddenly. What was it, a noise, a movement coming from the back bedroom—or was it his imagination? Lestinsky pulled his gun in case the killer was still in the house. He moved vigilantly to the bedroom where two bodies lay. A sudden noise led him to the large walk-in closet; there, a pair of legs jerked once. My God, another body!

Catching his breath, the deputy made his way to the kitchen. He picked up Joann's keys from the dining room table. "There's another one in the closet," he said, as he handed the keys to the detective.

Padgett walked Joann to the Cadillac and opened the door. Joann nervously reached inside for the pizza flier and handed it to the detective. He immediately got on his patrol car radio and read off the hand printed Florida license plate number BM 930 M and the temporary tag number D632939 which was written on the corner of the flier.

An investigator escorted Joann to the police station where she was interviewed further. Afterwards, she was taken to a motel in Inverness. She was to remain under protective custody for the time being.

Detectives remained on the scene through the night searching for evidence or clues that would aid them in finding the person, or persons, responsible for the horrifying murders of four. They had never witnessed such a brutal murder, such a hatchet job—ever, they noted.

Detective Thompson led three walks through the house that night. During the first complete walk-through, officers, including Deputy Bud Buddenbohm and the sheriff's K-9, Bo, were on the defensive, concentrating on what was around them. Was the killer lurking somewhere and watching their every move?

Citrus County Sheriff Charles Dean was quick in arriving at the scene. He joined deputies doing their second, more observant, walk-through. "Look at all these bloody shoe tracks," he commented. Officers spread out sheets of brown paper to protect the shoe impressions and any other matter that might have been left by the killer.

The third walk through was at a calmer pace, with Tim Whitfield, from the Hernando County Sheriff's Office, joining the team. In addition, Deputy Fred Johnson was called to video the surroundings.

Detective Thompson, flashlight in hand, walked down the dark highway about one hundred yards to where Joann had seen the Blazer parked. Reaching the area, he saw tire impressions left by a vehicle. Behind the first marks were tracks where someone had made a U-turn on the grass. Joann's Cadillac had apparently made the U-turn when she pulled in behind the Blazer to obtain the license plate number. Thompson returned to the house to share his findings with other investigators.

Deputy Buddenbohm and Bo searched outside for any trail that might lead to the killer. During the five-and-a-half-years Buddenbohm had been with the sheriff's office, he had worked the last four with Bo, a German shepherd police dog trained to track human smells by individual scents, including sweat, their deodorant and cologne, and other sources left in their paths. Upon arrival at Joann Sander's house, Bo had gone inside and sniffed everything, including the dead bodies. Also, the K-9 sniffed the house exterior, sheds, and surrounding grounds.

At about 3:30 a.m., footprints pointing toward the woods were sighted to the southeast of the house. Bo was aimed in that direction. The K-9 quickly picked up the scuff and followed it across the back yard and through a hole in a fence. Bo led Buddenbohm along the trail as it angled in a southwest direction toward the highway. There, the tracks came to an abrupt stop.

As dawn came, cops swarmed the 10 miles of rural area between Floral City and the Citrus-Hernando County line like vultures after road kill. "There's a madman running loose somewhere out there. No citizen or police officer is safe until he's caught," the sheriff's office announced.

Investigators learned that the license on the Blazer was for a boat trailer registered to John Barrett. The Blazer was registered to the International Auto Sales in Melrose, of which Joann's son Dorsey was half owner.

Padgett went to the motel to speak with Joann. Did she know her son owned the International Auto Sales?

Joann had a business card with Dorsey's name on it. But, she explained to the investigator, she was not really familiar with her son's goings-on in Melrose. She had not lived at the Big Ben Ranch since 1984. She thought that Doc Sanders owned a telephone beeper business that ran off an antenna at the Big Ben Ranch and the family belonged to a radio operators club. As for the International Auto Sales–Joann thought the car lot her son ran was located at the ranch.

Heading home

John Barrett's foot pressed the gas pedal. He needed to fly. Already he was speeding. He glanced in the rearview mirror. What he saw was like a tiny television screen. He didn't want to see the show anymore because he knew the whole story. He had seen it already. It was like he had watched the show on television as he committed the murders. It had seemed as if he were watching "Cops," or "Billy Jack."

He watched as the show played on. He was the star. He could still see the look on the last man's face when he saw what he had walked into.

While helicopter cops search, a killer runs

Paula waited anxiously. Finally, about 10 p.m., John stumbled through their mobile home doorway. He appeared exhausted. Paula peered at him, her tanned fingers raking through her long, now bleached, hair. "What happened?"

"Leave me alone! The deal went wrong. I got to get hold of Scott."

John got in the Blazer and backed from the yard. Scott Burnside's trailer was just a short distance north, at the paved end of Baden Powell Road.

The raping on Scott's trailer door was loud. When Tonya opened it, John glared at her. He had a piece of pipe in his hand.

"I need to talk to Scott." John held onto the pipe and walked past her. Then he and Scott quickly disappeared into the bedroom.

Something was wrong. Tonya knew it. She waited on the couch and stared at the television. She heard voices in the bedroom. She could tell by Scott's tone he was upset. She got up and quietly walked to the bedroom door.

"You fucked up," Scott yelled. "You fucked up. Let me think. We got to get rid of all that shit."

Tears streamed from Tonya's eyes. When the two men came from the bedroom, she asked, "What's going to happen now?"

"Nothing's going to happen now. I'll take care of everything. Everything will be all right." Scott put his arms around her shoulders. "Don't cry." He hesitated. "I wish you hadn't been here to hear this. You get out for a while. Go to a friend's house. I'll meet you later at the Chicken Factory" (a restaurant in Hawthorne, the next town over).

As Tonya left the trailer, it was like a magnet drew her attention to the window of John's Blazer. Then she gasped. If only this were a dream. She closed her eyes. But when she opened them, the scene was the same. She glared through the Blazer window in horror at a Rambo-type hat, gloves, a gun, and an ax–right there on the passenger seat.

Later, though still distressed, Tonya met Scott at the Chicken Factory. She cried the 10-mile drive to the Barretts' trailer. It was shortly before midnight when they went inside.

Through the night, the men laughed and joked about the whole thing. But Tonya couldn't stop crying as John described how he had blundered the carefully planned job. Four men were dead but Joann Sanders was still alive.

Eddie Murphy's "Harlem Nights" played in the VCR while John's joking about the murders got louder and louder.

Tonya tried to concentrate on "Harlem Nights." She didn't want to hear about the murders. How could they find these bloody details so amusing? How could they laugh when she felt so sick? All the times they had talked about getting rid of Joann now seemed so distant. They had never stopped to think what they were doing? What they were talking about? What might happen? She couldn't hold back any longer. Her tears became sobs. But the men kept laughing; and Paula didn't seem moved. "It isn't funny," Tonya cried, finally. "What's going to happen now? Everything's gone wrong."

The following day, John went to see Paula at the Suwannee Swifty. "They said for me not to worry about anything. They said everything is taken care of," he explained.

"That's a relief," Paula said.

"Just one thing, though. We got to get out of town for a few hours."

At about noon, John, Paula, and the kids went to Crescent Beach, along the Atlantic Ocean. When they returned to Melrose that evening, they stopped at the Jiffy store. As John pumped gas into the Firebird, Dorsey and Scott wheeled up beside him. They both seemed to talk at the same time. "I'm telling you there are helicopters flying all around the ranch. Don't go back home for Christ's sake. They're looking for the Blazer."

The Barretts left Melrose immediately and drove the 30 miles to Gainesville. They rented a room at a motel near Interstate-75.

Then they drove to a Burger King where John used the pay phone to call Scott.

Sunday morning, John met Scott and Dorsey across the street from the Suwannee Swifty store at State Road 20 going into Gainesville. Dorsey sat in the car while John and Scott stood at the back of the Firebird and talked. Scott handed John some money.

"This should get you somewhere. Get a post office box and we'll send you more money later," Scott advised.

Paula pulled away from the Suwannee Swifty. She really didn't know where she was going. She drove to Interlachen, a one-stop-and-go-light town a few miles southeast of Melrose. Then she drove on up to Starke, about 20 miles north of Melrose.

"We ought to get out of the state," Paula said.

"No reason to leave. Scott got rid of the gun. Dumped it from a boat. That stuff will never be found. By now it's at the bottom of the Gulf of Mexico. There's no way the cops can ever get me for this."

"We can't go back home," Paula said.

Paula drove to a shopping center in Starke and stopped at a Wal-Mart. While loading the trunk with new merchandise, one of Paula's friends pulled up beside her. She glanced at all the clothes Paula and John had purchased for the children. "Why are the kids in swim trunks? Why aren't you at work, Paula?"

"An emergency came up," John said. "We're going out-of-town for a few days."

Joann leaves the Big Ben Ranch

Joann Sanders believed she was the one the killer had been after. On past occasions, she believed her ex-husband had hired somebody to spy on her. She and Doc had fought bitterly while married. The last fight, in 1984, had resulted in Joann entering a shelter for battered women. Later, she bought the little stucco house south of Floral City in order to be near her parents. She went out a lot and had many friends.

The sad part of her life after she left Doc, however, was that her relationship with her sons became more and more distant. The boys had remained in their father's custody. They would visit her on Christmas, sometimes, and stay for only two or three hours.

Cops at the Big Ben Ranch, Withers talks

Once authorities learned the person who had committed the quadruple murder had driven a vehicle registered to a car dealership in Putnam County, they turned their focus in that direction. Detective Marvin Padgett quickly got on the telephone and called Captain Clifford E. Miller Jr., chief detective at the Putnam County Sheriff's Office. Padgett informed Putman investigators of the Citrus County case and its connection with the car lot in Melrose.

Soon afterwards, detectives looked from the window of the sheriff's airplane onto the thickly wooded rural countryside as they flew over Melrose and surrounding areas, including the Big Ben Ranch. The main thing investigators hoped to see was the green-and-white Blazer that Joann had described.

Not only did Citrus County officials fly over portions of Putnam County looking for the Blazer, on Sunday they went to the Big Ben Ranch to talk with members of the Sanders family. They talked first with a man in his 80s (father of Doc Sanders) and John Sanders (the youngest son of Doc and Joann).

"Do you know a John, besides yourself, that's connected with your family?" a detective asked.

"Yes sir." The young man started to count on his fingers as he named off several people named John.

Soon Dorsey and Phillip Sanders, along with Scott Burnside, showed up at the ranch. Padgett told the three men of the murders. They didn't show much reaction. It was like they were receiving information that was not of any great consequence or significance.

"Do you know why anyone would go to your mother's house and kill people?" Padgett asked.

"I don't know," Dorsey answered, looking about the room.

"Dorsey, how do you get along with your mother?"

"I don't really like being around her. She's quite a drinker. I don't like her like that."

"Do you know a man called John that's connected with your family?"

"Yes. I know several men named John."

"Do you know a John who drives a Blazer?"

"Yes. I sold a Blazer to John Barrett."

"Is he a customer at your business?"

"He's our part-time mechanic."

"Does he have a tattoo?"

"Yes. I think so."

"Where does he live?"

"On down Baden Powell Road. The road makes a turn to the right around some big liveoaks. The pavement ends there. Just keep going south. There are two trailers down there. John Withers lives in one and John Barrett lives in the other."

Turning his attention to Scott Burnside, Padgett asked, "Did you know about the murders over at Floral City?"

"Yes, I heard about them."

"How did you hear?"

"A guy came in at the car lot and told me about it."

Based on information obtained from the three Sanders brothers and Scott Burnside, investigators believed John Barrett was the target of their hunt. They left the Sanders ranch and drove east down Baden Powell Road. They veered to the south, zipping down the dirt road until they reached the brown doublewide trailer.

Of all the areas being watched, John Barrett's home moved to the top of the list. Investigators obtained a search warrant for the trailer. Once inside, officers got the idea the Barretts had skipped town in a hurry. Food was left on the kitchen cabinets and the air conditioner was still cooling.

Investigators looked for weapons that might have been used in the quadruple murders, but found none. Searching the clothes dryer, officers removed clothing that matched garb Joann Sanders had said the stranger named John had worn the day of the killings. Officers also found "Billy Jack" books, a brief case, a shirt with bloodstains, a bloody towel, and a loaded two-shot Derringer.

While some officers remained at the house, others continued the search by air over the county for the green-and-white Blazer. The air unit probed the grounds around Barrett's trailer, hovering over a pit located at the back portion of the land. Investigators explored the wooded areas around the property, venturing by foot into the thick, jungle-like hammocks. Among the searchers were Citrus County Sheriff Charles Dean and Major Buddy Mortimer, who had tromped into the woods about 400 feet east of the trailer. "We found the Blazer. Over here," they yelled. The vehicle was nearly all hidden by tree limbs and other foliage.

Noting a crazed murderer was still at large, investigators worked quickly. On Monday, they obtained a warrant to search the International Auto Sales. They reviewed sales and employment records. Again, authorities interviewed Dorsey.

"Have you heard or seen anything of John Barrett since the murders?"

"John and Paula were at the Jiffy store Saturday," Dorsey said. Officers though Dorsey was hedging.

"Which Jiffy store?"

"The one on the corner." Dorsey pointed east, toward the store less than a block away.

"Are you sure that's all you know?" an officer asked.

Dorsey nodded.

Meantime, investigators patrolling along Baden Powell Road in the unmarked cop car wheeled onto the driveway at the mobile home next door to the Barrett's trailer. A man appearing close to the description authorities had of John Barrett was getting into a vehicle. The detective's car spun close, blocking it. An officer got out and flashed his badge. The man stood still, trembling; a puzzled look appeared on his thin face.

His name was John Withers, his identification showed.

"Do you know John Barrett?"

"Yes sir."

"Do you know anything about four men being murdered in Floral City?"

"No sir."

The officer looked suspiciously at John Withers. "Are you sure?"

"Yes sir."

"Didn't you go with John Barrett to Floral City?"

Withers told Padgett he had gone with John Barrett to Floral City on an occasion to repossess a car.

But John Withers did not reveal to detectives all he knew and Withers realized that it was only a matter of time until he would be brought into the case. That worried him. He had not killed anybody and he didn't want to get any blame.

Withers asked his mother-in-law what he should do about his knowledge of the murder plot. "Tell the police," she advised. "If you're that worried about it, tell them what you know."

On August 10, Withers made a telephone call to detectives and later that day he met with authorities. This new information was forwarded to officials who had left the state tailing John Barrett.

On August 13 and 14, detectives served a search warrant on the Big Ben Ranch. Investigator George Simpson, who had worked in the ID Section at the Citrus County Sheriff's Office for five years, was ordered to search all the property, out buildings, and vehicles, on the entire ranch.

Investigators combed the ranch, beginning with the main house, and then moving on to the guest cottage, a large pole barn, and the ranch-shack where Dorsey lived on the other side of the road. The pole barn, directly behind the main house, looked like a junkyard with old cars, pieces of cars and all-terrain vehicles strewn around. Inside the building, Simpson observed different types of tools and gadgets including a welding table and galvanized pipe that had been cut at one end with a torch. A piece of this pipe,

Simpson thought, could have been used to build a gun silencer. That would explain the bits of steel wool found in the house in Floral City. On the welding table, Simpson noted a drill with metal shavings around it. In the same area there was a tap-and-dye set, the type tool one would use to carve threads on an object so it could be adapted to another object.

Down the road about a mile away, between the barn and the house, Simpson discovered a parked truck. Inside were scrap pieces of steel wool, like the matter scattered about in the house in Floral City.

Simpson also conducted a search for shell casings that would match the casings found in Joann's house. The area was like a shooting range. Bullet holes had been left in trees and in parts of abandoned cars over the years, but the ground was cleaned of any casings matching the ones fired by the murderer's weapon. In fact, there were no casings on the ground at all. It appeared the area was cleaned after target shooting.

While Detective Simpson searched the grounds, Detective Thompson searched inside the house. Thompson was especially interested in a computer room that contained a lot of radio equipment and a police scanner. With the scanner, Thompson realized, anyone listening would be right up on police calls. The listener would have first-hand information about the destinations of patrol helicopters.

The search for John Barrett moves to Ohio

John, Paula, and their five children arrived at John's parents' home in Middletown, Ohio, on August 6. The following day, John asked his brother to give him a ride to a nearby cornfield. "I'm in deep trouble with some friends in Florida," John said, clutching a green duffel bag. "I've got to hide out for a while. Drop me off down the road a piece."

Upon his return home, John's brother received a telephone call from a Florida investigator. "John Barrett is wanted for murder. We believe he killed four men here," said Sheriff's Sergeant Bruce Lovett.

Later that evening Joe confronted Paula. "What's going on, Paula? I had a call from Florida. The police there say John killed some people. Is that true?"

Paula was trying to get her baby to sleep so she could go shopping for hair dye. She was in a hurry to change her hair from blond to black. She really didn't have time to talk about the murders. "John was hired to make a woman disappear," she explained.

"Did he kill anybody?"

"He said he killed them. They were in the house and he got scared. He said he killed them to get them out of the way. John said there's no way the cops can get anything on him, though. The weapons used were dumped into the Gulf of Mexico."

But cops in Citrus County were warming up the sheriff's plane to head north. Assistant State Attorney Anthony Tatti, the assigned prosecutor for the case, noted more travel arrangements would be necessary. "In order for all the investigators working on this case to fly in the single engine Cessna 210, they would have to hold out their arms and flap like oars," he said, and arranged for some officers to fly to Ohio aboard a commercial jet.

Shortly before 7 p.m., after Florida authorities had arrived in Hamilton, Butler County Sheriff Holtzberger used his cellular phone to call the Barrett home. "Come outside, Paula," he ordered. "We want to speak with you."

Paula appeared at the door, and then detectives went into the house and questioned John Barrett's father. "We feel your son might be here. Mind if we search the house?"

"No, I don't mind. He's not here."

"Where is he, Paula? We know you came here together. Do you want a murder rap hanging on you?"

"He's not here. I dropped him off in Cincinnati. He's taking a bus to Detroit," Paula said.

In searching the house, officers considered that John Barrett might be hiding around any corner and that he was extremely dangerous.

John Barrett's brother led authorities to the cornfield in nearby Warren County, near King's Island Amusement Park, where he believed John was hiding-out. Officers, using police dogs and a military-equipped helicopter, began a manhunt over the countryside. After a six-hour search by Ohio and Indiana law enforcement, a tip from a resident led investigators to a different area near the town of Hamilton.

John Barrett calls on an old 'friend'

A shabby-looking stranger on Kathy's front porch startled her when she got home from work at about 5:30 p.m. on August 8. The man needed to shave and comb his hair. She approached him cautiously. He said his name was John Barrett. He claimed he was an old friend of her husband's and asked if he could wait outside for him. Though apprehensive, Kathy nodded.

Donald got home about an hour later.

"What you doing in Ohio, John? Visiting your kin?" Donald asked.

"Hanging out on vacation. Visiting my parents."

"How you making it? Still with Paula?"

"Everything's good," John paused for a moment. "Sure, I'm with Paula. We've got five kids all together. I've got more than I ever had in my life," John bragged. "I've got property, a trailer, two cars, firearms. My kids wear British Knight shoes."

"Sounds like you're doing good, John."

As they caught up on old times, two of Donald's friends, Tim and Anthony, came over. The guys all laughed and talked loud. They decided to pick up a couple cases of beer and go fishing at the Little Miami River behind the trailer park.

Kathy watched them go, and then she wandered about in the yard picking up litter. A grocery bag lying on the lawn near an aluminum shed caught her eye. How did it get there?

As she lifted the bag, a huge hunting knife fell out. Peeping inside, Kathy found camouflage clothing and food. She wondered if John had been camping out in the woods near her house. Her heart pounded. She didn't want that skuzzy man hanging around. She didn't want him with her husband. She had to do something. She had to tell somebody before the man returned.

Kathy hurried next door to talk to a friend about the bag of camping-type goods and the shabby man. Perhaps she could advise her on what to do.

"Is your mother home?" Kathy asked when her friend's teenage daughter came to the door.

"She's asleep."

Kathy told the girl about the stranger. "I don't want to take this bag back home," she whispered. "I'm afraid for that big knife to be around the house. I'm afraid of that John guy." She looked at the girl in the doorway. "Please, will you make sure your mother gets this stuff? Tell her I'll talk to her about it later."

While Kathy was at home trying to decide if she should check with the local police about the suspicious looking man, her husband and friends were out with him fishing and drinking beer. After downing two cases, they went bar hopping in town. It was getting late by the time they stopped at Hogies. John had a wad of money in his pocket and didn't mind pulling it out when beer was ordered. They got into a game of pool. John backed up to a corner so he was out of sight when some cops came in. The lawmen left, then John and Donald sat at the bar and talked some more. They had a lot of catching up to do.

Suddenly, just right out of the blue, John said, "Well, I just killed four people in Florida."

Donald gazed at John, unsure whether he had heard correctly. "What?" he questioned.

"I got caught up in a whirlwind. They call me the golden-boy down in Florida. I killed four people."

"How'd you kill 'em, John? Did you shoot 'em?"

"No. I beat them to death with a hammer and a pipe."

"Why, John? Why'd you kill 'em?"

"I was contracted to kill one. I did one of them in, then the others came in and I had to kill them, too."

The men kept drinking and talking until the bar closed, then they went back to Donald's house. Donald asked Kathy to take one of his friends home. While she was gone, John sacked out on the couch and Donald went to bed.

Angry cops want John Barrett to 'fess up'

Police lights shined on the surroundings outside Donald's house but neither Donald nor John Barrett knew what was going on. Both men were drunk beyond comprehension. Donald, unaware that John was being hunted by authorities and that cops had been tipped off about a strange person being at his house, was combative as armed police officers swarmed into his bedroom, getting him out of bed and taking him into custody. Was he being arrested for getting drunk? he wondered.

John, who was passed out on Donald's couch, was cuffed and escorted to a patrol car before he could even shake off sleep.

Detective Padgett, who had been on John Barrett's tail all the way from Citrus to Putnam and on to Ohio, went to the patrol car where John was locked inside. He compared the suspect with a photograph, and then checked his arm for tattoos. Sure enough, there was Mighty Mouse.

Once detectives got John behind jail bars, they wanted some facts.

"There's a lawyer in there," an officer said to Barrett. "Want to talk to him?"

"Yes."

Before the attorney went into the interviewing room, authorities filled him in on what the case was all about. Then the lawyer conversed with John. He advised him not to talk. Regardless of what the attorney had advised, Padgett wanted truth out of John. He had come too far and had worked too hard on this case to let it ride. He informed the attorney of such and went back into the interviewing room.

John was restless. The alcohol cluttering his mind added to the mental anguish, making the long hours of questioning seem even longer. He would take the lawyer's advice. He would exercise his rights to remain silent. If only that detective would leave him alone. If only he had the chance to think for himself without the cop's constant badgering. He looked up as the door opened.

"Listen," Padgett said. "We want to talk to you as a witness."

John glared at Padgett. The cop just wanted to talk to him as a witness. Yeah. Sure. He remembered what the cop had read, the card warning, where it said they can and will use everything he says against him. "I'm going to follow the advice my lawyer gave me," John said. "I'm not going to talk to you."

The detectives looked at each other and Padgett picked up a cigarette lighter and flicked the fire toward him. John put a cigarette in his mouth and held it to the flame. The nicotine tasted better with each drag. At least he could have his cigarettes. He would collapse for sure if they took them away. He took another drag, and then blew smoke out slowly.

Padgett kept talking. Didn't the detective hear what he had said, that he didn't want to talk to them, that he was going to exercise his rights? He would block out the conversation. He would block out everything they were saying. But then, what was it the cop said? Something about Paula? They better leave Paula alone!

"I just want to make sure it's okay with you if I come back in here three days from now and tell you something has happened to Paula."

"What you mean?" John asked, anxiously.

"Like, if Paula's dead. If they've cut her head off. We know you didn't go down there to kill somebody on your own. We know somebody sent you down there, John. Do you think those people are going to let everything go now?"

John thought about what the cop said. Would the guys really hurt Paula? No. They liked Paula. Joann Sanders was their problem, the one they wanted dead, not Paula.

The cop reached for his hand. "This is the hand you held the gun with, isn't it John? This is the finger you pulled the trigger with, isn't it John?"

John was tired. Why wouldn't they just go away? He needed rest. He had a headache. If only he could get some sleep, then he could think. Right now everything was a blur. The cop kept asking questions, questions he already decided not to answer. It was none of their business what he did, what he was thinking. If only he could rest for even a minute. He felt his head start to drop, then suddenly it was moving up; the cop was holding his head in his hands, raising it up. He tried to look away, tried to ward off the cop's angry glare. Again the cop's hands were on him, manipulating his head, turning it toward him, toward a video camera in front of him, its light blinking—a camera with which they were taping his every word, his every move.

He was tired of this crap. He was tired of the cop ordering him around, like he was his superior. He would ignore him. But how could he? Now the cop stuck his face right in front of his. What was he saying, anyway?

He needed a cigarette. He reached for the pack. The cop pulled it away. There was a smirk on his face.

John took a deep breath. What did they want to hear? That he had killed those guys? Did the cops think he would confess? Did they expect him to admit he had screwed up the job, that he was supposed to have killed Joann Sanders, but that he had killed everybody else at the house instead?

Scott had assured him that everything would be all right, though. Scott had promised to take care of everything. But where was Scott now? Why hadn't somebody bailed him out of jail? He had to get out of this mess. Perhaps if he told them something, just a little something, they would let him get some rest. He'd

have to drive back to Florida soon. He had to get some rest. He
needed a smoke. Again he reached for a cigarette.

The cop caught his finger. Then John started talking about something,
he didn't know what, the long drive back to Florida, perhaps.

"Shut up," the cop said. "You know, John, I've just about
decided what kind of guy you are. I think you would kill your own
children." The cop was angry now, and loud.

John glanced at the camera. He was still being taped. He made
tears come. He'd let people know the kind of treatment he was
getting here.

"How is it you can go out drinking beer with your buddies
and brag to them about killing 'all those people' but now you
can't even look me in the eyes and admit it?"

This was getting to be too much. John felt a quiver in his
stomach. He had to get out of this room. He had to get out of the
spotlight. He had to get some rest. "I think I'm going to be sick,"
he said.

"Well, go ahead and be sick. Throw-up if you want to," the
detective said.

That was all right. He'd use the video in court against these
cops. He started crying harder. He needed rest. He needed to see
Paula, to talk to her. He needed to talk to Scott. He needed a
cigarette. He needed a cigarette in a bad way.

"It was just like watching TV," John said, finally. "It was just
like watching TV."

More arrests made in the quadruple murder

In only a matter of days after the quadruple murder,
investigators had begun to look at the slaying as a murder-for-hire
scheme that had blundered. Detectives worked around the clock
putting together bits of information that connected more people
than just John Barrett to the case. Once John was jailed in Ohio, a
thick plot began to surface.

On August 9, the very next day after John was arrested. Doc and Dorsey gave Phillip, Doc and Joann's middle son, power of attorney over all the family's business dealings.

Upon Paula's arrest on charges of conspiracy to commit murder and accessory after the fact of murder, she sang loud and clear; but many words to her song were lies. Paula wanted to save her butt and told detectives what she thought they wanted to hear. Yes, she said, John had been hired to kill Joann Sanders. He was to receive payment from Dorsey and Scott.

As information and evidence piled up, it appeared to authorities that Dorsey Sanders III and Scott Allen Burnside had hired John Barrett to kill Joann, and on August 11, arrest affidavits were prepared for the two.

On August 12, with arrest warrants in hand, investigator Jerry Thompson set out to arrest Dorsey and Scott. Thompson sent two deputies to Doc Sanders' Key West residence, where officials expected the two might have fled. Investigator Robert Horton, of the Dade County Sheriff's Office, reached Key West the evening of the 12th, located the residence, and then went to a motel for the night. He returned the following morning to watch the comings and goings. Horton noticed a white van leave the residence.

Horton stopped the van. The person driving identified himself as John Sanders and said he had been sent to Key West to run the family's beeper business. Horton couldn't locate Dorsey or Scott.

August 13, Thompson went to the Big Ben Ranch looking for the two wanted men. Doc and Tonya were there, but Dorsey and Scott were nowhere around.

Then on August 15, the Sanders' airplane pilot called the Putnam County Sheriff's Office to tell authorities that Dorsey wanted to turn himself in. The pilot then drove Dorsey to the sheriff's office. Dorsey was booked on four counts of first-degree murder, conspiracy to commit murder, and assessor after the fact.

While Dorsey decided to face the music, Scott skipped town.

John travels back to Florida

Conversation between detectives and the man accused of slaying the four men was kept at a minimum as the commercial airliner flew through clouds over Kentucky, Tennessee, and Georgia. Detective Marvin Padgett sat on the seat next to John Barrett. He had seen the results of just one night of horror blamed on this man and had no intention of letting him loose for even a moment.

The following morning, John appeared before Judge Richard Tombrink at a special hearing called at the Hernando County Jail. Standing there shackled to six other convicts, John looked at the room of reporters and photographers. "Would you ask the reporters to leave?" John requested.

Tombrink refused. Cameras continued clicking.

No jail time Paula

Paula Barrett would not go to trial. She made a deal with the prosecution to plead guilty to accessory after the fact of murder, for which she was promised five years of probation. Also, she would testify in the upcoming trials. She would be excused from testifying against John Barrett. A woman didn't have to testify against her husband. Even though she and John were not legally married, she would receive the same recognition.

By cooperating, her children might even be returned to her from the State of Ohio. They had been taken when she was arrested. After Paula was extradited to Florida and then released from jail, she stayed with her grandparents. Her parents gave her a 1984 Chevy Cavalier to drive. And for money, she sold blood plasma for $25 a week in Gainesville.

She had contact visits with John on Tuesday evenings from 9:30 until 11. Regardless of the plot to kill Joann and the murder of the men, Paula said, "John cares about people."

The Verdicts

In July of 1991, almost a year after the murders, a jury in Ocala convicted Dorsey Sanders III of conspiracy to commit murder and four counts of first degree murder, for which he was sentenced to life in prison. He will be eligible for parole after serving 25 years.

As dawn came to the long stretch of islands separating the Gulf of Mexico and the Atlantic Ocean, on the Friday morning the jury had given its verdict, Doc Sanders was at his home in the Florida Keys awaiting news of the outcome. But while the jury was deliberating, a judge was signing a warrant for Doc's arrest on the same solicitation, conspiracy, and murder charges.

In August of 1991, in St. Petersburg, John Barrett was convicted of four counts of conspiracy to commit murder and four counts of first-degree murder. After an emotional outburst by John's mother, during which she pleaded with jurors not to kill her son, the jury recommended John be sentenced to life in prison. In Inverness the following month, Judge John Thurman went against the recommendation and sentenced John Barrett to death in Florida's electric chair.

For a couple years after the murders, cops tracked Scott Burnside to Minnesota, Kansas, Texas, and Washington, D.C., even to a South Sea island. Then detectives lucked out. They followed Scott's mother to the Cook Islands, some 1,800 miles northeast of New Zealand. Detectives arrested Scott at the airport where he was seeing his mother off after her visit. On Good Friday, 20 months after Scott left Putnam County, he was finally in custody. Scott was brought back to Citrus County and convicted by a jury for conspiracy to commit murder and four counts of first-degree murder. He was sentenced to life in prison. He will be eligible for parole after serving 25 years.

In April of 1993, an Ocala jury deliberated for more than 14 hours before bringing back a verdict of not guilty in the case against

Doctor "Doc" Sanders. During closing arguments, Doc's attorney, Mark Shelnutt, implied that the jurors must have felt like the television viewers in 1986 who watched as Geraldo Rivera blasted open a vault that supposedly contained gangster Al Capone's hidden treasure.

"Remember what happened when the wall was knocked down?" Shelnutt said. "There was nothing there."

STORY 9:

Rumble

At The Old Publix

Ken: They were just kids fighting and it got out of hand

My editor met me as I entered the newsroom the morning of May 19, 1990. "Have you heard what happened last night?" he asked. Ken Melton was pacing, almost in the same spot.

"A kid was killed. There was a riot. We have to be careful how we handle this," he said, anxiously. The dead boy was white. Word was, several blacks killed him.

I stood by my desk for a moment, and then with notepad and pen in hand, I left the office for the two-minute drive to the Brooksville Police Department.

A fight had broken out during the night. Teenagers who had been friends had suddenly separated into two clicks, one made up of whites and the other of blacks. They had vowed violence on each other. Within only a couple of minutes, a white teen was clubbed to death with boards that had been pulled from an old building located in The Subs, an un-incorporated district on the south side of town. In the city's early days, the area dubbed The Subs had been know as The Colored Subdivision.

As the days, weeks and months passed, and as a handful of young black defendants were eventually charged with murder, townspeople, both white and black, hung onto every prayer that Brooksville would overcome the tragedy.

For months, I read police reports, covered court proceedings, talked with people, read court depositions, and reported on the case for the *Daily Sun-Journal*. The following account is as true to the facts in the case as I can present.

Poolside party turns to violence; cops were in and out of the picture

A poolside party was in full swing at the Candleglow Apartments to celebrate the twenty-first birthday of a disc jockey from WWJB, the local radio station.

It wasn't that all the young people in Brooksville were invited, and it wasn't that they weren't. Those who heard about it made up their own minds whether to go. The enticing factor was a keg of beer there for the taking.

During the first part of the evening, everything was cool between the racially mixed crowd. As they drank beer from the keg and the liquor they had brought with them, they became loud. Neighbors called the police several times over a two-hour period. But no one was arrested and the party continued. Minors kept drinking.

Suddenly, two white teenagers got into an argument over who had been seen with whose girlfriend at a different time and place. Then another white teenager decided his friend needed help, so he butted in.

There was more noise. The cops came again. This time everybody scattered. Within minutes, the Old Publix parking lot, a few blocks away, was buzzing with some 100 white teens.

(The site, at the Hernando Plaza, was referred to as the "Old Publix" because the empty storefront had previously housed a Publix supermarket. Since the store had closed, teens often went there to hangout.)

A police car pulled in soon after the youths had arrived.

"We're not doing anything," someone said.

"Okay. You can stay here as long as you're quiet and nobody complains."

As the patrol car drove away, some teens pulled out their hidden beers.

A car loaded with black teens drove up. And then a shiny black truck driven by Chuck, a white teen, wheeled onto the lot, its tires squealing as he spun around in a doughnut. "He's going to get us run off again," somebody said.

"We'll see," said Kenny, also white. A group of Kenny's friends followed him to Chuck's truck.

That is when the fight started. Kenny and Primp, a black teen and Chuck's friend, went at it. The view of who did what first varies according to who gives an account of the incident. When the two stopped fighting, about five minutes later, a handful of white teens took off their shirts and started after Primp. Primp quickly got back into his friend's car. Somebody kicked at the door and tried to pull him out. Someone yelled, "Nigger, get out of your car. We're going to kick your ass." Someone else yelled, "Haul ass nigger."

As Skip put his car in gear and started to pull away, someone from inside yelled, "We're going to come back and kill you. We're going to get our Uzis and we're going to come back and blow you away. You whites are trash."

At about 12:30 a.m. the cops came again. "What's going on? Who was fighting?" they asked.

"No one was fighting. Everything's cool," the youths lied. So the cops again left and went about their wee-hour business.

Getting together in The Subs

Sometime around midnight, 15-year-old Michael was hanging around outside the Elks Lodge in The Subs. It looked as if a lot of his friends were getting together at Howard's Café, a popular nightspot just a couple blocks from the Elks. Michael and 15-year-old Dominic decided to check out the action.

Once at Howard's, they joined the group of excited black teens who had gathered around Primp. Primp had gotten a cut on his wrist and another on his shoulder during the scuffle with Kenny. Now, the talk was of getting even with Kenny. Tyrone arrived in his grandmother's little gray Datsun 210. Talk was loud and uncontrolled. They started "pushing-up," trying to get Primp mad.

They were deciding what to do about the situation when Chuck pulled up in his big-wheeled truck. Since Chuck and Primp were close friends, Chuck was about the only white person really welcomed in The Subs. Chuck had not asked Primp to get involved in the argument he had with Kenny at the Old Publix, but he had never-the-less. Now, it was his duty to make sure everything was cool with Primp. Chuck didn't want to see more fighting.

He brought his truck to a stop in the midst of the commotion. "What's going on here, man?"

"Everything's cool," Primp said.

While Chuck conversed with Primp, one of the guys standing nearby spit beer onto Chuck's face. Some others passed by him and knocked their fists on his truck. "Why'd you do that?" Chuck wined.

"Chuck, you better get out from here now," Primp warned.

Chuck knew trouble was brewing in The Subs. He drove straight to the Oak Hill Apartments parking lot, across the street from the Old Publix, where some of the whites had moved after their last encounter with police. "There's something going on down in The Subs. You're too close to The Subs here. You better move on." Nobody was paying Chuck any attention. "Okay, if you're not going to leave, don't say you weren't warned," he said, then sped away.

Meanwhile in The Subs, youths pulled boards from the side of Howard's Café to use as weapons in the rumble that lay ahead. In two different vehicles, the gang headed back to the Old Publix to even the score with Kenny.

They saw Kenny's group had moved across the street to another parking lot. They wheeled onto the Old Publix parking lot and stopped behind the Dollar General store for a brief chat. Then they drove along a private trail-like road hugged by bamboo and trees, which ran alongside the Oak Hill Apartments complex. About a half-a-block up the trail, they parked by a group of mailboxes.

With boards resting against their shoulders, like soldiers with shotguns, they formed a pack and tromped along the jungle-like trail through the thick growth of bamboo.

911 called; cops where are you now?

Robert had recently lived at the complex and still had friends there. He was out front and heard Chuck give the warning that trouble was brewing in The Subs. Though a lot of the kids left, Robert, like many others, didn't believe anything bad would happen. Then he saw cars drive by with guys hanging out the windows. They were yelling, "You whites are going to die," (Robert said, later).

A few moments later, teens from the vehicles appeared out of nowhere it seemed, right out of the bamboo, on foot and carrying boards.

Kenny knew he was the person they wanted. He was the one who had fought Primp earlier in the night. He reached into the back of a nearby pickup and pulled out a chain, then slapped it against the side of the truck. The chain broke.

"You want us man? Then put down the chain, white boy," somebody yelled.

By then, Robert knew something was going to happen. The best thing to do would be to leave.

Another of Kenny's friends, Bryan, saw trouble was at hand. He had heard the guys yelling from the cars as they passed. He had seen them drive up the road and park near the mailboxes. Bryan, who had a broken leg and was on crutches, kept his eyes on the pack as he made his way to his friend John's apartment and stood outside. Bryan didn't want any trouble.

Russell Coats was standing behind Robert. "You aren't going to do this," he said to the pack. "We're all friends here. We went to school together. We party together."

About that time bottles started flying. Youths, both white and black, were getting hit with various objects. Kenny slung the chain, leaving himself without a weapon. Then he took off running. He grabbed a crutch Bryan extended to him as he ran past John's apartment.

John had just arrived at his apartment, from his disk jockey job at the skating rink and was emptying his waterbed, when several girls rushed in. "Get in," he said, and quickly locked the door. He dialed 911.

Bryan hobbled to his car. He didn't want it messed up. He drove a few feet up a narrow road and pulled near the trash bin. Some of the blacks and Kenny ran in front of his car. Kenny still had his crutch. Suddenly Bryan couldn't believe his eyes and ears. Tyrone reached into a car, pulled out a revolver and held it to Kenny's forehead. Kenny quickly stuck his arms up.

Some others were about five feet from Kenny and Tyrone. Somebody yelled, "Shoot the cracker. Give me the gun. I'll blow his f—ing head off."

Bryan had to do something immediately to prevent a shooting. He didn't even have time to think. His hands suddenly hit the car horn. And with the abrupt sound, one of Tyrone's friends jumped from somewhere and grabbed the gun. Kenny ran.

Bryan, too, saw his chance to escape. He started backing up, and then put the car into drive. A bottle went through his back window. As he stepped on the gas peddle, he heard somebody yell, "Wait!" Bryan stopped long enough for two teens he didn't know to jump into his car. As he spun away, he looked back. Several blacks were running after the car. He drove a short distance, and then realized he couldn't leave his friends.

Bottles were being slung. Youths with boards were swatting at whites as if they were flies. Kenny hit several black teens with Bryan's crutch. (They later reported to the hospital, located within a short walk from the commotion. One black received at least 14 stitches in his head.)

Jacky, who resided in apartment number 25, was somewhat used to teenagers, both white and black, partying at the complex. This night, she could hear a lot of unusual noises. She tried to ignore all the yelling and screaming. But the noise became louder and louder, until she couldn't ignore it anymore. She got up to look and saw a group of young people, white and black, near a car making loud remarks and arm motions. Suddenly there were gunshots.

Breathlessly, Jacky stepped back, knocking over a lamp and pushing her child abruptly to the floor. "Stay down," she screamed, and crawled to the telephone to dial 911. When the operator answered, she cried for help. Police were needed at once at the Oak Park Apartments. A fight was going on. Shots had been fired.

Kenny grabbed his girlfriend's hand and pulled her along so fast that they almost flew to John's apartment. The door was locked. Kenny banged, and then started kicking. He backed up, ran, and kicked again, this time knocking the door down. The door jam pulled from the wall, then the drywall crumbled.

"Do I have blood on my head?" Kenny asked. He was scared. So scared he could barely think. "Am I shot?"

Robert, still outside, was scared, too. He didn't know which way to go. People were running everywhere. Bottles were flying. Boards were banging. He heard a noise. "Phu-ff." Then again. "Phu-ff." The noise was coming from a gun. Someone was shooting at them. He ran. Russell Coats was behind him. They ran from the parking lot, cutting between apartments and heading toward the adjacent woods.

The whites quickly disappeared and the only one left was Russ. (Michael said in his deposition.) They took off after him. He wasn't sure who, but the one faster than him caught Russ after Russ had darted between two rows of apartments.

Then someone else swung a board at Russ and hit him in the face. He fell. He didn't get up then. He couldn't. All the guys started hitting Russ with boards. Russ didn't move again.

Michael backed from the huddle. He saw some girls he knew from The Subs. He ran as fast as he could to the car and jumped through the window.

Jacky heard cracking sounds coming from near her kitchen. In the darkened apartment, she crawled to the window. She saw several black youths with clubs. She also saw a white boy. The white one threw up his hands and said something like: "Hey man."

One of the blacks was taller than the others. He raised his club and swung it back, and then she couldn't see the white anymore. She still heard a muffled sound. She still heard cracks. She saw an arm with a club still moving. She heard a voice over and over saying: "I told you not to f—with us."

Then someone said, "Let's get out of here."

Robert's heart beat fast. Reaching the woods, he stopped. "We made it Russ," he said, turning. But Russ wasn't with him. He looked around. Russ had disappeared. Glaring between two apartments, Robert saw a huddle of teens with boards. They were swinging them in downward strokes. It looked as if they were slapping them against the ground, or the sidewalk. There were loud noises, like they were hitting the concrete. Robert couldn't make out who the people were in the huddle, but he knew it wasn't an object being struck. It was somebody.

They're beating someone, Jacky whispered to herself. They're beating the hell out of someone. "I said, let's get out of here," one again said.

As the pack took off, Robert ran from the woods toward the spot the huddle had just left. As he got closer, he saw the person on the ground–his face flooded in a pool of blood–was Russ. Robert sank to his knees. "Russ," he cried. "You're going to make it. You're going to make it. Just hold on."

Things were happening so quickly. Jacky heard screaming teens coming from every direction. She stepped out of her apartment. Someone cried out, "Call an ambulance. Russ is hurt. I think they killed him." She didn't move for a moment. It was hard to focus her eyes and her mind. "Oh, God," she cried.

She grabbed at her phone. She had to tell the police to hurry. She had to tell them that a kid had just had his brains beaten out and they needed to get an ambulance there. Again she dialed 911.

Jacky went outside. A group of teens surrounded the person on the ground. Someone yelled for a blanket and she hurried to fetch one. Others were just screaming. Soon, the Brooksville Police wheeled up to the apartment complex and shooed everybody away from Russ.

City prepares for a hard time

Local folks found teens having a gang fight here a bit hard to believe. Some news media called the incident a racial riot. The Brooksville Police denied any such.

The incident "did not start out to be racial," said Police Chief Ed Tincher. "It ended up that way."

A motorist called the police saying there was fighting at the Old Publix. "By the time officers arrived, the fighting had stopped, however, the kids were ordered to leave the shopping plaza," Tincher said.

"Some of the white group left and went to Oak Park Apartments. Two or three vehicles of young blacks arrived at the apartments and got out of their cars and attacked the group of whites. Some ran. Some stood their ground and fought. Then a youth discharged a gun. Then everybody ran. The victim (Russell Coats) cut between two duplexes. He either fell or was attacked by six people who beat him in the area of the head until they caused his death." The chief took a deep breath and exhaled.

"Whether or not this will have affect the future of the black and white citizens in this city and county, only time can determine.

Some people with self-serving interests are trying to make this a racial incident. I'm saddened by that."

Even Brooksville City Manager Jim Cummings made a statement to the press: "It's a horrible nightmare. No one should have to die like that. It's inconceivable. The behavior of both groups of young people Saturday morning was uncivilized. That's not the way civilized groups act." Moreover, he said, "There's absolutely nothing to support that the killing was racial. The more intelligent and logical members of our community, regardless of color or race, will approach this with calm. They will allow the justice system to work. A stable community belongs to all of us. Not just a select group."

The following Monday night at the City Council meeting, Mayor John Tucker said he wanted to form a committee of residents that would include white, black, and Hispanic to study and give input to any problem facing the city or county before it had a chance to surface. Tucker put the proposal before other councilmen and they agreed.

The mayor called the killing of Russell Coats a "tragic accident, something that can't be ignored" and he noted the incident did have racial tones to it. In the weeks following, such an alliance was formed. Civic groups held public picnics for black and white people to join together in harmony. Local ministers and bishops proclaimed "Prayer Days" and called for brotherhood and peace in the "confused and hurting" city.

Perhaps city officials made light of the racial overtone in the beating death of Russ Coats, but not Gene Coats, Russ' father. Mr. Coats called Hernando High School where his son had attended classes. He asked school officials to announce that no blacks would be tolerated at his son's funeral. (Later, Mr. Coats called the school and apologized to the innocent black youths.)

The announcement was made. On Tuesday, May 22, about 300 white teenagers attended the services at Turner Funeral Home, packing the facility beyond its capacity. The teens later attended the cemetery service. At the gravesite, the minister spoke of the

Lord's promise of strength. After his sermon, someone called out, "An eye for an eye."

A total of eight young black males were indicted for first-degree murder for the beating death of Russell Coats. A grand jury in May indicted seven. An eighth youth was indicted the following February.

The grand jury also indicted 19-year-old Kenny, who had fought with Chuck on the evening preceding the rumble, on misdemeanor charges of disorderly conduct and aggravated battery for his involvement in incidents the evening before Russ was slain.

In the presentation handed to the court along with the indictments, grand jury foreman Sanford Goldman noted the grand jury believed Coats' death was a direct result of a lack of moral restraint, self control and parental guidance of both groups of young people that met in the parking lot at the Oak Park Apartments. Goldman further stated that he did not consider Coats' slaying a racial incident just because it involved black and white people. Many of the kids involved in the incident were friends before Coats was murdered and are friends now, he said.

"The incident could have occurred between a group of kids from anywhere, for example, from different countries. In this case, it involved white and black kids. This could happen anywhere."

Even with so many city figureheads saying the incident was not racial, it was hard for the people of Brooksville not to worry that a major riot might break out at any minute during the days following the slaying. Residents, both white and black, seemed to walk on eggshells. Although city officials tried to keep things calm, some of the major news media continued to headline racial tones. There was news out that the city was in the palm of terror.

And then news that the Ku Klux Klan would come to town to rally in the wake of the teen's slaying made the city tremble. At the time, Sheriff Thomas Mylander said he didn't anticipate any violence from the community, but that the outside agitators could cause problems. People like the "Klan and the Skinheads use such tragedies as this as a vehicle to get themselves heard," the sheriff said.

Mylander, like Chief Tincher, denied the fatal incident was of racial merit. It was a situation that occurred "after stupid things came about and got out of hand. You are always going to have kids disagreeing. You are always going to have adults disagreeing. But give some common sense about what you're going to do. We had a tragedy here. We don't need any more. Look at the situation. Really, just look at the situation."

By this time, it looked like the KKK would come to Brooksville. The sheriff requested that residents say to the Klan: "Yes, we have a problem, but, hell no, we don't need you here."

An emergency city council meeting was held June 11 for the city to decide if officials should ask for a court injunction to prohibit the Klan from demonstrating in the city for a "cooling off" period of 45 days. Both the police chief and sheriff expressed great concern about the Klan entering the community.

Chief Tincher said the police had several tapes of recorded calls made of from Tony Bastanzio, Klan leader in central Florida, containing his threats. The Klan leader said he would come to Brooksville and "raise hell," Tincher said.

Tincher further noted that, because of conversations he had had with Bastanzio, he feared the leader might bring in a vehicle loaded with weapons.

Sheriff Mylander said he was worried about the safety of the residents and police officers that would have to deal with the organization's presence. City officials, including the sheriff and police chief, went before the Board of County Commissioners to ask for their support in obtaining a court order that would prevent the Klan from demonstrating in the county for 45 days.

"I feel there is a danger in this individual coming to town," Mylander said to the commission. Although the tragic incident had taken place in the city, "It could be just as devastating should the Klan rally in the county," he said.

Commissioner Richard Kellingsworth asked Mylander what he would do if he didn't get the support of the commission on this.

"I have the authority to use any method I feel is necessary to protect the community. I would go to the judge myself. I am truly afraid of what will happen if the Ku Klux Klan comes here," the sheriff said.

"There is absolutely no question of the threats made by this individual—on tape. He has directed his intentions," City Manager Jim Cummings injected.

Upon receiving the support of the County Commission, authorities presented the matter to Judge John Booth on June 13. Bastanzio, accompanied at the hearing by another member of the Klan organization, said the reason he planned to visit the city was because Russell Coats had his civil rights violated.

"I told him the father (Gene Coats) doesn't want him (Bastanzio) here," Tincher said. "Mister Coats has gone on television and apologized to the black people not connected with his son's death because he had demanded they stay away from his son's funeral."

"Most of that is true," said Bastanzio. "However, the issue still stands."

Bastanzio, Tincher said, has stated to officers that Brooksville would be a good area for two of his people to get arrested to "challenge the law" by wearing hoods to cover their faces, which would be a violation of the Florida Statutes.

"The eye-for-an-eye, tooth-for-a-tooth thing is here," said Tincher. "There have been threats, like the burning of a house and other acts of violence. There have been reports from kids that the Klan is going to march on the schools.

"You are trouble makers," Tincher said, glaring angrily at Bastanzio. "You are like the gasoline that's poured on the fire before it's lighted."

The Klan was banned from the county for the 45 days, as requested by authorities.

After the "cooling off period," on August 8, the Klan obtained a permit to rally in the city. And so came the Klan, the Neo-Nazis and the Skinheads. An army of police and sheriff's deputies from three counties lined the streets with shields and weapons. Media from newspapers, radio and television from all over the country were everywhere. The Guardian Angles, too, were seen around the courthouse square.

Only about 30 white Klan supporters and a few black hecklers showed up for the rally. Some whites and blacks on the streets seemed to be there out of curiosity.

The event authorities and residents had dreaded since the death of Russell Coats went with nothing more serious than tacky jesters from Klan supporters and obscenities from black agitators. The Klan had said it would come to town in protest of the slaying of the white teenager, but that didn't seem to be the topic. Actually, there didn't seem to be a topic at the rally—just a lot of rattling on.

The outcome

A jury found Kenny, who had been indicted by the grand jury on charges of disorderly conduct and aggravated battery, not guilty. However, at the time of the fight on the Old Publix parking lot, Kenny was on probation for stealing a gun, a crime he had committed at age 17. However, the judge reserves the right to punish a person on probation if he gets arrested, even if the jury finds him innocent of the charges. Judge Jack Springstead exercised that privilege and sentenced Kenny to serve four-and-a-half years at the Department of Corrections (DOC) at the Florida State Prison in Starke. Kenny, with time gained by working and good behavior, served only a fraction of the sentence. He was out of prison by the time the other defendants went to court.

Primp was the only defendant to go to trial on first-degree murder charges. The other defendants accused of killing Russell Coats entered into plea bargain agreements with the State Attorney's

Office. Michael was first to enter a plea. The agreement, signed by Assistant State Attorney Patricia McCarthy, Michael's defense attorney L.R. Huffstetler, and the defendant, called for special conditions in which Michael would plead guilty to manslaughter and receive a sentence of nine years in the DOC. Michael would provide a "full and truthful" sworn statement to the State Attorney's Office, submit to and pass a polygraph examination if asked to do so by the state, and cooperate and testify truthfully at all hearings, depositions and trials concerning all co-defendants involved in the death of Russell Coats. A manslaughter conviction carries a maximum 15 years or a fine of $10,000, or both.

After Primp was convicted of third-degree murder, the other defendants entered plea agreements, most pleading guilty to third-degree murder.

Russ' father, Gene Coats, called a press conference at his home to announce his disappointment in the outcome. He believed some of the youths would likely be walking the streets within a couple of years. And they were.

STORY 10:

They Killed For

A Hunk Of Crack

Chad Greenwater turned off the lime-rock road onto a dirt trail not far from Brooksville. On that hot, sticky night in the wee morning, Chad was wishing he were anywhere other than this rural area. He was driving through a parcel of property owned by his mother on his way to take a friend home. It was about 1:30 a.m.

A short distance down the trail, the car rounded a bend through a heavily wooded area. That was when Greenwater saw something lying in his path. From a distance, it looked like a dog with its tail sticking up and wagging. When he got closer, though, the object appeared to be a piece of carpet.

"Somebody dumped an old rug," Chad muttered, annoyed that people often used the property as an illegal dumping ground. A few feet closer, however, he saw it was something more than an inanimate object. He stomped his foot on the break pedal.

"Jesse, look there!" he exclaimed to the fellow on his right. A man lying in the road was struggling to raise his head. "Jee-ze!" Chad drawled. "There's blood everywhere! Looks like somebody beat him up pretty bad."

Speechless, Jesse Arnold just sat there and stared at the man.

"Whoever got him might be out here somewhere. I ain't taking no chances," Chad said, quickly shoving the Ford Taurus into reverse. He backed into the edge of the woods, shifted into drive, and then stepped on the gas pedal. Dirt flew behind the car as it turned and sped down the trail back toward the lime-rock road. Chad drove straight to his home, less than a mile away, and dialed 911.

An Emergency Medical Service unit and deputies from the Hernando County Sheriff's office were on the scene within minutes after receiving the emergency call. A medical technician pronounced the man dead at 1:55 a.m. on Wednesday, July 1, 1992.

Crime scene technician Gary Kimble, of the sheriff's forensic section, arrived at the scene soon after being called in. Kimble and other technicians began to check the area for anything that might be a clue that would lead to the killer.

Kimble studied the dead man's body. He was young, black and clad only in shorts. He lay face down in the dirt. At a glance, Kimble could see numerous injuries on the victim's body. He looked over the scene. Taking out his pad, he made a special note of tire tracks near the body with at least three different tread designs. He also observed that a pair of dark-colored rubber boots, commonly worn by concrete workers, next to the body.

Sergeant Mark Rivenbark and Detective Scot Bierwiler reported to the scene, looked it over, and then went to Chad's home. The investigators told Chad they wanted to check his automobile.

"Go right ahead. I have nothing to hide," the young man said. Then the lawmen radioed for a wrecker truck to tow his Taurus to the sheriff's impound lot.

Chad and Jesse agreed to go to the sheriff's office later that evening to give statements. They would be interviewed separately so that investigators could see if their stories matched.

Both men had said that the man on the trail was alive when they found him. Meanwhile, Kimble escorted the body transport unit to Leesburg, in Lake County, where the required autopsy would be performed.

At the sheriff's office, a check of the victim's fingerprints identified him as Henry Lee Presley, born May 23, 1969. Records indicated that he had been on probation for drug use. The postmortem examination by Dr. Janet Pillow of the Fifth District

Medical Examiner's Office revealed that the victim had been shot
at least four times—in the leg, arm, head, and torso. One bullet
had lodged in the right knee, one entered and exited the victim's
head, and two entered the right side and exited his back. Dr. Pillow
noted that the two gunshots to the victim's right side appeared to
have caused his death by severe internal bleeding.

That evening, as agreed, Chad and Jesse arrived at the sheriff's
office to be interviewed. Detective Bierwiler asked the men for
details of where they had been on June 30th, prior to finding the
body on the trail. Chad said they had been visiting with friends
most of the day. He had picked up Jesse and given him a ride to
his job at Pizza Hut about 4:30 or 5 p.m. Then Chad went to see
another friend's new house in the northern part of the county.
Afterwards, he visited his mom. He picked up Jesse from work
about 7:30 p.m. and they went to a friend's house where they
"just hung out" for a while. They later went to shoot pool.

Upon leaving the pool hall, Chad drove Jesse to the wooded
area to show him 19 acres that he owned. That area was not far
from the site where Presley's body was found.

"Did you ever get out of the car and walk on any of the
property?" Detective Bierwiler asked.

"No," Chad answered. He said that after showing Jesse his
property, he turned off the lime-rock road onto the dirt trail. That
was when they found the man lying in the trail and called
authorities.

Bierwiler asked how close Chad's tire tracks were to the spot
where they saw the body. About 15 to 20 yards, Chad answered.

Bierwiler asked if he had stopped anywhere else on the way to
or from visiting his friend in northern Hernando County. Chad
said that he had stopped at a Texaco service station on U.S. 19.

The day after the body was found, Detective Tom Holley and
several other investigators conducted a neighborhood canvass in
an area in Brooksville, known locally as The Subs, where lots of
crack cocaine exchanges hands. Arrest records showed that Presley
had lived and hung out there. Several witnesses told detectives

that on the previous night they had seen a black man getting into a large, light-colored van, which they believed was occupied by a white man and his wife.

Another witness said the man who had gotten into the van was Henry Presley. Yet another witness told officers she had last seen Presley about 1:00 or 2:00 a.m., on Josephine Street, one of the main drags in The Subs. Presley had walked up behind a white van. Shortly afterwards, she heard three gunshots.

"I'm sure it was Henry," she said. She remembered that Presley had been wearing yellow shorts with a flower design and some type of brown slide-on shoes. He had been shirtless.

During their canvassing, detectives turned up a woman friend of Presley's who said he had come to her home on the evening of June 30th to stay the night. She said the last she saw of him was at 11:30 p.m. The two had gone to bed together, but when she got up to check her baby about 1:30 a.m., Presley was gone. The woman said that whenever Presley stayed the night with her, he often went to a neighbor's home to bum a cigarette in the middle of the night. So she naturally didn't think too much about his absence.

"He's not been doing any drugs," the woman told cops. "He's on probation. He had drug screening yesterday evening." Presley had done drugs in the past, she said, and sometimes he would buy and sell crack cocaine to earn some money. Several other witnesses told the detectives they had heard gunshots coming from the area where the van was parked. Following the shots, the van sped away, heading west on Summit Road and out of The Subs. The same witnesses said that the van was often seen in the area.

News of Presley's death quickly spread. A man who would not give his name called the sheriff's office and said a rumor was going around that the people in the white van had killed Presley. Deputies had no way of contacting the caller after he hung up. They didn't know whether he was a witness to the crime.

Meanwhile, since the sheriff's Intelligence Division had contacts with confidential informants in The Subs, Detective

Bierwiler was able to obtain the name and phone number of one he thought might have information about the murder.

When detectives contacted the informant, she said she had indeed known Presley. The informant told officers she had heard, through talk in The Subs, that Presley sold crack to certain white folks who often drove an older-model work van. She gave Bierwiler the address of an apartment where drugs often were purchased. The informant had heard that the woman, who sold crack to Presley, was afraid the people in the van would try to harm her so she left the dwelling and walked down the road. She was dressed all in pink, the informant said.

Detective Bierwiler put out a BOLO (Be On Look Out) alert for her and soon she was picked up and brought to the sheriff's office for questioning.

Another man told Detective Bierwiler he had been in a white van on one occasion. He had seen a man in the vehicle, about 30 years old, with reddish bushy hair and a beard and mustache. The man who usually drove the van had light-brown curly hair, was clean-shaved and in his 20s. The woman who was usually with the two had light-colored shoulder-length hair. The van was an older-model white Chevy with large tires in the rear. It had a loud exhaust and only two seats. There were wooden racks on both sides in the back loaded with tools.

This witness said there were two people currently locked up in the Hernando County Jail on drug charges who could possibly provide the names of those in the van.

Detective Mark Gongre went to the jail to check out this new information. One of the inmates gave him the names Danny, Debra, and Fuzzy. He said they lived close to the Gulf of Mexico in the well-to-do Hernando Beach area.

Once investigators had these first names they had no trouble putting last names to them. There were numerous reports on file of domestic violence at the residence with folks having those first names and fitting the given descriptions. Detectives showed mug shots of the three to several people who previously had been in the van. They picked out two faces they said were familiar.

The mug shots identified were of Debra Ann Durso and Drew "Fuzzy" Johnson. There was another man who usually traveled with Debra and Fuzzy. The probes didn't run across his photograph.

When the detectives learned that Debra Durso and her husband owned a Chevy van, they set up surveillance at the couple's Hernando Beach home.

About eight the following morning, Sergeant Rivenbark received a telephone call from a man who said he lived in Hernando Beach. Having seen a lot of patrol cars cruising the area around the Durso home during the night, the caller asked if the cops were looking for Barry Durso. "That's possible," Detective Rivenbark noted. "Do you have any information?"

"About six yesterday morning the van was parked on a vacant lot across from my house," the caller said. "That van has never been parked over there before. Barry found his van parked on the vacant lot yesterday morning. He said someone had used it, then washed it out with soap and water."

Following that telephone conversation, Rivenbark contacted Detectives Mike Owens and Rick Kramer, who had set up the overnight surveillance at the Durso residence. Rivenbark directed the detectives to talk with the man who had called and provided the new information.

Owens and Kramer went to the caller's Hernando Beach address and interviewed him. The man said he had spotted the van about 6:30 a.m. on the vacant lot and called its owner. "Apparently, somebody had a party inside the van and somebody threw up," the witness said. "(The owner) said the van had been driven until the gas register needle was on empty."

The owner had left his house about 7:15 a.m. to go to Brooksville. When he returned, his van was gone.

Detectives inspected the vacant lot and discovered some worn-down tire tracks. These tracks had different types of treads with a definite pattern, much like the tracks at the scene where Presley's body was found the day before.

The sheriff's forensic section was contacted and told of the possible tread match. Technician Kimble went to the vacant lot and took casts of the tracks. While he was there, he was notified by radio that a white van was spotted heading toward the site. Kimble left the lot and pulled into a nearby driveway, so not to warn the occupants that police were on their trail.

About 10:00 a.m., detectives followed the white van to a swimming pool company office in Spring Hill, halfway between Brooksville and Hernando Beach, where they stayed for about 15 minutes. Keeping their distance, detectives continued their pursuit for more than an hour. Finally, they stopped the van and took the men inside into custody. They brought the pair to the sheriff's office while a tow truck was called to take the van to the sheriff's impound lot.

The occupants, Barry Durso and Drew "Fuzzy" Johnson, were questioned at the sheriff's office while other investigators took photographs of the van and its tires.

While the forensic technicians were making casts of tire tracks at the vacant lot, a neighbor walked over and identified himself as an ex-New York cop. He said Barry had come to his house on the evening of June 30th, close to midnight, saying that somebody had stolen his vehicle. "He asked me to drive him around to a few local bars to see if we could spot his van," the witness said. "I told him maybe he should call the police and report the van stolen. But he wouldn't do it."

During an interview at the sheriff's office, Barry Durso agreed to allow detectives to search his van. He asked that the officers be careful in handling $300 worth of swimming pool tiles he had just purchased, and that his paycheck, which was left inside the van, not be messed with. In another room, Detective Tom Holley was interviewing Fuzzy Johnson about his whereabouts during the last couple of days.

Johnson recalled that on June 30th, he and Barry were building a swimming pool for a homebuilder in Tampa. Johnson said that on the way home that evening in the work van, he was "joking the whole way back" with Barry. "I said, 'I bet two bucks Debra won't be home when you get there." Johnson said he thought that Debra Durso was running around with another man.

Sure enough, Johnson said, Debra was not home when they got to the house. Then Johnson and Barry went to a warehouse to pick up some swimming-pool tiles they would need the next day. While out, they gassed up the van. Suddenly, they heard the van take off. Barry, Debra's husband, ran outside yelling for them to stop.

About 8 o'clock the next morning, Barry appeared at Johnson's house and said that he had found the van. Already late for work, the two men loaded their ice chest and work clothes into the van and headed to Tampa.

Johnson noticed the front of the van had been washed out, and when he mentioned it Barry said, "I think somebody threw up in here."

That afternoon, while they were working on the pool, they discovered various objects missing from the van, including Durso's black-and-orange rubber work boots. That evening, the men spent the night at the home of one of Johnson's relatives in New Port Richey to avoid driving to Hernando Beach then all the way back to Tampa the following morning.

The next day, the partners got off work about 8 p.m. On the way home from Tampa, they stopped in New Port Richey at the Health and Rehabilitative Services (HRS) to pick up food stamps. "While I was in the food-stamp line, the guy in front of me had a copy of the *St. Petersburg Times*," Johnson said, noting he couldn't help but notice the headlines about a man's body being found. A caption in the story noted, "with a pair of rubber boots." Johnson said he grabbed the newspaper from the man's hand and read the article.

After waiting in line for about an hour and getting the food stamps, Johnson and Barry went back to the van. "I'm not going to take the fall for this. I'm not taking the rap if some bullshit happens 'cause of these boots. I'm not going down. I've been in prison," Johnson said to Barry.

During the police interview, Johnson admitted that he had been in The Subs on several occasions to purchase crack cocaine. The detectives wanted the names of the dealers he had bought from. "We've already found some people who say you are a crack buyer," Detective Holley informed him.

"Am I getting nailed for that?" Johnson asked.

"We're not dope cops," Holley said. "We're working on something else. We want some names."

Johnson was jittery about giving drug information to the police. However, Holley assured him that detectives had already been asking questions, and that several others had already picked him from a photo lineup.

"We didn't exactly pick you out of a phone book," Holley informed the nervous man.

Fuzzy Johnson offered several names, but he never mentioned the dead man, Henry Presley.

Detective Holley asked Johnson if he had ever been in any fights in The Subs. Johnson said that he had when he and Debra had gone there to buy crack. When questioned further, Johnson admitted that on two different occasions, he had even been beaten up while purchasing the illegal substance.

After interviewing Johnson, detectives Holley and Bierwiler went to the next interview room to question Barry Durso. "Basically, whatever Fuzzy told y'all is the same thing I'm going to say," he said.

"We'd like to hear it out of your mouth," Bierwiler noted.

The man said when he got home on Tuesday night, June 30th, his wife Debra was not there. Johnson stayed over that night. They had watched a Jane Fonda movie. During the night, someone took the van. Thinking that Debra had probably taken it, Barry said he got a neighbor to drive him around to different bars at Hernando Beach looking for it. The next morning about 6:30, he got up and went to his kitchen. He lit a cigarette. He looked out the window and his van was parked alongside a vacant lot near a neighbor's house.

Barry went right to the van. The motor was still warm. He checked his gas gauge and saw that about a half a tank of gas was missing.

"Fuzzy told us you had to clean something out of the van," Detective Holley said. "Are you forgetting this? Are we just having to pull it out of you, or what?"

Barry said it appeared somebody had thrown up on the dashboard and that it had been partly wiped up. He told of going to work that morning, after finding the van. Everything was normal. "We just worked our butts off," he said.

When questioned about what he wore at work, Durso hesitated, and then said he wore whatever he needed to. "I got so much stuff in that van it's ridiculous."

"You got boots?" Detective Bierwiler asked.

"Yeah, I had a pair of black boots."

"Where are they now?" Bierwiler asked.

He didn't know the whereabouts of his boots. They were in the van the last time he saw them, probably a couple of weeks before, he said.

The detectives asked Durso questions about his wife, Debra. Where was she on the night of June 30th?

Did she always go away for days at a time? Did she run around with other men? Durso really didn't want to talk about his wife. They had their arguments and she went out. He even had accused her of sleeping with other men, but Debra was a good girl, he said.

During the interview Durso said he was starting to feel uncomfortable with the conversation. He wanted to leave the sheriff's office. He said he needed get all his tools together. "I got to work," he declared. After a while he said, "This is weird!"

That day, a call came in to the sheriff's office for Detective Bierwiler. The anonymous caller said he had seen a white van matching the description of the van being sought by the authorities. It was parked at the residence of a man named Wayne Trapeo during the early morning hours of July 1st. Someone had been cleaning the vehicle, the caller said. Following up on this information, the detectives picked up Trapeo for questioning.

While other detectives were trying to locate Debra Durso, technician Kimble returned to the sheriff's processing garage to secure the white van. In order to make room for the van, deputies released the Ford Taurus, which had been driven by Chad Greenwater when he and his friend found Presley dying in the dirt trail.

At the sheriff's office, Detective Mark Gongre interviewed Wayne Trapeo. "Just run through it with us real slow," Gongre instructed the man.

Trapeo said that Debra and a man named Danny Garner, whom he had never met, had come to his house in the early-morning hours of July 1st. "They woke me up and asked me if they could wash out the van. So I say, 'yeah, no problem'."

Trapeo helped the couple clean out the van, but he had not been with them earlier, he said.

After cleaning the van, Debra asked Trapeo if he would drive the van to her house. She was afraid to go home because her husband would be angry with her. Trapeo agreed. However, instead of taking it all the way to the Durso home, he parked it on the nearby vacant lot.

Trapeo allowed Debra and Danny Garner to stay at his home the rest of the night. About half past six the following morning, he heard a knock at the door. Seeing Barry outside, he warned Debra and Danny. The pair quickly hid. "One hid behind my water heater. I got a big air compressor, and the other one hid behind that," Trapeo said. "I went to answer the door. Barry came right in and walked through the house. He looked in all the rooms. But he didn't spot them."

Debra and Danny went to bed and didn't wake up until about two o'clock in the afternoon. That evening, the two told Trapeo they were going to lay low at a friend's house in Aripeka, a small fishing village in the marsh lands along the Gulf of Mexico.

A search warrant was served on Trapeo's residence. From there detectives took into evidence numerous items which they believed had been removed from the van, including some blood covered boards, a white bucket spattered with blood, and a bloody cushion. In a trash container, lawmen found four empty shell casings. One casing was right at the top and clearly visible when the lid was opened. The three remaining were near the bottom. That evening, cops also searched the home of Danny Garner and found a silver-colored 357-caliber revolver, a box of ammunition, and a dark-colored shirt wrapped around the gun.

From the van, searched at the sheriff's impound lot, a number of items were taken into evidence including blood samples, clothes, and towels that had been stuffed between the two front seats, a crowbar, and the vehicle's tires.

As the detectives obtained statements from people who had been in contact with Debra and Danny the day after the killing, mounds of information began to pile up on the two suspects.

Detectives learned the couple had tried to borrow a friend's car shortly before midnight on June 30th. The friend had felt "uncomfortable" about lending them his car because he could see a stainless steel revolved sticking out of Danny's waistband. The friend drove them to a Circle K convenience store, left them there, and went home.

Another man said he had seen Debra and Danny on July 1st about 8 p.m. at the Beach Bar in Hernando Beach. The two had talked about Danny killing a black man who had cheated them out of a piece of crack cocaine. They asked the guy if he would drive them to the dirt trail site to see if the body was still there. The man agreed. As they drove there, Debra and Danny asked if he had gasoline they could use to burn the body to destroy the evidence. "I thought they were stoned," the man said to Detective Holley. But when they reached the dirt trail, they saw the crime scene tape and hurried away.

In questioning Trapeo, Detective Bierwiler learned the address where the two suspects were hiding. A team of deputies was sent to set up surveillance there. While watching the house, lawmen saw a cab pull up to the residence. Danny and Debra got inside and the cab and it pulled away. A short distance down the road, officers stopped the taxi, took both suspects into custody, and brought them to the Pasco County Sheriff's Office. The taxi driver told police the pair wanted to be driven to the nearest Western Union Office.

Detective Holley, Sergeant Rivenbark, and Assistant State Attorney Anthony Tatti went to the Pasco County Jail to interview the suspects. When the two were read their rights, both asked for an attorney.

They were held on charges of attempting to flee justice while authorities prepared a probable cause affidavit charging Daniel "Danny" Garner and Debra Ann Durso with first-degree murder. Arrest warrants were issued on July 3rd.

To avoid a trial, Debra Durso pleaded guilty to manslaughter and was sentenced to 12 years in the Florida Department of Correction.

At Danny Garner's trial his attorney tried to convince the jury that Garner had killed Presley in self-defense. That just didn't fly with the jury. Garner was found guilty and was sentenced to life in prison. He will be eligible for parole in 25 years.

During closing arguments, Assistant State Attorney Don Scaglione walked across the floor and stood before the jury. "And now you're going to hear from Henry Presley," Scaglione declared. "He's going to speak to you from the grave."

Scaglione brought out a picture of the victim showing ample evidence that he had struggled in the road before he died.

State Attorney Investigator Jane Phifer spent evenings and weekends helping Prosecutor Scaglione prepare the case against Garner. Phifer studied Henry Presley's character and prepared his profile. Presley had been known to use drugs, a practice that placed him in contact with his killers. He was not known to be a vicious person, but rather a gentle man. "He would have never gotten in that van if he thought he would have been harmed," Phifer commented, recalling the case.

He knowingly would have never traded his life for a hunk of crack cocaine.

STORY 11:

Granny Killer

On The Loose

Spring Hill is a conglomerate of houses, strip malls, and restaurants dotting sand hills that cover much of the southwest portion of Hernando County. Nights are mostly quiet. People usually patronize restaurants that feature a happy hour with two-for-one cocktails and a buffet of free food.

In the early evenings, some seniors proceed to recreation halls where they do country line dancing, square dancing or join up with a round-dance group.

Retired people make up much of the "Nature Coast," some being widowed women who live alone. They had, for the most part, considered the area safe until suddenly somebody's granny was slain.

Within a few nights the unincorporated area became know as the "granny killer's territory." A monster was on the loose. The villain stalked, raped, murdered and then burned elderly women.

The Hernando County Fire and Rescue service answered a call to an address on Melrose Street, August 7, 1993, where a fire was raging. About the same time, crime scene technicians from the sheriff's office were also on the scene. Upon arrival of both teams, the home was too hot to allow entry.

Finally sheriff's technicians Russ Knodle, David Still and Larry Stringham went inside and began an investigation. With the use of high technology light instruments, they searched for clues that might suggest whether the fire was deliberately set.

The burned body was that of 80-year-old Sophia Garrity. She had lived at the residence alone.

Arson specialists from the sheriff's office ruled the fire accidental. Officers noted there were signs of an electrical short in wires leading to the television and in the ceiling space above the bedroom. Arson specialists said the fire had probably started due to a portable fan found inside the bedroom. But Detective Mark Gongre, who was investigating Garrity's death, not the cause of the fire, noted suspicious incidents at the 15-year-old block house. Soot lined the inside window frame in the woman's bedroom. This led him to believe the screen had been removed prior to the fire.

When questioned later, firefighters could not remember if they had removed the screen or if they had raised the window. A stain near the bed also looked suspicious. Fire investigators later noted the stain was most likely caused from alcohol. Garrity was reported to have suffered from chronic leg pains and rubbed them nightly with the flammable substance.

Detective Jim Holbrook talked with some of Garrity's neighbors. They all sympathized, saying she was a really nice lady.

In the wee morning hours of August 18, the fire rescue and sheriff's deputies answered a call to an address in Brookridge, a deed restricted retirement community of well-kept mobile homes with its own recreation facilities. A fire was raging. Once the fire was put out, the charred body of Ruth Goldsmith, 70, was found in her bedroom. Fire authorities ruled this fire too, as accidental.

But Detective Scot Bierwiler started pounding on doors in the neighborhood. He asked about the victim. Who were her friends? Did she have family? He found out the victim's best friend, Lydia Riddell, lived two blocks away. He went to tell her what had happened to her friend, Ruth Goldsmith. Riddell took the news hard, letting her emotions go.

Two weeks later, in the early morning hours of September 2, a neighbor of Riddell's woke up from the sofa where she had fallen asleep watching "The Commish," on television. She saw the reflection of flames on her living room window. Looking out, she saw a fire raging at the 79-year-old Riddell's home. Breathlessly, she grabbed the telephone and called the guardhouse to report the fire. The gate attendant called the fire department and firefighters were dispatched at 1:14 a.m.

Upon putting out the fire, firefighters found the body of an elderly woman, later identified as Lydia Riddell. Riddell's hands were bound with duct tape behind her back and what appeared to be remains of a nightshirt was pulled over her head.

Somebody had broken into Riddell's home. The intruder had come through a utility shed attached to a screened-in room. The intruder had cut the screen to gain entry into the mobile home. Riddell's 1990 Pontiac 6000 was missing from the carport. A BOLO (Be On Look Out) for the car was sent out to law enforcement officers. Shortly afterwards, Detectives Bierwiler and Carlos Douglas were notified that deputies had found the car on a lot on nearby Fitzpatrick Drive.

Arriving at the lot, they found the car backed in between some tall pine trees. Bierwiler found two sets of footprints around the car, one of bare feet and the other of sneakers. Crime scene technicians took impressions of the prints. The vacant lot was lined in back by a chain link fence, separating the Brookridge community from Grove Road.

Detective Bierwiler didn't waste any time asking questions throughout the neighborhood to see if anybody had heard or seen anything suspicious. He asked people if they had seen Riddell's car on the streets or on the lot where it was found. He talked with numerous people; but no one had seen anything.

With Riddell's car having been taken, her mobile home broken into, and her body bound with duck tape, raped and dead, detectives were sure they had a homicide on their hands. They compared the deaths of Riddell and Goldsmith. They were too similar to be a coincidence. Both fires had started in the master bedrooms and had destroyed the rear corners of their trailers.

In addition to the incident's being similar, detectives learned the women had been good friends prior to moving to Florida from

Philadelphia. Both had attended the same church in Spring Hill. Detective Mike Owens wondered if the women had been slain by somebody they both knew.

Medical examiner Dr. Janet Pillow, who performed the autopsy on Riddell, noted the body was too burned to determine a cause of death, but since the woman's hands were bound behind her with duct tape and what looked like the remains of a nightgown pulled over her head, she classified he death as a homicide.

Less than a month after Riddell was slain, a long-time friend of 87-year-old Lorraine Alice Dawe called Dawe's phone number. For two days, Dawe didn't answer. The friend, who had a key to Dawe's home, said to his wife, "I had better go over there and see if she's all right. Alice doesn't stay out overnight."

In Dawe's bedroom, the friend found a mound of blankets and pillows on the bed. Two feet were sticking out. He touched her foot; it was cold. This time Dawe, a former speed skater, was not her cheerful self. She was dead, her body wrapped in a bedspread, with pillows stacked on top like a pyre.

Sheriff's technician Dave Stringham was in charge of the scene. He took vacuum sweepings, which he later sealed and sent to the Federal Bureau of Investigations (FBI). Technicians Ken Locke and Russ Knodle found several fingerprints in the garage, car, on the screen and in the bedroom.

The canine unit from the Citrus County Fire Prevention Office (just north of Hernando County), made up of Deputy Fire Marshall Rodney Bloomer and Princess, a 3-year-old black Labrador retriever, was sent to the Dawe home. Princess found traces of flammable liquid on a rug beside Dawe's bed. In this case, the fire had gone out before destroying evidence.

Sheriff Thomas Mylander beefed up patrol. Air officer Tom Nowlin flew over the west end of the county in the sheriff's helicopter spotlighting down on vacant property and fields looking for anything suspicious.

Toward the end of September, Mylander announced that a serial killer, one who preyed on elderly women, was on the loose.

He warned residents to be extremely cautious. Elderly people were advised to put in alarm systems and buy dogs. He suggested elderly, single women pair up until the killer could be found. Mylander announced the last two slain women had been sexually assaulted. All the women's bodies had been found in their beds. The four women were all single and lived alone. All killings had involved fires.

As the horrible news blazed over West Hernando County, elderly residents got their names listed with the Spring Hill Alert Residents Patrol (SHARP), a daily check-in phone watch. A local martial arts academy offered free self-defense classes to seniors. Owners of local pawnshops reported elderly people were rushing to purchase guns.

Phone calls from people fearful of even their next-door neighbors flooded the sheriff's 911 system. Sergeant Frank Bierwiler, Scot Bierwiler's father and spokesman for the sheriff's office, was getting numerous calls from news media all over the United States. He advised callers that the sheriff's office was working around-the-clock on the investigation. They wouldn't stop until they had found the serial killer.

Detectives checked every lead and finally thought they had found something. Their investigation led them to Gerald Bush, a man about 30-years-old who walked the neighborhood day and night wearing blue jeans and a button-down shirt. He would stand out front of his residence on occasions and just look around. Late at night, he was seen carrying a duffel bag while loafing along the streets. He would go up to anybody's house if they had a light on, regardless of the time.

People in the neighborhood considered Bush a "peeping tom." One neighbor said Bush was extremely infatuated with knives, always talking about them and telling what a violent person he had been in the past.

Checking Bush's record, Detectives Bierwiler and Douglas found he had been arrested several times on drug charges. In fact, the detectives learned Bush was in jail at that very moment.

Bierwiler and Douglas went to the jail to interview Bush. His answers to questions asked during each interview were conflicting. He said he lived in Spring Hill with his parents. He had been looking for work. His dad was ill. He said he wasn't using drugs.

Later in the interview, Bush said he was using drugs and that when he was on crack cocaine he would stay up all night wandering the streets. Also, he said that during the time frame of the killings, he had been out walking in areas where some of the murders had occurred. Bush said he would go to different houses, regardless of the time, and talk to the people living there. Detective Bierwiler thought Bush was very vague and deceptive with his answers.

More than being concerned he might be a murder suspect, detectives thought Bush seemed worried his mother would find out he had a drug problem. He didn't want her to know because she was already burdened with so many problems due to his father's illness.

But he would keep changing his stories. First he would say he didn't know any of the murdered women. Then he said he knew two of the ladies from Brookridge, that he had seen them at the nearby Assembly of God Church.

Then he said he had never been in Brookridge. Then he said he had been in Brookridge looking for a vacant lot to purchase, one that he and his parents could put a mobile home on. He said he was never in any of the murdered women's houses; then he said he might have been in their houses. His story continually changed during each of the interviews with Bierwiler and Douglas. The detectives asked Bush if he would go with them and allow them to search his home.

"Sure," he said.

Bierwiler, Douglas and Knodle conducted the search. They found numerous pamphlets from local churches and a map marking off locations. When questioned about it, Bush said he attended different churches to meet people and make new friends.

A roll of duct tape on a stool propped against the bedroom door grabbed Bierwiler's attention, since one of the murdered women had been bound with duct tape.

"What do you use this duct tape for?" Bierwiler asked.

"For packaging. And stuff like that," Bush said.

There was something wrong with this man, detectives agreed. He would be talking about one subject then his words would just wander off and he'd start talking about things that weren't even pertinent to the questions. "He's definitely not a typical, normal person," Bierwiler noted in his report.

After the interview, detectives took Bush back to jail. He would be easy to locate if they wanted to question him further.

As October approached, news of the vicious attacks on elderly women in Spring Hill had spread across the nation. Reporters from national television networks and radio came to Hernando County to cover the story.

On Friday, October 8, Sheriff Mylander said detectives were checking leads, but there was still much work to do before the case was solved. He would not say if any real suspects were being investigated. Upon speaking with the NBC crew preparing for the evening news show "Dateline," Mylander said he didn't want to release information known only to the killer, or say anything about the investigation that would tip him off.

During the investigation, detectives talked with numerous people in Spring Hill. Detective Mark Rivenbark called on a man named Claude Millhouse. Upon checking bank accounts of Lydia Riddell and Ruth Goldsmith, detectives had found checks written to Millhouse. Millhouse explained that prior to the murders of the women, he and a relative, Mike Kaprat, had done handy work for the women. Kaprat had even dated the granddaughter of Sue Garrity, the first victim.

Detective Tom Holley questioned another man known to have done some yard work for some of the victims. The man was very cooperative. After the questioning, Holley didn't consider him a suspect.

During the investigation, more information surfaced about Gerald Bush. A neighbor told Detective Douglas that Bush had shown up at his house the night of the fire at the Goldsmith home.

"He was all sweaty and agitated. He asked if he could borrow $50. I told him I didn't have $50. But he was persistent. He just wasn't going to leave until he got some money. So I found $50 to give him."

"What time was that?" Douglas asked.

"It was before midnight," the neighbor said.

Douglas made note of the neighbor's conversation and filed it in his daily report.

Detective Rivenbark had been at the FBI office in Quantico, Virginia, when Dawe was killed. Upon returning to Hernando County he received a telephone call from Detective Tom Holley. It was about 9 p.m. on the 29th of September.

Holley told Rivenbark he had been assigned to work the night shift taking phone calls that had been pouring in about possible suspects. He received a call from a woman saying authorities should investigate a man who had been seen in the area named Mike Kaprat.

The following morning, Rivenbark studied over a stack of supplemental reports piled on his desk. In them, Detective Holbrook had documented information about Kaprat. Rivenbark went to Detective Bierwiler. "Look, here's a man now who we haven't given much thought to. But its time we probably give him some consideration."

Rivenbark prepared a request for the forensic science section to locate Kaprat's fingerprints and check them with prints found at the Dawe residence.

Investigators found fingerprints of Edwin Bernard "Mike" Kaprat III on record. Kaprat had been charged with beating a man to death in Tampa in 1991. That charge was later dropped for lack of evidence. Tampa police had originally arrested Kaprat because he used the murdered victim's credit cards two hours after the victim was beaten to death and his body dumped in a mangrove thicket on the Courtney Campbell Parkway. (The parkway crosses Tampa Bay to connect Tampa and Clearwater. Mangroves are state-protected shrubs that help prevent the shores from washing away during storm surges.) There was no physical evidence linking Kaprat to the murder, however, Kaprat eventually pleaded guilty to forgery and dealing in stolen property for using the dead man's credit cards. He received two years house arrest for the crime.

Kaprat became the prime suspect in the gruesome granny killings, leading detectives to set up an around-the-clock surveillance on him. Detectives and undercover cops didn't let Kaprat out of sight, even while he commuted to Tampa to his job making boat propellers for tugs and shrimp boats. Detectives kept close enough they could make an arrest whenever the order came.

In the wee morning hours of October 3, Kaprat was walking on a road in Pasco County, just south of Hernando County. In order to keep tabs on him, an undercover cop picked him up and gave him a ride. Kaprat told the cop his girlfriend was mad at him because she found a bite mark on his back. While Kaprat talked, he chain-smoked, crushing out his cigarette butts in the ashtray.

By October 7, detectives were ready to move with search warrants that had been prepared for Kaprat's girlfriend's house in Pasco County, his family members' homes in Spring Hill, his car, and his person. The warrant prepared for his person ordered hair and other body samples to be collected to send to the FBI.

On Friday night, October 8, 1993, 10 weeks after the bizarre killings had started, Kaprat was on his way from Tampa to Hernando County. Detective Rivenbark gave the order: Stop him. Nothing more needed to be said. Detectives made their move.

Patrol cars whirled upon the suspect on Waterfall Drive, just north of Spring Hill Drive, stopping a car driven by the 250-pound man with long dark hair and a dragon tattoo on his left arm. His identification showed him to be 29-year-old Edwin Bernard Kaprat III.

Rivenbark wasn't far away. He whizzed to Waterfall Drive. Joining other officers, Rivenbark told Kaprat to sit down at the rear of the patrol car.

"Mind if I smoke," Kaprat asked.

"No problem," Rivenbark said. "We need to talk. Will you go with us to the sheriff's office?"

Kaprat agreed to go but asked that officers make sure his car was secured.

At the sheriff's office, Bierwiler and Douglas advised Kaprat of his rights. Then the two detectives conducted an interview.

Detectives learned Kaprat was familiar with the area where the murders had occurred. One of Kaprat's family members lived next door to Alice Dawe, and across the street from Sophia Garrity. On occasions, Kaprat and another family member had been to the older women's homes to do odd jobs for them.

Kaprat was indicted by a grand jury in October of 1993 for first-degree murder for killing the four elderly women, sexual battery, arson for setting fire to their homes, burglary and burglary with battery.

While on trial for the Riddell murder, portions of a taped conversation Kaprat had with detectives shortly after midnight Oct. 9, 1993, was played to the jury. At first, the interview was casual, with Kaprat asking the muscular detective Douglas if he worked out at the gym. Then Bierwiler asked Kaprat if he knew about the rapes and killings of elderly women in Spring Hill.

"I wish I did know," Kaprat said. "I think they should be put down. The death penalty, as far as I know, is still in effect in the state of Florida," he said. "Just like people who rape people. I think they ought to be castrated."

At first, Kaprat said he had never been in Dawe's home. Then Douglas asked, "Why do your fingerprints appear on her car? This is some serious shit."

"Look man, I was not at her house. I mean, not really, Kaprat said. He had considered purchasing her car, that was probably how the fingerprints got there, he said.

"How did they get on her window screen?" Douglas asked.

"I sat with her for tea," Kaprat said.

"What about the cigarette butt found in her bedroom?" Douglas asked.

I broke into her house and went to the bedroom to look for jewelry. I did not touch her. I did not hurt her," Kaprat said.

"I got one other question for you. How did your cigarette butt get on that lady's body?" Douglas asked.

About two hours into the four-hour interview, Kaprat said to Douglas, "What if I was to take a swing at you and your partner shot me? That would be cleaner; that would be quicker. My name, my family's name, wouldn't have to be dragged through the mud. You could say, 'Suspect resisted arrest'."

In the interview, Kaprat said he had parked his car just outside the Brookridge subdivision and hopped the security fence to get inside. He admitted he had sex with Riddell and made her perform oral sex on him. He also admitted being responsible for two broken bones in her back. He said he had stomped on her back because she was having a heart attack. He said he was putting her out of her misery. "Just like I wish one of you all would shoot me and put me out of mine."

"I'm gonna go up there (to death row) and fry like Ted Bundy," Kaprat said.

After Kaprat was sent off to the state prison in Starke to await his appointment with the electric chair, the people of Spring Hill breathed easier. But Kaprat never made it to the electric chair. He was slain by an inmate in a prison fight a few weeks after he was transported to Starke.

STORY 12:

Killer Left Body

For the Dogs

In the back lands, animal and fruit farms with singlewide mobile homes are pretty much hidden with trees. A crime committed in remote areas of Hernando County might possibly go unnoticed for days. That is, unless somebody starts looking.

When William "Billy" Van Pelt was murdered, the crime drew attention when a friend couldn't get in touch with him.

Billy, a 46-year-old pig farmer and dog breeder, was a friend to everybody he came in contact with. But he lived alone and answered to nobody. His trailer was set back where folks traveling the closest blacktop road a mile or so away would never know it was there. A dirt road trailed from the highway to his home place. He didn't need much. He would sell a hog for butchering once in a while, and producing a good litter of registered rotweiler and snauzer dogs brought in more money than he really needed. He found rotweilers popular with country folks and the prissy snauzers perfect for people living in apartments in the Tampa area. His business was flourishing. He had enough to eat and plenty money to spend.

Comings and goings at his trailer were mostly by business associates involved with either pigs or dogs. Strangers rarely found their way to his place.

Farmers living near Billy saw him outside his trailer every day. He always fed his animals at their regular eating times and did this-and-that around the yard. He spent a lot of time with the dogs and went on a regular route around the city of Brooksville to gather slop. Picking up scrap foods, thrown out by restaurant kitchens, was a job that needed daily attending. Restaurant folks wouldn't hold throw-outs for him long.

When Billy's neighbor, Sally Whitehead, didn't see him for several days, she started wondering where he was. If he had gone out of town for one reason or another, he would have asked somebody to care for his animals. Even the gate to the yard was left open, thus allowing several hogs, Rotweilers and Snauzers to roam the countryside. Whitehead had known Billy for several years. He wouldn't allow this.

Sally tried several times to enter Billy's yard. She wanted to knock on his trailer door, but each time she tried, the dogs moaned and groaned so much they frightened her off.

Something's got to give, Sally determined. She could see the entrance to the trailer was closed. Sasha, one of the rotweilers, was stretched out by the door. Each time Sally started toward the residence, the dog would growl angrily. Sasha was a vicious animal. And Rambo was inside glaring out a window. Rambo, an extremely aggressive rotweiler, was usually left outside to guard.

Sally walked backwards around Sasha and the other dogs. She was afraid that at any moment Rambo would break through the trailer window. She knew he wanted to chew her up and he would if he got out. She tried to bully her way around the dogs for several days, finally she knew the only thing to do was call the law.

Tom Brooks, a sheriff's deputy found his way through the winding country roads to Billy Van Pelt's residence. Once there, he radioed for back up. He could not get to the trailer with the angry dogs roaming the area.

Brooks waited in his patrol car while a unit from the Hernando County Animal Control arrived to subdue the animals. He looked around the property. It was a pure mess. Several rotweilers ran around the cruiser barking and growling. Cows and pigs roamed about the yard.

Once animal control arrived and got the dogs under control, Brooks went to the trailer door. When no one answered his knock, he entered. What he saw was hard to grasp. He turned and hurried back to his car and relayed to the sheriff's office what he had found.

Several officials, including the sheriff's Crime Scene Unit and representatives from the animal control were on the scene when Detective Rick Kramer arrived at the trailer. The site was horrifying. A man's body was lying stomach down on the kitchen floor in stinking body fluids, including dried blood. Maggots covered the floor and what was left of the man's badly decomposed body. Dog droppings, along with some of the man's body parts, were scattered about the trailer. Officials speculated the remains had been carried about by the hungry rotweiler that had been shut up in the trailer for several days.

Crime scene specialist Lawrence Stringham photographed areas of the scene. Luminol sprayed in the hallway showed evidence of blood. Such items as swabbing from the kitchen floor, a book showing how to grow marijuana, a pornographic book, several used disposable syringes, six pairs of adult diapers and seven pairs of women's underwear, a telephone, and a shoe box and lid were gathered as possible evidence.

Detectives found a circular hole at the base of the dead man's skull, but due to the decomposition of the body and the heavy maggot infestation, details of what had happened to Billy Van Pelt were unclear.

Once detectives contacted the medical examiner's office and the body removers came and bagged Billy's corpse, detectives left the scene until the following day, since it was getting late and lighting in the small trailer was poor.

The following day, crime scene technician Dave Still went to Leesburg to attend Billy's autopsy. Still took into evidence the T-shirt, blue-jean shorts, and white underwear Billy had worn. Medical Examiner Janet Pillow removed three projectiles from his head.

Back at the sheriff's compound in Brooksville, Still processed Van Pelt's 1977 Chevy pickup truck. And upon returning to Van Pelt's trailer, he found a .22 caliber automatic Marlin rifle. However, he was unable to find any fingerprints.

The day after the autopsy, Kramer went to the trailer. He took into evidence the victim's address book, business cards, driver's license and various papers that might help in finding whoever had intruded into this man's home and killed him.

While crime scene officers performed their jobs, Kramer started talking with people who had known the victim.

Kathy Tuttle considered herself Van Pelt's best friend. They were both in the dog-breeding business and often worked together. The last time she had seen Billy was on Monday evening. He had promised to come to her house the following day, then again on Sunday, which would have been Father's Day.

"I'll be back tomorrow," Billy had said upon leaving her house that last time. "I need some shots for the dogs." He usually got shots from Tuttle, who purchased large quantities at a time.

Friday came and Tuttle still had not heard from Billy. She had tried numerous times to call him on the phone but his line was always busy. By Friday night, Tuttle had begun to worry. She stayed up until 1 p.m. trying to call Billy. Still, the busy signal was all she got. Finally, she called the telephone company and asked the operator to check the line.

Tuttle was still trying to get a hold of Billy by phone on Father's Day. She planned what she would say when he answered. She would just wish him a happy Father's Day and say, "from an old dog," or something like that. She would just joke with him. But when she dialed the number, the line was still busy. Then she started calling police departments and hospitals to see if Billy was in either. She couldn't find him anyplace.

On Monday, Tuttle went every place she knew to look for Billy. She traced his steps. He had told her of a new slop pick-up account he had obtained from the Golden Corral restaurant in

Brooksville. She finally called the restaurant and asked a friend to help her find Billy.

Then when she called the sheriff's office, she was hit with the bad news. "I'm sorry, Kathy, your friend's already gone," an investigator said. She hung the phone up and went into a state of hysterics.

Upon talking with detectives, Tuttle told of people who knew Billy. There was a fellow who once lived in a trailer back in the woods. His name was Ivan Morales. Tuttle had met him when she went to Billy's trailer and gave him Rambo. Rambo was still young at the time, but the dog was mean; and even though she had raised him from a puppy, he was too vicious for her to handle. Morales had come walking up out of the woods while Tuttle was at Billy's trailer that day. She instantly noticed the stranger had a power over animals. Rambo growled and showed his teeth at Morales, but after about an hour or so, Morales had complete control over the animal and walked right up to it.

"He was like a master with animals. He had a pet panther. I knew it was against the law to have a panther unless you have a special permit. I don't think he had a permit. But that captured beast was his pet, just the same," Tuttle said to Detective Kramer.

"And when he came walking up out of them woods, he went right up to Rambo and walked around him. Then he began to fool around with Rambo. They became friends right away. I couldn't believe anybody could get so close to that high-strong dog. I never could get that close to him. Even when I came to visit Billy after that, Billy would make Rambo sit in the hall while I was in the kitchen. Rambo's always been vicious."

Tuttle had seen Morales a few times after that with Billy. Once they drove onto the parking lot at a convenience store where she had stopped. Another time she was at Billy's and he came there with a woman and a baby.

As the case began to develop, detectives learned there were several people who had the opportunity to kill Billy Van Pelt. He had lived by himself, but people stopping by for marijuana was not unusual. He had even had a marijuana plant growing in his trailer.

In the Florida Department of Law Enforcement laboratory in Tampa, crime lab analyst Terrance A. Lavoy concluded three bullets that had been removed from Van Pelt's body were fired from a .32 caliber handgun.

Detectives learned of Jason and Irene Wright, a couple in the dog breeding business, did a lot of dealings with Billy.

When Kramer first arrived at the Wrights' home to question them about Van Pelt, Irene Wright was the only person there. Kramer asked if they had guns. She said they did, and showed him several.

None was a .32 caliber, like the gun used in the crime.

Later, Irene told her husband of Kramer's visit and showed him the weapons she had presented to Kramer.

I have another gun, Jason said. You didn't show him the .32 caliber handgun I have hidden. He'll find out about it and want to know why you didn't let him see it.

Right away, Jason Wright called Kramer. "I have another gun," he said. "My wife didn't know I had it put away." Kramer returned to the Wright's residence and picked up the gun to turn over to the crime technicians for processing.

Kramer made other calls trying to find leads in the investigation. He even checked the local meat company where Billy Van Pelt had his hogs butchered.

But most of all, Kramer was investigating any possible involvement the Wrights might have had in the slaying. At this point, Irene Wright was Kramer's number one suspect. Since the slaying, Irene had obtained custody of the victim's dogs from the animal control service, saying she planned to sell the canines and give the money to Billy's mother.

A neighbor of Billy's told Kramer that the Mexican man, Ivan Morales, who had lived back behind Billy's place, had lots of dealing with Van Pelt. She remembered an article a few months back which was published in the *St. Petersburg Times* saying Morales had been arrested for having "an illegal wild cat, or something like that," she said. "He helped Billy with his pigs and dogs. He had a wealth of knowledge about those animals. I think Billy would give the Mexican marijuana for helping him," she said.

Kramer learned Morales had moved somewhere near Tampa, 50-or-so miles south of Brooksville. "I better have a talk with him," Kramer told his supervisor, Sergeant Mark Rivenbark.

Kramer went to the area where Morales had moved. Upon contacting neighbors in an effort to locate Morales, he found nobody really wanted to talk. Finally, Morales's brother directed Kramer to a tiny camper in a nearby back yard.

"We're investigating the death of Billy Van Pelt," detectives informed 38-year-old Morales after asking him to step from the trailer.

"Billy's dead? I can't believe it."

"When was the last time you saw him?"

"Just a few days ago. Billy came down and picked me up. I went up there to help him with his hogs. He was supposed to come back down here on the weekend. He was to take me back up there with him to do some work. He never showed up. I haven't heard from him since."

"You sure that was the last time you saw him?"

"Yeah. But, I don't understand why you're talking to me about it. I been arrested for a couple killings before, for this and that, but I didn't kill Billy."

"You want to give us permission to search your house and car?"

"Sure you can."

"Would you be willing to take a polygraph exam?"

"Sure I would. I didn't kill Billy."

At the sheriff's office, officials set up a polygraph and were making plans to pick Morales up and bring him in for testing. Kramer had spoken with Morales since the initial interview and he had still agreed. In the meantime, detectives were busy following up with a lot of other information and interviews regarding the case.

Detectives went back to pick up Morales, but he was gone. "He left town a couple weeks ago," neighbors said.

Upon talking with people in the vicinity of the Van Pelt place, Drew Pierson, who lived in a barn near Billy's trailer, said he had seen Morales doing work for Billy the weekend cops believed the killing occurred.

Another acquaintance said Billy had been at a dog show and had heard Irene and Jason Wright "bad-mouthing" the victim.

Still another neighbor said he had seen Morales and given him a ride in his pickup truck about the time the murder occurred. He had taken him down the road a little ways from Billy's place. Morales had come from the dirt trail entrance leading into Van Pelt's property. Morales's wife had been waiting in a car alongside a nearby dirt road. Morales had lots of money on him at the time. He had paid the neighbor $35 he owed him. He then got in his car and drove off, going east on a dirt trail alongside a power lines right-of-way. There are dirt trails leading in every direction out there, the neighbor said.

October came and detectives still didn't have any real evidence in the case. Then a serial killer started raping and murdering old ladies in Spring Hill, which grabbed up most of the detectives' time before the case was solved.

Once cops had the "granny" killer in custody, detectives returned to the Van Pelt case. Kramer learned the Morales family was staying in Texas. He contacted Morales's wife Betsy. She said her husband was still willing to take the polygraph test, but it would have to be done in Texas. "Poppy (her pet name for Morales) doesn't want to come to Florida because he knows there are warrants out for him there," she said. "Y'all think he killed Billy."

"There isn't a homicide warrant out for Ivan," Kramer said. "The warrant is for violation of probation. He broke his probation. Remember, he's still on probation for having a wild cat illegally."

Kramer then notified the sheriff of the county where Morales was living in Texas that Morales was a suspect in a homicide and asked him to keep his ears and eyes open.

Kramer didn't go to Texas then, but continued to investigate the actions of other suspects, mainly Irene Wright, who had already hired a lawyer to defend her should she be arrested for Van Pelt's murder.

In the meantime, a confidential source called the sheriff's office to tell everything she knew about Ivan Morales. He had worked with her in Sumter County at the Salvage Kingdom, a shelter that housed wild animals. Morales had been trying to get a license to handle exotic cats, she said.

"He called me from Texas," she said. "He said he bought some land out there and was going to raise animals. He says he's working for a zoo out there. He says he's going to kill the owner of the shelter here because he didn't give him enough work-hours to get a license to have panthers." Detectives notified the zoo owner that there might be a conspiracy to kill him.

As the investigation continued detectives learned Morales had been in Atlanta, Georgia, and had been arrested there for stabbing his wife.

But Morales denied the accusations. He claimed he had not done the stabbing. "I was parked along the roadside and was out of the car taking a leak. A black man stopped and robbed Betsy and stabbed her while I was relieving myself," he said.

Cops in Atlanta didn't believe Morales's story, but turned him loose anyway when Betsy dropped the charges against him.

The following April, Kramer got a call from an acquaintance of Ivan and Betsy Morales. "They're back," she said. "They're living in Tampa. Ivan is trying to get up enough money to go back to Puerto Rico. And you know what else happened officer? Ivan stabbed Betsy when they were in Atlanta. He stabbed her a bunch of times, but she's still alive. They're still together."

Detectives knew they would talk to Morales, but there was no physical evidence to charge anybody with Van Pelt's slaying.

Irene Wright was still a suspect in the shooting, but not even the Colt .32 automatic that Kramer had taken from the Wrights could be used as evidence, according to results from a test performed by the Florida Department of Law Enforcement. It had been test-fired into the water tank in the laboratory, and then the bullets recovered. The particular firearm could not have fired the bullets that killed Van Pelt, noted Terrance A. Lavoy, FDLE crime lab analyst in firearms.

On April 22, due to a rotation of job assignments, Kramer was transferred to another duty and Detective John Cameron was assigned to the case. The investigation continued but with no physical evidence. Undercover cops kept a close watch of Ivan and Betsy Morales as well as Irene and Jason Wright.

Betsy was selling crafts at a flea market near Tampa. Detectives learned she was looking for dried cow skulls to decorate and sell as western ornaments. An undercover cop posed as a cow-skull salesman and went to the Morales' home and had a long conversation with Betsy. Nothing came from it.

Then suddenly in October, it was like a cat was let out of the bag. Betsy Morales was caught shoplifting at a Home Depot. Officer Judy Cashwell, a police officer in Tampa, made the arrest.

"Will somebody go out to my car and tell my husband I'm being arrested?" Betsy pleaded.

"Poppy, you get me out of jail," Betsy called as police escorted her from Home Depot. "Don't you leave me there, Poppy. I don't want to go to jail."

But this was Betsy's second arrest in two days. The day before she had been arrested for driving on a suspended license.

While Betsy was in jail begging that somebody bail her out, Morales was making plans to go to Puerto Rico to live there with his sister. He was selling marijuana to raise cash. He gave Betsy's dogs to her father and signed his children over to one of Betsy's relatives.

"Did you know Ivan is leaving the state?" Detective Cameron asked when he and Detective Michael Nelson went to the jail to interview Betsy.

"He's not going anywhere. He's trying to get up enough money to get me out of jail," Betsy said.

"You're father says Ivan has a girlfriend. They're having an affair. He's leaving for Puerto Rico on flight 1213 out of Tampa."

Detectives told Betsy that her husband planned to leave October 22. The two-day interview with Betsy included showing her pictures of Morales with another woman and a copy of the airplane ticket.

"He even gave your children and your dogs away," Cameron said.

With this news, Betsy was both mad and hurt and decided to get even with her husband. She told detectives that Morales killed Billy. He killed Billy to get money he owed him. Betsy said Morales had then traded the .32 caliber revolver he had used to shoot Van Pelt off to two black men in Tampa for some crack.

Detectives arrested Morales at a Days Inn located just off I-75 near Tampa on a warrant for violation of probation. During an interview with Morales at the Hillsborough County Sheriff's Office, Detectives from Hernando County played a portion of Betsy's tape.

"I don't have to listen to it anymore. I did it. I killed Billy," Morales said.

In his confession Morales showed detectives, by pointing to his own head, where each of the bullets had entered Van Pelt's scull. With this confession, detectives were able to obtain a warrant charging Morales with first-degree murder. Detectives transported him from Tampa to the Hernando County Jail, near Brooksville.

Morales told Detective Cameron about two previous murders for which he had been convicted. He had killed a man at a beach hotel near the Gulf of Mexico in South Florida over a crap game. He had also killed his first wife while he was living in New Jersey. She was 18 years old and pregnant at the time of the killing. He was convicted and served some time for those two murders. He told detectives he had also been involved in more than 40 other homicides, including that of a police officer.

Detectives checked his story. They found some of the incidents had actually happened, but other people were convicted of the crimes. Some leads went nowhere.

Awaiting trial, Morales was allowed to make phone calls from the jail. He called Betsy and they chatted at length. They made up. Betsy said she would come to the jail to visit him. But before she could get there, she was picked up on a warrant for the second time for driving with a suspended license. She was taken to jail. While there, she asked to see detectives working on the Van Pelt case.

Her husband, Ivan Morales, didn't kill Van Pelt, Betsy said, and confessed to the slaying. The story she had to tell went something like this:

On the day of the killing, she and "Poppy" had gotten up early in the morning and decided to leave the city and take a nice ride in the country. They decided to drive to the area where they had lived previously. They stopped at a convenience store near Brooksville where she and the three kids got sodas. Poppy got himself some beer. They were near the spot where they had lived and decided to call on Billy. He owed Poppy money and they needed it.

Morales parked the car a short distance from Billy's trailer. This was the area where they had let their cows roam. There was a special place in their hearts for the backland. He decided to sit in the car with the children and drink beer while Betsy went to collect the money.

Betsy slipped her gun in her purse and walked across the field.

Billy met her outside, because she couldn't get close to the dogs. They greeted each other and made small talk.

"I got a new litter," he told her of his rotweiler pups. "Come see." They went to the pen and she held a couple puppies. Then she asked him for $60 he owed Poppy.

He said, "Sure, I got the money. Come on in the trailer."

He put Rambo in the back bedroom and got the money for her.

"You want to smoke?" he asked, rolling marijuana.

They were smoking when Billy got fresh. She tried to get to the door. Billy quickly locked it so she couldn't get out. She yelled for Poppy to come, but he didn't hear her. All the time, Billy was getting "rougher and rougher."

He wouldn't turn her loose. He raped her right there on that "nasty, dirty old floor." He didn't even remove her clothes. He just pulled her baggy shorts to the side.

"I was shaking really bad. I was just shaking like a leaf. I was terrified."

She opened her purse and stuck her hand inside so it rested on a small .38 caliber revolver Poppy had purchased for her.

Billy turned back toward her. "I thought he was coming back at me. I had my finger on the trigger, even before I finished getting the gun out of my purse. I just pulled it out. I shot once. And then I shot two more times.

She ran out the door then, just as her husband was coming toward the trailer.

"I killed Billy," she yelled.

"Poppy wanted to go take a look, but I told him not to." So they got into their car and left. They rode around for a while, and then stopped at a store near Bushnell (the next town north of Brooksville) to wash up in the restroom.

Betsy said she traded the gun for crack cocaine a couple days later.

Detectives didn't buy Betsy's story.

In December 1995, a jury convicted Morales of the first-degree murder of Billy Van Pelt. During his trial, as Morales sat chained hand and foot, his emotions ranged from tears to laughter and jokes.

Upon taking the stand during the penalty phase of the trial, Morales broke down and cried. He said the jurors had made a mistake, that he had not killed Billy Van Pelt. He said he forgives them and he loves them, however, and asked them to sentence him to death in the electric chair because he could not live the rest of his life locked away like a caged animal.

Morales said he had killed the other two people he had been convicted of in the past. But, he said, "I had no reason to take a life. I did take two lives. One was my wife. I will never forgive her . . . uh . . . forget her," he said of the 18-year-old pregnant woman.

Morales has admitted to killing two people prior to the execution-style slaying of Billy Van Pelt, Assistant State Attorney Don Scaglione said to jurors. Then he mentioned the incident when Morales reached across his children in a crack cocaine-enhanced rage to stab Betsy 13 times." Scaglione also told jurors how Morales would impersonate police officers to rob cocaine dealers. "Ivan Morales is a convicted, cold-blooded, pre-meditative murderer," Scaglione said.

Morales's defense attorneys tried to paint a different picture of Morales, calling him a victim of child abuse, married to a manipulative wife, and had fallen to drug and alcohol addictions that had ruined his life. Morales's family members testified that Morales had been severely abused as a child. His siblings said both their parents would beat, burn, urinate on, and sexually abuse them.

Defense attorneys called Morales a victim of what abuse does to a person, while prosecutors referred to him as a killer, a liar and evil.

Morales said, "I am an animal."

Judge Jack Springstead, upon receiving a recommendation from the jury, sentenced Morales to live in prison, with no chance of parole, for 25 years.

STORY 13:

She Awakened To A Gunshot

In The Night

Julie Leacock woke up on the sofa where she had fallen asleep the night before. Though she was taking strong pain medications, her mouth hurt. She had recently had her teeth pulled and was suffering from swollen and bruised gums. She took a couple more pain reliever pills and got her three children off to school. Once that was done, she went into the bedroom to wake her husband, Steven. If he didn't get up soon he'd be late for work. She shook him but he wouldn't wake up. He wouldn't move.

Julie got in her van and drove down the road to her neighbor's house. "Fred, something's wrong with Steve. I can't wake him up. Will you come over?"

"No problem," he assured her.

Inside the bedroom at the Leacock's trailer house in a rural area in Hernando County, 31-year-old Fred Angel looked at Steve. "You're not going to wake Steve up," he said. "Steve is dead. My mother is a nurse. She's seen people die in their sleep like this. I think he's had a hemorrhage." Fred picked up the telephone and dialed 911.

The morning of March 19, 1997, Detective Robert Libengood went to the trailer on Moon Road. He talked with Julie. She was in a daze, not crying, not even inquisitive. She just sat there, not saying anything.

Julie explained that her husband wasn't too healthy and had suffered from a heart problem and chronic back problems.

She had not slept with Steve the night before. She had slept in the living room to be near her son who suffered from asthma. She had not heard anything unusual during the night.

Several detectives talked with Fred, who had come to the Leacock's home when Julie fetched him that morning.

Fred had known immediately that Steve was dead, he said. He saw a hole in Steve's head with blood coming out.

After talking with investigators, Fred walked outside the trailer where a couple neighbors had gathered. They gossiped about the situation.

"I think he had a brain hemorrhage," one said. "That vein busted in his head and made the hole."

Could be from a bullet, another said. He mentioned Steve and a neighboring landholder having trouble over a fence. He had heard Steve complaining about dogs and goats coming on his property.

Mickey Moran, an investigator for the medical examiner's office, arrived at the scene about noon after receiving a "signal 7" call, meaning there was a dead person at the residence. He spoke with a deputy on duty, got logged in, and entered the house where several crime scene officers from the sheriff's office were collecting evidence.

The first thing Moran saw was a white male lying dead in bed. Rigor mortis had already set in. He checked the body over carefully. Good God, he thought, this man must have been dead for 12 or so hours. Wearing rubber gloves, Moran pushed hair on Leacock's head apart to see where the wounds were. When he did, gunpowder residue got on his gloves. This indicated a gun aimed at Leacock's head had been fired from close range.

Seeing what looked like a bullet hole going into Leacock's head, Moran rolled the body over and found the bullet exit hole. There was blood with residue indicating that part of the bullet had gone into the pillow.

In all, Moran spent about half-an-hour with the body, then he turned to Deputy Libengood. "There's a bullet hole in the back of his head. It goes from right to left directly above the ears. The gun was fired close to the head."

With Steven being found on his left side facing the wall, his attacker had to have acted from the right side of the bed. "That's what I think," Moran said.

Moran took photographs, videotaped the scene, and called Taylor Transport Body Removal to come pick up the corpse and take it to Leesburg, in Lake County, for an autopsy.

Julie and Moran stood outside the trailer. She mentioned Steve had gone to the hospital the day before with an illness. "Can I find out what that hole in his head is all about?" she asked. "We'll find out what happened after the autopsy," Moran assured her. He knew he had not mentioned the hole in Leacock's head to Julie but figured she had seen it when she was trying to wake him earlier that morning.

The next day, after detectives learned Steve Leacock had died of a bullet wound to the head, Julie and Fred were brought to the sheriff's office for more questioning. Even though detectives hadn't found a suicide note, neither Julie, Fred, nor Jason was suspected of killing Steve. Cops just needed answers to more questions.

Detective Libengood gave Julie a ride to the sheriff's office in an unmarked cruiser. Her car was inside the crime scene tape.

At the sheriff's office, Julie smoked often. She asked for something cold to drink, explaining about her recent trip to the dentist that had left her mouth throbbing. While being interviewed, Julie said she was hungry and ordered a stuffed baked potato from Wendy's because it was soft and she could roll it around in her mouth with her tongue without feeling too much pain. She certainly couldn't chew.

Julie went on to talk about Steve's friends. She recalled a couple motorcycle-rider friends had been visiting Steve the night before. The guys had hung out and smoked marijuana. One had not taken off his helmet so she hadn't seen much of his face. They might have come back to the trailer and done something to Steve, but if that were the case she didn't see nor hear them, she said.

Julie had gotten the kids off to school before getting dressed that morning. She drove her oldest son to class, and then came home and got her two younger children dressed. A friend from down the street came by the house and drove the kids to the elementary school in town.

"I was up two hours and didn't notice Steve moving. I thought he was sleeping and didn't go in the room. I wore the same clothes to take my son to school that I had slept in," she said, still in a bit of a daze.

Everybody got tired as the day passed. The cops and the witnesses were at the sheriff's office for 12 intense hours. Libengood watched Julie while she took cigarette break after cigarette break. She never finished her potato so it was there on the table during the whole interview.

As time passed, Libengood and other investigators talked to Steve and Julie's children. They said their mom and neighbor, Fred, were "close." The kids said they and their mom visited at Fred's house often, but that their dad never went with them.

After some probing by investigators, Julie revealed names of some people who knew Steve and might know something about what had happened to him. One was an acquaintance named Jason Greenwell; another was Julie's cousin, Sammy Coppola. The two lived together at Weeki Wachee, an area near the swamplands bordering the Gulf of Mexico.

Detective Tom Holly obtained a search warrant and visited Greenwell's home. Investigators knocked on Greenwell's back door and when he answered, announced they were coming in.

Low-and-behold, detectives found a gun, a .9 millimeter Ruger, the same type weapon that had been used to kill Steve.

Earlier that evening, while detectives were looking for Coppola for questioning, they got beeped from the sheriff's office. It seemed Julie had called and left a message that her cousin, Sammy Coppola, was sleeping at her mom's house. Cops could talk to him there.

At about three o'clock in the morning, several detectives stayed at Greenwell's residence while others went to speak with Coppola.

At Julie's mom's home, detectives went to wake up Coppola. "Will you come with us to the sheriff's office and tell us what you know about the shooting death of Steve Leacock?"

"I don't know anything, but of course I'll go with you," Coppola said.

While Steve's friends and family were being interviewed at the sheriff's office, other detectives were canvassing the dead man's former neighbors.

One said she had driven by Julie's trailer the morning of the shooting. She did not know Steve had been shot. Julie looked terribly stressed so she offered to drive the children to school. Julie seemed pleased she had stopped to help. "Normally, she doesn't let the kids ride in my Camero. But, this morning, she gave them a big good-bye kiss. She acted as if she would never see them again. She made a big, dramatic deal of it."

When she left with the kids, Julie followed her in her van. "When I turned to go down Sunshine Grove Road, she turned in the opposite direction. I think that's when she was going to Fred's house."

Cops asked the neighbor about Steve. What kind of man was he? Was he good to his wife? Good to the kids?

The neighbor swayed as she talked. "Steven was a demanding person. He gave his oldest son lots of chores. But he was never physically violent."

Detective Libengood drove to a restaurant where Wanda Wallace, Sammy Coppola's girlfriend, worked. He told her that an unidentified source had seen her car at the Leacock's home the night of the shooting. But Wallace said she had been working the whole night of the incident.

When she had arrived home from work that day, Sammy told her about the shooting, she said. He told her Steve had been shot. But Wallace didn't believe it, "not for one minute."

"Come with me and I'll show you," he had insisted. So she, Sammy, and Jason Greenwell drove to the Steve's house. She couldn't believe what she saw—all the crime scene tape pulled around the house and police cars in the yard. Then she realized Sammy wasn't kidding.

Later that evening, detectives located Jason Greenwell at a country bar across from his home near the gulf. He was extremely intoxicated. They took him in to the sheriff's office for questioning and found he was "pretty mad, not very jovial." He was much too intoxicated to talk for quite a while.

Also, detectives interviewed Herb Smith, another of Steve's neighbors. Herb had gone out of his house to see what was going on that morning when he saw several cars at the Leacock place, he said. "Fred came out and said Steve had been shot, there was a small hole in the back of his head. I said, 'you got to be joking.' If everybody was home, why didn't they hear the shot?"

Herb had not heard the shot from over at his house, he said. Even if he had, "I wouldn't pay any attention to it. There's always somebody shooting around here, practicing, you know." He hesitated. "I thought Steve was a nice guy, you know. I mean, the guy would give you the shirt off his back. A prime example is when I bought a car from him. Like he could have got a lot more money than what I paid for it. And he had four brand new tires sitting there mounted. I asked him how much he wanted for the tires and he says, 'Oh, take them'. He says, 'What are neighbors for?' He gave me practically brand new tires to go with the car. Another time, the neighbor next door blew a motor in the car and Steve went and got a motor for him. Steve helped him put it in. And you know, things like that. I don't even know if he charged for that. That's the way Steve was," he said, looking up at detectives from the interview table.

"Fred came out and said, 'He's been shot'," Herb continued. "When the ambulance got there, they were going to take the body and Fred said, 'Well, what about the hole in his head? You know, the hole in the back of his head.' I guess the EMS didn't even notice it. So he noticed it. He brought it to their attention, I guess."

Jason Greenwell, 48, had been arrested on a felony charge in North Carolina when he was 18 years old, so he could not legally to own a gun. In addition, he had recently gotten out of jail for a DUI violation. He had first met Steve when he and 29-year-old Sammy Coppola had helped him work on his trailer. Steve was tearing out old wall covering and putting up drywall. That was the only time Greenwell had come into contact with Steve, but he had met Julie twice and had known Sammy for a little more than two months.

Sammy recently had stayed with Steve and Julie until Steve kicked him out. Now he was living part time with Greenwell and part time on a boat docked along the Gulf of Mexico. "I let Sammy stay at my house one or two days a week," Greenwell said. "I wasn't allowed to let anyone live there." Every now and then, he'd bring Wanda Wallace over, he said.

Greenwell recalled a time when Julie brought Sammy a note from Steve saying if he didn't finish hanging the drywall, Steve was going to take back the car he had given him. That's all I know about that, Greenwell said.

The night after the shooting, Jason Greenwell, Sammy Coppola, and Wanda Wallace had gone out drinking in bars in the nearby fishing village of Aripeka. They shot the bull, so to speak, just talking a lot of crap—weather, games, and sports. They had started drinking at eight the morning before. They returned home later that night, and then Greenwell went to another bar in the area to give Sammy and Wanda privacy. When he came home, the couple was in Sammy's room. Greenwell went to his room. The next morning Wanda went to work and he and Sammy went drinking. And, "yes," Greenwell told detectives, he owned a .9-millimeter Ruger. And yes, both Sammy Coppola and Wanda Wallace knew he owned it. Sammy had even helped him clean it before.

After that first interview with Greenwell, detectives paid him other calls. There wasn't enough evidence to hold Greenwell for murder, but he was charged with felony possession of a firearm.

Upon his canvassing Leacock's neighborhood, a neighbor told Detective Scott Brockew that she had been in bed reading her mail with her window open at about 10:30 the evening of the shooting and had heard a "pop." She thought it was a gunshot but she couldn't be sure.

Brockew later talked with Wanda Wallace at the sheriff's office. He asked what she had done during the two days prior to the murder. She said she had worked, but Brockew found discrepancies in two interviews conducted with her. On the second interview, Brockew thought Wallace told nothing but lies for two straight hours. When "pinned down," she couldn't even say when she had eaten or washed her clothes. Brockew thought Wallace couldn't recall true facts because she was trying to fabricate things.

She started talking about Steve Leacock, saying he was "loud and boisterous" and that he liked his beer. But, she said she "kind-of" liked him. She appeared confused as she rambled through events of the two days.

"Look," Brockew said. "This is only two days. You need to recall yesterday and the day before."

"I'm under a lot of stress from work," Wallace said. "I'm a waitress. I have financial difficulties. Anyway, I was in bed the whole time the night Steve was shot. The morning after the murder Sammy woke me up when the alarm clock went off. He said I was going to be late for work.

At this point, detectives considered Greenwell and Wallace suspects. And everything in Julie Leacock's story didn't quite add up. She had said she had not changed clothes at all the morning after the shooting. But one of Julie's kids said his mother had slept in a Florida Gators T-shirt. Yet when detectives interviewed her, she was dressed in black shorts and a black shirt.

The child said he woke his mom up from the couch and she went into the bedroom and changed clothes. Also, he said one of his younger siblings had asked where was their dad and their mom, Julie, had said, "He has gone to Pinellas to work." She told them not to go into the bedroom. The kids said they usually went into the bedroom before school to wake up their dad and tell him goodbye and give him a kiss. But on this morning, "Mom said, 'don't bother. He went. He's gone.'"

Some "flags" were beginning to rise in the heads of detectives. They were speaking with Julie Leacock. "If you were in our shoes right now, say you're investigating this case, what would you do? Where would you go? Who would you look at?" Detective Libengood asked her.

That's when she brought up her cousin, Sammy. She said she had actually awakened when she heard a gunshot the night of the shooting. She had seen her cousin, Sammy Coppola, running out of the house with a gun and saying, "he's done." She had been frightened but just didn't know what to say to detectives when they interviewed her. She said her husband had been abusive to her and that was why Sammy had shot him.

So she had heard the shots. So she had knowledge of the shooting and had not given detectives any assistance at all. Now, all of a sudden, she was saying her husband was abusive and that her cousin had killed him.

Finally, Julie started to talk. She said, Sammy told her to stay on the couch, that her husband was "done." So, out of fear, Julie said she followed her cousin's advice. She lay there all night with her head under the pillow, afraid to move. She had been too frightened to tell detectives this previously. Also, she had been too relaxed with the medication she was taking for her aching mouth to think about the consequences.

Detectives went to Julie's mom's house in the early morning and found Sammy sleeping. They took him in for questioning. In about two hours after arriving at the sheriff's office, Sammy confessed.

Sammy Coppola's story was that Julie had been hounding him, begging him, to get a gun from Jason Greenwell, who had recently gotten out of jail.

Sammy said that while he had lived with Steve and Julie, he had an affair with his neighbor, Becky Rineheart, who was married. Becky had since gone to live in North Carolina. Steve had not approved and had told the woman's husband of the affair. Julie told Sammy if he would get a gun and kill Steve, he and Becky could move into the house with her (Julie).

When Steve informed Becky's husband of the affair, he became extremely angry and had beaten Sammy. Sammy and Becky had ended up living in the woods together. Julie said, "Look, if we get rid of Steve, you can see her. You guys could live in my house. Get a gun, get a gun."

Sammy called Becky in North Carolina and said, "Hey, Julie would let us stay with her. Julie is offering to let us live in her trailer, but I have to get rid of Steve."

Something has to be done soon, Becky agreed. That's when she told him she was pregnant with his baby.

"How do you know it's my baby," Sammy asked.

"Because my husband has been fixed."

That was all it took. "Steve is done," Sammy said.

Sammy stole Jason Greenwell's gun. The night before the shooting, he went to Julie and confronted her while she lay on the couch in the home she shared with Steve. He said, "I'm here to do it. You want it done?"

"Yes," she said.

Sammy went into Steve Leacock's bedroom, put the gun behind Steve's ear, and pulled the trigger. After he killed Steve, he went into the living room and told Julie it was "done" and he left the house.

By the time Sammy confessed, detectives working on the case were really tired, but they drove right out to the Leacock place and picked up Julie. Holding another interview, detectives, who had slept little since the killing had occurred the day before, were literally falling asleep. But the case was closed. On interviewing Julie again she said, yes, she had hounded her cousin Sammy Coppola a bit. She confessed that she had not liked her husband, that he was abusive, and that she had wanted Sammy to kill him. But she never really expected he would do it, she said.

Upon presenting the case to the jury, Assistant State Attorney Don Scaglione recalled a neighbor had thought perhaps Steve Leacock had died of a heart attack.

It was a heart attack, Scaglione said. "Obviously, a heart attack. A bullet in back of the head kind-of makes your heart stop."

In the summer of 1998 both suspects were convicted of killing Steve Leacock. In May, Julie Leacock was sentenced to 30 years each to run concurrent for second-degree murder, criminal solicitation to commit murder in the first degree, and accessory after the fact. In July, Samuel Augusta Coppola was sentenced to 35 years for second-degree murder and 30 years for criminal solicitation to commit murder in the first degree and assessor after the fact. Coppola's sentences are to run concurrent.

STORY 14:

Killers Claim Rock Star

And

Bodyguard Fame

A telephone call came in at the Pasco County Sheriff's Office from police in Clayton County, Georgia, on Tuesday, December 22, 1992 reporting the discovery of a 1986 Chevrolet in a motel parking lot there. The car was registered to James M. Boyington of Zephyrills, Florida. The Clayton County police thought it might have been involved it in a robbery that had occurred at the motel.

It was 8:54 a.m. when Deputy Melbourne B. Eakley, on routine patrol at that hour, was dispatched to Boyington's residence to see if anyone was there. No one answered Eakley's knocking. The officer walked around the duplex. The curtains were all drawn shut. Doors and windows were closed tightly.

Later the same day, a Teletype from the Georgia authorities confirmed that the automobile they had found–the one registered to James Boyington–was involved in a robbery. After receiving the information, Pasco County officers were again dispatched to Boyington's residence. This time, one of Boyington's neighbors obtained a key from the landlord so the officers could enter the duplex.

Inside, Patrolman Eakley and Sergeant Melford Griffin eye's wandered about the room, at the calendars of nearly nude Chippendale-type men on one of the kitchen walls, and at a telephone laying broken in the hallway in front of the bathroom.

Officers entered the bedroom. It was in complete disarray.
The bed sheets were messed up. A lamp was knocked over. Drawers
were pulled out from a chest. Clothes and broken items were
scattered about the floor.

Then officers saw a sliding interior door off its track. When
they went to check it, they gagged at what they saw inside. The
decomposing body of a white male was in the closet, lying in a
fetal position, wrist and ankles bound with gray telephone cord.
Tape covered the man's mouth, apparently to keep something in
place inside.

While sheriff's deputies in Florida were conducting their
inspection of James Boyington's dwelling, trying to figure out why
a man had been left bound, gagged, and stuffed inside the closet
in this quiet Florida neighborhood, the police in Jonesboro,
Georgia, were looking for two individuals responsible for robbing
a man named Jack Green in a motel room.

In the wee hours of Tuesday, December 22nd, Green called
the Jonesboro Police Department to report that he had been robbed.
He said he had been stressed out and had gone into a bar where
about six men whom he did not know were drinking. After downing
two drinks, he suddenly felt dizzy and could barely walk. It was
almost 2 a.m., time for the bar to close, and everybody started
making plans to go to another bar, one that stayed open until 4
a.m. As the bar closed, everybody left. Green, who was too tipsy to
drive, walked over to a nearby Waffle House for a cup of coffee.

When Green came back to his car, a man he had seen inside
the bar earlier walked up to him and asked if he was okay. The
man said he had a room at the motel near the bar and offered
Green a place to rest until he was able to drive.

Green took the man up on his offer and accompanied him to
the motel. Upon entering room 208, he saw the man had a
roommate. An ice chest filled with beer was in the room. From the
number of empty beer cans there, he got the idea the men had
already been partying for some time. They offered him a beer and
he accepted.

Green was a clean-shaven young man with a short haircut. He was smartly dressed, his attire set off by a black-leather bomber jacket. One of the men remarked about Green's neat appearance: "You look like a police officer."

Still dizzy, Green tried to focus his eyes. Both men had sore-looking noses. They had tried to punch earrings through their own nostrils, they explained when they caught him staring.

One of the pair identified himself as James Boyington and declared he was carrying a .45-caliber gun strapped to his leg.

After a while, all the drunken talk about guns began to frighten Green. He decided to leave the motel room. As he did so, the man who called himself James followed Green outside and demanded he stay. Green insisted on getting inside his car, but James started pushing him. The other man, who called himself Cliff, tried to calm James down. Unable to get free from James, Green went back into the motel room.

Things were a blur to Green. He could barely make out what was happening. Then he realized one of the men was threatening him with a .45-caliber handgun. Green was unaware of what followed. The last thing he recalled was removing his clothing and going to bed. When he woke up, about 6 a.m., the two men had left the room with all his clothing. When he looked outside, he saw his 1992 Oldsmobile had vanished. Green quickly called the police.

Upon checking all the cars on the motel parking lot, police found a car with Florida plates registered to James Boyington. When they checked the motel records, however, the officers found no Boyington registered there. Their next step was to call the police in Pasco County, Florida.

Back in Zephyrhills, Florida, investigators had been summoned to James Boyington's residence where the bound and gagged body had been found stuffed in the closet. Crime scene Officer Brian MacMillan arrived and put up yellow tape to preserve the scene until other technicians could arrive. Then Paul Tidd, a crime scene supervisor, arrived and started checking the apartment.

Crime scene technician Gary Kimble, from the Hernando County Sheriff's Office, was also summoned to Pasco County to lend a hand at the apartment. Officers lifted fingerprints and went over the residence with a lumalite, a device that can detect matter invisible to the naked eye. The crime scene was also vacuumed for fibers that might help identify individuals who had been in the apartment during the deadly struggle.

Supervisor Tidd assisted Investigator Brian MacMillan in collecting different materials he thought might have a bearing on the case. The fact that the bedroom closet sliding doors were off their bottom track suggested a struggle might have taken place inside the closet.

Neighbors and family of 62-year-old James M. Boyington identified his body.

Dr. Joan Wood determined the cause of the victim's death as asphyxiation. When the tape-gag was removed, it was discovered that a sock had been stuffed inside his mouth. He had died as a result of struggling against his bindings. It was determined he had been dead since Saturday, December 19th.

A neighbor told investigators he had recently seen Boyington's car parked outside his home while Boyington was away on a cruise. Another neighbor had seen Boyington return by taxi about 3:30 p.m. on Saturday, accompanied by a younger, blondish man, but the neighbor did not know the young man's name.

A friend of Boyington's said he had often seen young men entering and leaving the victim's apartment. The witness saw two young men enter the apartment a couple of weeks before the murder. One of the men had curly hair and a mustache and beard, and was wearing a baseball hat. Another had what the witness described as a crooked eye. The pair had been in and out of Boyington's duplex often, the friend said.

Through questioning Boyington's friends, relatives, and neighbors, the investigators learned the gray-haired Boyington was considered a very gentle man who would never have hurt anybody. He loved classical music, the opera, and enjoyed eating out in fine restaurants. At home, he would snack on chocolate-chip cookies or cake brought to him by neighbors. "He seemed like a lonely man," one of the neighbors recalled.

"He has been taken advantage of by people after his money," another neighbor told the investigators.

As the sleuths checked into his background, they learned Boyington had grown up and lived most of his life in Maine. Six years before his murder, he'd retired as manager of the men's department in a retail store in Boston, then moved to Florida to live the good life in the quiet bedroom community just northeast of Tampa.

But ever since he had moved to the Sunshine State, there had been a stream of young men in and out of his duplex, according to his neighbors and relatives.

"They were frightening," some said. "They were bleeding him. I think he was afraid."

Unfortunately, nobody seemed to know any of the visitors' names.

Boyington had often told his relatives that he feared for his own life. "I may not be alive long enough to take the trip," he had said, referring to his planned Caribbean cruise.

Even though he had feared the worst, Boyington did take the cruise. He left on December 12th and returned on December 19th, the Saturday when, according to the medical examiner, he died.

During their probe, investigators' attention was drawn to a man named Buster Kethean, a transient who may have been involved in a recent burglary in the neighborhood. It was known that Kethean sometimes slept in a nearby abandoned building and often hung out at a park frequented by homosexuals. Kethean– or just about anybody else from the park–could have entered Boyington's residence without raising a lot of suspicion.

Upon inspecting Boyington's apartment, investigators were unable to find his wallet or credit cards. Deputies notified banks

to flag Boyington's accounts. By doing this, if anyone tried to use
the cards, police would be notified.

All the while, in Jonesboro, Georgia, police searched the motel
room where Green was robbed. They found various papers
identifying two Florida men: 25-year-old Clifford Curtis Jarvis
and 30-year-old Brian Walter Kipp.

Detective Chris Buttler of Georgia's Cobb County Police
Department had Boyington's automobile brought to the Georgia
Bureau of Investigation crime lab to be held there until Florida
investigators could have it picked up.

During the investigation in Florida, detectives conducted
extensive interviews. They learned Kipp had met Jarvis on
December 19th, when Jarvis had invited Kipp to stay at his place
for the night.

That night, Kipp and Jarvis went to Boyington's residence.
Detectives believe Kipp and Jarvis had planned to rob Boyington.
Cops theorized that while the two men were visiting Boyington,
they bound and gagged him, then stuffed him in the closet. Marks
on the inner part of the door indicated Boyington might have
been alive when he was left inside the closed and had struggled to
get out.

Meanwhile Kipp and Jarvis took Boyington's credit cards and
fled to Georgia in Boyington's Chevrolet.

The case picked up steam when Sergeant-Major Morris Tolar
of Georgia's Cobb County police received a call from an employee
at the Cumberland Mall in Atlanta informing him someone was
trying to use a credit card that had been flagged by Citibank.
Lawmen asked if the clerk had gotten the credit-card imprints. He
said he had. The numbers on the card imprint matched the
numbers on a credit card police were looking for—one belonging to
James Boyington.

When officers went to the Cumberland Mall, the store clerk
described the man who had tried to use the credit card as being
obnoxious. He was carrying a CD player, the clerk said. He had
been there only minutes before the lawmen arrived. He had been

with a man wearing a gray shirt with the Embassy Suites Hotel and the name Holley stitched on it.

The clerk said the man with the credit card did not have any identification, and when the clerk went to process the card, he saw it had been flagged in the computer. Thus, he refused to honor the card and called the cops.

Sgt. Tolar had been briefed on the Florida case. He knew the killer might have stolen the flagged credit card from a murder victim. Florida officials had also said the robbery and murder might have occurred after a homosexual liaison. They told Tolar the same suspects might have been involved in a similar incident that had occurred in Clayton County, Georgia (which is two counties south of Cobb County), where Jack Green was robbed in an incident that also involved homosexuality.

Detectives hurried to the Embassy Suites Hotel. Outside, they saw a man who fit the description given by the mall clerk. The man was wearing a gray shirt bearing the hotel name and the name Holley. Detectives approached him and started talking. Dave Holley, who was a bellman, told them he had driven a man who called himself Boyington to the mall; it was a hotel courtesy to drive customers to the mall. Holley said the man had claimed to be a rock star.

Holley accompanied the "rock star" into several stores where he tried to purchase some items with a credit card. Holley said the man was obnoxious, rude, and made racist remarks. Holley tried to persuade him to go back to the hotel. Finally, the man agreed, saying he needed to get back anyway. He had a concert to play that night, he said.

Upon checking the hotel register, detectives found the name James Boyington was indeed in the register book. This individual had guaranteed the room with a credit card in that name. Detectives found the 1992 Oldsmobile registered to Jack Green in the parking lot.

With a suite in the elegant hotel being registered under the name of the man found dead in a closet in Florida, police believed they were dealing with some mean characters. Sgt. Tolar immediately called for backup. Extra units had already been assigned to patrol the mall area during the holidays because of the increased likelihood of auto thefts and robberies. At the hotel, police got together with management for a briefing about the suite where the suspects were staying.

Tolar wasn't taking any unnecessary chances. The Clayton County police had already told him the suspects might be armed with a .45-caliber handgun.

Before making any moves, officers developed a plan on how to take the suspects. The arrangement resulted in Tolar and several officers accompanying Holley to the suspects' suite. Other officers followed, covering Tolar from behind.

As previously mapped, Holley knocked on the door. It opened. Holley quickly moved aside from the doorway, enabling officers to view the suspects inside.

With guns drawn, officers rushed into the suite. "Get on the floor!" they ordered.

"Can I help you? What's going on?" one suspect asked.

"Identify yourselves," Tolar demanded. His gun and his eyes were fixed on the suspects. The lawman could detect the heavy odor of liquor wafting through the room. An opened bottle of Jack Daniels sat on a nearby table. A checkbook, some change and a cigarette lighter near the liquor bottle led Tolar to believe someone had emptied his pockets there. A CD player was on another table in the sitting room. Tolar remembered the store clerk at the mall had said the man trying to use the flagged credit card had been carrying a CD player.

"What the hell is this?" asked a suspect. "Somebody's going to get their ass sued."

"Identify yourselves," Tolar demanded again. Meanwhile, another officer went up to the suspects and cuffed their hands behind their backs.

"James Boyington," one of the pair said. The other suspect identified himself as Cliff Jarvis.

"I know what this is all about," said the suspect using the name Boyington, making light of the situation. "This is all about that credit-card stuff over in the mall. I can explain that."

The man using Boyington's identification said he was a rock star and that Jarvis was his driver-bodyguard. He said Jarvis had been in charge of keeping up with all his identifications, but he had somehow managed to lose his picture ID. "That's why I have no picture identification," he said. He also declared he was supposed to play that night with the popular rock group Twisted Sister.

Now Jarvis spoke up. He told police the information his friend had given was true. "I'm his driver. And we lost his driver's license. He doesn't have any picture identification. I do all the driving for him. He's a rock star."

"I'm supposed to play again in Atlanta tonight," the counterfeit Boyington said. He paused for a moment, and then asked for a cigarette.

Officers had not planned to conduct an interview during the arrest, therefore steered clear of any questions about the Florida murder or the assault on Jack Green in Jonesboro, Georgia. They were there, they informed the suspects, because of the possible misuse of credit cards.

As in some other states, in Georgia, police can arrest a suspect on probable cause regardless of the nature of the crime. In this case, the man using the name Boyington was the man police believed had been using the stolen credit card.

In due course, Jack Green positively identified photographs of Jarvis and Kipp as being those who invited him into their motel room and then would not let him leave. Upon searching the motel, police also found items belonging to the suspects. An identification found on the parking lot, too, belonged to Kipp.

After being taken to a police substation at the Cumberland Mall, the man who police believed was Brian Kipp maintained he was James Boyington, and that he was a guitar-playing rock star. In any case, cops just let him continue making his outlandish claims.

Both suspects talked up a storm. But the rock star-and-bodyguard fantasy soon got to be too much for Clifford Jarvis. He finally spilled the beans.

Jarvis, who had bleached hair and whose nose appeared to be broken, said he only did what his friend Kipp told him to do. Kipp beat him often, he said. Kipp had recently beaten him up so badly Jarvis ended up with a badly broken nose and his face was left with a mound of bruises. Jarvis began to cry. Kipp would beat him up if he didn't do what he wanted him to do, he said. "Kipp made me do it," Jarvis told police.

Georgia's Cobb County authorities arrested Clifford Jarvis and Brian Kipp, detaining them until Florida lawmen could arrive.

In Pasco County, Florida, on Christmas night, Detective Pierce called Detective Randy Scott Belasie. "Pack your bags. We're going to Georgia," he said. Because it was during the holidays, the two could not get a commercial flight to Atlanta, so they decided to drive to Cobb County where the two suspects were being held. Pasco authorities also sent a wrecker to Georgia to bring Boyington's vehicle back to Florida.

The two suspects were later returned to Florida on a governor's warrant for first-degree murder.

A local grand jury indicted Clifford Jarvis and Brian Kipp for first-degree murder on January 19, 1993. The pair stood trial in the fall of that year in two separate proceedings before different juries. On November 19, 1993, Brian Kipp was sentenced to 22 years on a second-degree murder conviction. Clifford Jarvis was sentenced to life on a first-degree murder conviction, with a mandatory 25 years to be served.

STORY 15:

Couple On The Run:

Caught With Gun In Her Panties

In the slightly rolling countryside in Central Springs, Florida, where mobile home parks house a lot of retired people, residents don't really expect crime to come calling. But it happens all too often in the Tampa bedroom communities.

On November 16, 1995, when Detective Allen Proctor was notified of a slaying at a mobile home in a trailer park on Wise Road, he raised his brows. Not only had an elderly woman been killed, but her caretaker was dead, too.

Detective Proctor drove the short distance from Dade City to the trailer park where he met with other detectives and crime scene technicians.

Inside the residence, Maudeline Bailey, 84, sat slumped over dead in a bloodstained chair. A few feet away, Alice Durfee, 57, lay dead facedown on the floor in a pool of blood with her hands palm-up next to her head.

It appeared to the detective that the woman on the floor had been shot in the back of her head. Walking through the house, Proctor noticed dresser drawers in the bedrooms had been pulled out and clothes left hanging from the edges.

Proctor went outside and conversed with a team of officers who had arrived at the residence.

The two women had been discovered dead by a neighbor. Maudeline Bailey's daughter had asked the neighbor to walk over to the trailer and check on Mrs. Bailey and her caretaker, Alice Durfee. Mrs. Bailey's daughter had been trying to contact her mother since she arrived in Miami for a business convention.

At first, the daughter didn't think much about the phone being unanswered. The caretaker played on a bowling league and her mother could have gone with her. That would leave nobody home to answer the phone. Mr. Bailey had entered the hospital two weeks previously.

But then, having made numerous calls home over a couple of days, the daughter had become quite worried and contacted the neighbor.

It was getting dark and crime scene tape was already up when technician William Joseph arrived at the home. Joseph spoke briefly with Detectives Proctor and James Medley. He put covers on his shoes and slipped his hands into crime scene gloves to avoid contamination and to keep from destroying any evidence.

Joseph walked up the ramp and onto the screened porch. The door was ajar. He reached up and opened it from the top to prevent destroying any prints that might be there. Inside, he flicked on a light.

Entering the front room, the technician walked toward the dead women. Mrs. Bailey's hair was covered with blood, still he could see the exit wound on her head. Taking a closer look, he saw the bullet had entered the left side of her head in the rear, leaving an open lesion from which blood escaped and rolled down the chair and splattered onto the nearby lamp.

In a drawer in the bedroom, Joseph found identification, including driver's license, social security card, and papers in a wallet identifying the older woman as Maudeline Bailey. But he didn't find any identification for the caretaker.

Joseph went through normal crime scene procedures, including using a shop vacuum and doing sweepings to pick up hair and fiber which might be used for evidence. He also attempted to lift prints inside the residence.

Joseph finally left at 1 a.m. and returned after a few hours sleep. That morning, he found prints from the yard that appeared to have come from two different pair of shoes. He collected bloodstains from a handicapped accessible ramp leading from the ground to the screened-in front porch.

Inside the house, Joseph got down on his hands and knees to search for a projectile. Finding a bullet, he photographed it in place, and then put it in a brown paper bag. He also collected samples of blood from the lamp.

Meanwhile, it was learned that Alice Durfee's car, a 1990 Nissan, was missing and had been presumably taken by the killer or killers. A nationwide bulletin to be on the lookout for the Nissan was put over the wires.

Autopsies revealed both women had been shot in the back of the head. Maudeline Bailey, once, and Alice Durfee, twice.

Detectives didn't have any real suspects. They followed up on a number of tips and questioned several individuals. Their efforts went nowhere.

Far from the murder scene and the little town of Crystal Springs, Lynne Grace Lenton, employed by Revenue Canada Customs Border Services, at Emerson, Manitoba, peered into the window of a dirty 1990 Nissan that had just crossed the border into Canada. Inside were a man and woman.

"Do you have any handguns, firearms, mace, pepper spray, or stun guns in the vehicle?" she asked the male driver.

He got out of the car and stood with his back to Lenton. "We don't have any handguns in the vehicle, do we?" he asked his female passenger.

The young woman looked down to the floor of the car and put her hand down in-between the two seats. Then she peeked up at the man and said, "No, we don't have any handguns."

Suspicious, Lenton sent the couple to Immigration for a thorough inspection. The driver moved the car to the side of the building, as directed. When asked, he identified himself as Alex Hoffman and said he was going to Canada to see his sister.

Robert Steven McCarthy, a peace officer with the Royal Canadian Mounted Police, found a .22 caliber pistol in the vehicle. McCarthy arrested the driver under the Customs Act because the gun had not been declared upon entry to Canada.

The young woman traveling with the man had been standing just outside the room. She came in, identifying herself as Alice Durfee, the owner of the vehicle. "What's going on?" she asked.

McCarthy explained that her companion was under arrest and would be appearing before a local magistrate. He handcuffed the suspect and escorted him to a police car. He started to drive away, then stopped. He was having doubts about the couple's identify. McCarthy stopped behind the vehicle the couple had arrived in and took another look at it. Paying closer attention to its contents, he noticed various credit cards and prescription bottles with labels made out to Alice Durfee and Maudeline Bailey.

At this time, the woman using the name Alice Durfee was free to leave. However, she didn't have any driver's license, so she was not allowed to take the car.

William Frederick John Hemings, commander for the Emerson Detachment, and member of the Royal Canadian Mounted Police, was informed the customs inspectors had seized a handgun from an automobile that had crossed the border. Hemings peeked inside the car and noticed a bag, bowling ball, and bowling shoes in the back seat. The vehicle also contained a walker used by handicapped people.

Hemings learned the young female was identifying herself as the registered owner of the vehicle and the male was said to be Alex Hoffman. The male had no identification. He said he had left his wallet at a truck stop just over the border in North Dakota. Hemings contacted operators at the truck stop but they said the wallet had not been turned in.

"This is odd," Constable McCarthy said. "A young couple bringing a walker with them to Canada on a holiday."

"Phone Florida. Find out about the registered owner of the car and the identity of the people we have in custody before we proceed any further," Hemings advised.

McCarthy ran information about the car through the computer. Soon he had linked the vehicle back to Pasco County, Florida. He called Pasco County authorities and spoke with Detective Proctor. A 1990 Nissan had been stopped at the border crossing at Emerson, Manitoba. The people in the car identified themselves as Alex Hoffman and Alice Durfee.

"You have somebody claming to be Alice Durfee?"

"Yes, we have Miss Durfee here," McCarthy said.

"That's impossible because Alice Durfee has been murdered," Proctor replied.

McCarthy reported back to Commander Hemings. "Take the woman into custody as a party to the offense of possessing the unregistered weapon," Hemings advised.

After the two were taken into custody, the woman claiming to be Durfee, still wearing the same clothes she was arrested in, was patted-down and taken to a different detachment in Altona, a 45-minute ride away. At the detachment, she was strip-searched. The female jailer noticed a bulge in her underpants. She asked her to remove whatever it was. The woman reached between her legs and pulled out a tissue paper wrapped gun and handed it to the jailer.

On November 17, Detectives Allen Proctor, Denney Campbell and James Medley left for Canada. After arriving in Winnipeg, they made the one-hour drive through a snow blizzard to Emerson. Once there, Rob McCarthy told detectives the woman was still using the name Alice Durfee.

Upon being interviewed by detectives, the woman told this story: Her name was Melissa Harris. She was present when the two women in Crystal Springs were shot. But she had not been involved in it. She was traveling with Earl Linebaugh. He had killed the women.

As detectives worked on the case, they uncovered numerous bits of evidence relating the suspects to the crime, including shoe impressions in the yard, fingerprints on property belonging to the slain women and witnesses putting the couple in the area during the double murder.

Witnesses had seen the couple walking hand-in-hand near the home. They remembered the two coming out of the woods with a blue backpack with a yellow patch on it, which was later found in the car in Canada. A neighbor said the couple asked if they could use his phone. He was uncomfortable about letting them inside his house, so he lied and said the phone wasn't hooked up. At the next home, that of Mrs. Bailey, Melissa was allowed inside to make a call.

Two different guns, a Jennings .22 and the H&R .20, had shot the two victims. The weapons were the same type as found in the car and in Melissa's panties. One of the bullets in Alice Durfee's head was from the same gun used to kill Maudeline Bailey. The other bullet was from the other gun.

A pillow had been placed on Durfee's head. Two guns, one on the bottom and one on the top, were pressed into the pillows and both triggers were pulled. "The two are married in crime," prosecutors said. The gun Melissa pulled from her panties was the second gun used to kill Alice Durfee, detectives said.

In the case against the two, the prosecution rounded up 42 witnesses and 52 pieces of evidence.

They learned: Earl Linebaugh and Melissa Harris first met in Jacksonville, Texas. Melissa, the mother of three small children, was separated from her husband. Earl had served time in prison, but he appeared nice to Melissa, even though, she told officials, "From the first time I met Earl he had a handgun on him. He claimed it was necessary to protect himself from enemies."

Earl and Melissa decided to gather Melissa's children, who were in the custody of Melissa's mother, and leave Texas. So the following day, Earl packed up his guns. He stole his father's camping gear and Melissa stole her cousin's credit cards. They loaded the guns, the stolen goods and the kids in a 1980 Ford and headed for New Mexico to visit friends before traveling across the country.

In New Mexico, the car broke down. They rented a U-Haul truck and left the car at a motel where they had stayed over night. Finally, they made their way to a relative's house in Orlando; there they left the children.

They planned to make Tampa their next stop. Earl pulled off the interstate about 50 miles north of Tampa and they talked about what they would do next. Having the overdue U-Haul in his possession made Earl nervous. He decided to dump it. So taking the camping bag, two guns, and a small bag of clothing, the couple set out on the final leg of their journey on foot, walking back onto the interstate and holding out their thumbs in search of a ride.

Soon a Highway Patrol car stopped alongside and a trooper told them they couldn't hitchhike on the road. He gave them a ride to a nearby exit. The couple got out of the patrol car and ventured off into the woods where they slept the rest of the night. They needed a car and cash. The next morning they walked the railroad tracks and soon reached a mobile home community.

The next stop was the home of Mrs. Bailey, and double murder.

In two separate trials, the suspects were found guilty of first-degree murder. Melissa Harris was convicted in December of 1997 and sentenced to life in prison. Earl Linebaugh was convicted in December of 1998. He, too, was sentenced to life in prison.

STORY 16:

She Listened To Kidnappers

Plot Her Murder

Back roads coiling between orange groves and thick Florida hammocks are usually hidden from people traveling on Interstate-75 as it cuts through the Withlachoochee State Forest. Local people, hunters, and game wardens use those roads mostly for innocent purposes—but not always.

Branch Everett, a mechanic from the quaint little town of Dade City, had just put a new radiator in his wife's car and decided to take it out for a test-drive on the afternoon of September 8, 1991. As Everett turned the car around to head back the way he had come, something peculiar lying a few yards down a sandy path caught his eye.

Everett stopped his car and started down the sun-baked trail. Getting closer, he knew what he saw: It was a body, a woman's body with her hands tied behind her back. Everett hurried back to his car and drove to the nearest community to call the police.

Authorities arriving from the Hernando County Sheriff's Office could tell right away the woman had been murdered. She was lying in the grass wearing a T-shirt and shorts, her hands bound behind her back with a rope. It was apparent she had been shot in the back of the head. There were no clues to her identity or why she was slain.

Sheriff's Detectives Carlos Douglas and Rick Kramer were assigned to the case. The two detectives had worked closely on other cases in the county and made a good team. Sheriff Thomas Mylander knew the detectives were capable of handling the job; he figured they would find out what had happened to this woman.

Tim Whitfield, investigator in the forensic science section of the sheriff's office was contacted by beeper, then directed to meet with Sergeant David Lee at the crime scene. Upon his arrival, Whitfield went to work, first by taking an overall view of the body and the surrounding area.

An ominous black cloud in the northern sky caught the cop's attention. The wind, already blowing harder than usual for this part of Florida, was suddenly picking up speed. Whitfield was concerned that any potential evidence might be destroyed in the coming rain.

Whitfield collected soil from underneath the victim's head and directed crime scene technician Ken Locke to help take still and video photographs of the body and the surrounding area. The two officers also photographed shoe and tire tracks that lay along the roadside.

Paramedics then placed the dead woman in a body bag and delivered it to the medical examiner's office in Brooksville, about 12 miles west of the crime scene, for a preliminary postmortem report. Other officials combed the area looking for anything that might lead to the killer.

At about 9:30 that evening, Sergeant Lee contacted the detectives and informed them that the body of a white female, about 35 to 40 years old, had been found near Ridge Manor. They were asked to come down to the county medical examiner's office in Brooksville to help make the identification. Once there, detectives wrote out a description of the victim, noting her fair skin, dark curly hair, and tattoos. She was wearing a ripped T-shirt that bore the words "Low Country Harley Davidson, Charleston, South Carolina," and a pair of military-type cutoff shorts unzipped halfway. A $1 bill and some change were still in her shorts pocket.

She was lying on the medical examiner's table face down and bound by a piece of rope looped twice around her wrists.

Whitfield finished his work at the crime scene then joined other investigators at the medical examiner's office. Using the lumalite, which makes certain types of evidence glow, Whitfield did a scan on the victim's body and clothing. While he looked for any types of fiber that could be used as potential evidence, Gary Kimble, a lab technician at the sheriff's office, rolled fingerprints from the victim.

Later that evening, Douglas and Kramer went back to the sheriff's office and issued an alert to other law enforcement agencies containing the victim's description in hopes she had been listed as a missing person.

There had recently been several homicides involving bikers in Sumter County, which joined Hernando on its northeast section. The victim may have witnessed one of those killings, cops speculated.

Early the next morning, the dead woman was taken to the medical examiner's office in Leesburg, about 60 miles east of Brooksville, for an autopsy. Several investigators went along to observe, including Douglas and Kramer.

The autopsy showed she had died from a .25-caliber bullet wound inflicted at close range to the back of the head. Excessive red, blue, and purple wounds on the victim's body showed she had struggled violently before death.

Meanwhile, at the sheriff's office, Detective Michael Owens got on the telephone and started calling tattoo parlors in Tampa and surrounding areas in hopes the woman could be identified by her tattoo.

While Douglas and Kramer were at the autopsy, Russell Knodle, a forensic technician, checked the victim's fingerprints. Her pattern classification was unusual. Knodle revealed his findings to officials at several different law enforcement agencies, including the Florida Department of Law Enforcement and the Federal Bureau of Investigation. Tampa authorities checked their print files and found they had a set of fingerprints taken from a woman who had previously been arrested there. Apparently, Mary Elaine Shearin was arrested for shoplifting in Tampa in 1977, so her prints were on file.

Knodle took the dead woman's prints to Tampa and compared the two sets. The prints matched perfectly.

Detectives Douglas and Kramer were still in Leesburg when they received word the victim had been identified. Now, after a quick trip home to freshen up, they would have to go to the victim's address to further the investigation.

Once in Tampa, Douglas and Kramer met with officers. At about 4:30 that afternoon, they went to the victim's address to speak with her relatives. Detectives learned that Shearin, the wife of a Vietnam veteran and the mother of two youngsters, had last been seen by family members in the early morning hours of September 8th. She had visited friends, returned home, drank a soda, and then went out again. She was last seen driving her yellow 1986 Cadillac Cimarron. Shearin had not been reported missing by family members because they had assumed she was visiting with friends in Tampa who did not have a telephone.

An all-points bulletin was put out for Shearin's Cadillac. At about 10 on the evening of September 10th, Sergeant Louie Potengiano, of the Tampa Police Department, radioed in that he had spotted the victim's Cadillac at a barbecue place. Officer John Preyer heard the call and started down 22nd Avenue, at about 45 miles-per-hour, toward the area where the Cadillac was seen leaving the restaurant. Near a busy intersection, Preyer slowed the patrol car while awaiting word on which way the Cadillac was about to turn. The Cadillac was heading west on Hillsborough Avenue. Preyer made several quick turns to head it off. At about the same time, several police cars arrived on scene, all with their police lights flashing, warning the driver of the Cadillac to stop.

Preyer whipped onto Hillsborough Avenue and screeched in front of the Cadillac. The driver pulled over near a gas station.

Preyer got out, drew his gun, and pointed it at the driver. The officer noticed the motorist had something in his hand.

"Drop it!" Preyer ordered. The driver dropped a set of car keys as another officer snapped handcuffs on him. Another man got out of the car on the passenger side. An officer handcuffed him, too. Both men were advised of their rights and told they were being taken to the police station for questioning. If they had done nothing wrong, they had nothing to worry about, they were told.

From the moment handcuffs were put on the two suspects, they were separated. There would be no way they could collaborate on a story.

Detectives Douglas and Kramer were contacted at their homes about 3:30 on the morning of September 11th and informed the murder victim's automobile had been stopped in Tampa. Detectives wasted no time in getting to the city.

At the Tampa police station, Kramer spoke with the suspect who had been driving the stolen vehicle. The suspect, who had identified himself as Brad Crane, said that on the evening of September 7th, he had been hired by a couple to drive the Cadillac. Later that night, the two had dropped him off at a section of Tampa called the "projects," he said.

A couple of hours later, the man returned to the projects without the woman and hired Crane to drive him around in the Cadillac while he smoked crack, he said.

In another section of the police station, the man who had been riding with Crane when police stopped the Cadillac, identified himself as Oliver Engles. His story was altogether different from Brad Crane's.

Engles said he had spent the weekend partying with another friend and some prostitutes at an elderly man's house in Tampa. He had never met the man driving the Cadillac until shortly before police spotted them. His car had broken down near the barbecue cafe, so he had hitched a ride with the man in the Cadillac.

While detectives questioned the suspects, other investigators checked the Cadillac. Officers found it strange that the lining material inside the trunk of such a luxury automobile was badly ripped and torn. Officers also found pieces of rope in the trunk. This was valuable evidence if it could be matched with the rope taken from Mary Shearin's wrists. And last but not least, officers added to their evidence a small, chrome-plated .25-caliber handgun, found lying on the console.

In the meantime, other officers checked out the suspects' stories. While Engles sat in the patrol car, a detective talked with the elderly man who lived at the house where Engles said he had spent the weekend partying. Engles' story checked out. He was released.

Brad Crane's story, however, was proved to be a total lie. Detectives found out that Crane was not even the man's real name. He was actually 30-year-old Alfred Lewis Fennie.

During Fennie's interviews, he told several stories about what had happened in the early-morning hours of September 8th. Most of these stories turned out to be more lies.

Then finally, Fennie said his friend, 26-year-old Michael Antoine Frazier, had killed the woman. Fennie told detectives that Frazier could be found at Fennie's girlfriend's apartment since the girlfriend was Frazier's cousin. That night, detectives went to the restaurant where Fennie's girlfriend, 28-year-old Pamela Colbert, worked. She gave the officers the keys to her apartment where she said Michael Frazier could be found.

Tampa Police officers Jone Preyer, Matt Smith, and Robert Nasief went to the apartment. They saw Frazier, whom they recognized from a photo that had been taken during a prior arrest. Frazier was sleeping on the living-room couch. One of the officers snapped the handcuffs on Frazier before he even knew what was happening. Lawmen observed that Frazier had a serious wound on his arm, as if he had been bitten.

"How did you get that bite?" Douglas asked, after Frazier was brought to the police station for questioning.

Pamela Colbert's child had made the bite that had left deep teeth marks in his arm, Frazier explained.

While Fennie and Frazier were being held for further questioning, Detective Noblitt talked with Pamela Colbert at the restaurant where she worked. She agreed to allow detectives to photograph her child's teeth to see if the teeth impressions matched the bite marks on Frazier's arm. In the meantime, impressions were being taken of Mary Elaine Shearin's teeth at the medical examiner's office in Leesburg.

At Noblitt's request, Colbert gave him all the clothes Frazier had worn on the morning of September 8th.

"Fennie says you killed the lady," Douglas said to Frazier during interrogation.

Frazier denied he had been the triggerman. "Ask Pam," Frazier said. "Pam knows. She was there."

Detective Noblitt, who was observing the interview, could barely believe what he was hearing–Pamela Colbert was at the scene when Shearin was killed. Noblitt had already spoken with Colbert. She had seemed unaware about anything that had happened the night of the murder. "She was as cool as a cucumber," Noblitt would later say to other officers.

Noblitt decided to pay another visit to Pamela Colbert. "I need you to go with me to the police station to answer a few more questions," he said. The woman agreed.

Noblitt watched through a one-way mirror while Detectives Douglas and Kramer advised Colbert of her rights and began to interview her. And just as Frazier had promised, within two minutes, Colbert was nodding her head. "I'll tell you everything that happened," she said.

After putting together details and evidence, authorities charged the three suspects, Albert Fennie, Michael Frazier, and Pamela Colbert, with the first-degree murder of Mary Elaine Shearin.

Pieces of rope that had been used to tie Shearin's hands behind her back and pieces of rope found in the trunk of the Cadillac were sent to FBI Special Agent Joe A. Dizinno, an expert on bank robberies and kidnappings. Dizinno unraveled the pieces of rope to determine if they had once been a part of the same rope. He examined the color, thickness, construction, strands, and the paper core inside the rope contents taken from Shearin's wrists with the rope taken from the trunk of her Cadillac. When Dizinno unraveled the paper core, he made a positive physical match. "There is no doubt in my mind the pieces were once the same rope," he told investigators.

At the Florida Department of Law Enforcement headquarters in Tampa, Terrance A. Lauoy, a firearms analyst, examined the gun that had been found inside the Cadillac. Detectives believed it was the pistol used to kill Mary Shearin. Technicians fired the gun into a water recovery tank, then removed and examined the slugs. Markings on the bullet taken from Shearin's head and those fired into the water recovery tank matched. This proved to investigators that the bullets were fired from the same gun.

Imperfections inside the barrels of guns are never the same, even when constructed about the same time and at the same manufacturer. "When the bullet goes down the gun barrel, it picks up these imperfections. I have no doubt the bullets (that killed Shearin and the ones fired into the water recovery tank) were fired from the same pistol," Lauoy explained to investigators.

As detectives collected more evidence and more witnesses' statements, they put together the horrible story of Mary Shearin's grisly murder. Although all the facts of what actually happened would probably never be known, detectives believed the account Michael Frazier finally gave was closest to the truth, despite his apparently self-serving downplaying of his own role. "I'm not going to sit in Old Sparky (the Florida electric chair) for anybody," he told Detective Douglas.

Many people went to the low-income projects area looking to buy drugs. "Dope dealers stand on the street corners in the projects. When cars pass with people inside looking like they want to buy dope, dealers wave for them to stop," Frazier explained.

"When a car stops, the dealer will hop into the car and ride around the block and sell the person drugs," he continued. If there is no one in the area who looks suspicious, like a police informant, the transaction is done through the open car window, he said.

Frazier said that he and Alfred Fennie often stood on the street corners outside the projects. They pretended to have dope to sell. When somebody stopped, they would "beat them up and rob them," Frazier confessed.

Shortly after midnight on the morning of September 8, Frazier and Fennie decided they would go to the corner of Florida Avenue and Broad Street, a place where Frazier said he had sold dope on previous occasions. This was a place where the two often hung around waiting for a dope-buyer to rob. In the early-morning hours, the yellow-colored Cadillac pulled out of the projects. The men waved for the car to stop, then Fennie ran out in the street and jumped into the passenger seat beside Mary Shearin.

The idea was to sell Shearin drugs using the "buy-wait" method. This is when the drug dealer gets the money up front and the buyer waits while the dealer goes elsewhere to get the drugs. It was, of course, not unusual for the seller to never return with the drugs. "You ain't stealing," Frazier asserted, explaining that no one forced the buyer to hand over the money. "There ain't nobody going to chase you down in the projects."

Frazier said he ran over to the Cadillac. The plan was to rob Shearin. Frazier was not going to let Fennie take all the money. "I wanted to get my share of the money. Nobody's going to beat me out of the money," he told cops.

When Frazier reached the Cadillac, Fennie said, "Come on, get in the car and let's go." Frazier jumped into the back seat and they started off. At gunpoint, Fennie robbed Shearin of her purse and wedding rings then ordered her to drive around the corner. She did as she was told.

With the gun poking in her ribs, Shearin maneuvered her Cadillac into the dark, alley-like street. Fennie told her to stop there and ordered her out of the car. He demanded the number of her automatic bank teller card. She told him a number. Then, with the small chrome revolver pointed at her head, Fennie ordered

Shearin into the trunk of her Cadillac. Fennie closed the trunk. He then drove to a bank to withdraw money. But there was a problem; Fennie could not get the automatic teller to accept the number. Frustrated, he drove into a dark bushy area and ordered Shearin out of the trunk and into the back seat. While Frazier stood outside the Cadillac smoking a cigarette and listening to Shearin's pleas for mercy, Fennie held her down in the back seat of the car and raped her, Frazier said. Frazier could clearly hear what Shearin was saying, but, he said, "I ain't no freak. I wasn't watching."

Fennie was in the car with Shearin for about 15 minutes, Frazier said. Then Fennie pulled the victim out by her arms and stuffed her back into the trunk. Again, he demanded her automatic bank teller number. Shearin called off the same numbers she had given earlier.

Still wanting his share of any money they might get with Shearin's bankcard, Frazier accompanied Fennie to the bank. He would use his share of the money to purchase dope. Then he would sell that for more money, and with the profits, he would buy more dope. Frazier explained his plan was to have a good drug business going for a while without any worries.

Fennie and Frazier drove to a bank in downtown Tampa, but just as had happened at the previous bank, the automatic teller would not accept the bankcard. The men drove to another bank, but they could not make the card work there, either.

Now the men had no doubt that a problem with the bankcard existed. In anger, Fennie drove the Cadillac about two blocks down a street to an unlit area. He stopped, got out, and opened the trunk. He told Shearin she had given him the wrong card number. Again, she repeated the same number, pleading that it was correct. Fennie again slammed the trunk shut, locking Shearin inside.

Fennie got back into the Cadillac, and he and Frazier drove to a concrete company. There they stole four concrete cinder blocks, normally used for building block houses, from the back of a pickup truck and placed them inside the Cadillac on the back floorboard. The plan was to tie the bricks to Shearin's legs and dump her into a lake or river where her body would not be located too easily, Frazier stated.

Since neither Frazier nor Fennie had a driver's license, they decided to pick up Fennie's girlfriend, Pamela Colbert, who was also Frazier's cousin, and have her drive the Cadillac to a remote location where Shearin could be disposed of.

At daybreak, with Shearin still locked in the trunk, Fennie pulled the Cadillac near Colbert's apartment and Fennie and Frazier went inside. While Fennie talked with Colbert, Frazier went into the kitchen and got something to drink. Fennie picked up some leftover pieces of rope from a clothesline that Frazier and Colbert had recently strung outside Colbert's apartment and stuck them in his pocket.

Soon Frazier, Fennie and Colbert were on the way north on I-75. With the Cadillac moving smoothly up the highway, the trio inside played the radio and listened to music while they talked about killing the woman. Fennie wanted to kill Shearin because she had seen his face when he raped her. He must "do her in," he said.

"Look man, okay," Frazier claimed to have said, "I'd rather take my chances going to prison for what I've done. I don't have the heart to kill anybody."

"Then don't be around when it's done," Frazier quoted Fennie as saying.

Somewhere near Sumter County, Frazier looked back and saw three fingers sticking out of the trunk. Frazier warned Fennie that the woman was working her hand out of the trunk and might get the attention of someone in another car. Colbert exited the interstate at the next off ramp.

Colbert pulled into a dark area. Fennie got out and went over to the trunk. Moments later, he got back into the car and recited four numbers. "Memorize these numbers," he said.

Colbert then drove to a nearby convenience store and Fennie went inside. He was only gone for a little while, and then he returned. "There's a bank about four miles up the road." Fennie said.

But before trying the bankcard again, Fennie told Frazier and Colbert there was a matter that needed taking care of. Time had come to deal with Shearin.

With Fennie calling the moves, Colbert drove the car up a dark road to a wooded area and stopped. Fennie got out and opened the trunk. "Hey, help me get the lady out of the trunk," Fennie called to Frazier.

When Frazier grabbed the struggling victim, she managed to lock her teeth into the flesh of his arm, clamping harder and harder until blood poured from the wound. Frazier yelled, and breaking away, he hurried to the car, grabbed a towel and wrapped it around his arm. Shearin's teeth had cut deeply into his flesh, and the bleeding just wouldn't stop.

Still in the trunk, Shearin grabbed a crescent wrench and tried to defend herself against Fennie. But the wrench was no match for the gun aimed at her head.

Fennie ordered Shearin out of the trunk and made her bend over the car. Reaching into his pocket, Fennie pulled out the rope he had picked up at Colbert's house and tied Shearin's hand behind her back. Then Fennie led Shearin down the dirt and a grass path. All the while, she was crying out for help. A few minutes later, Frazier told cops, a shot was fired, and then Fennie came running back to the car alone.

"Let's go," Fennie said, jumping into the front passenger seat.

The trio got back on the interstate to look for the bank that the convenience store clerk had mentioned. When they arrived, they found a sheriff's patrol car parked outside. "Don't stop," Fennie said. Colbert kept on driving.

A little way down the interstate, the three got off at a restaurant and ate breakfast. Colbert paid the bill. She also paid for a baseball cap for Fennie to wear when he went to withdraw money with Shearin's bankcard.

After finishing breakfast, they drove back to Colbert's apartment. They decided Fennie would keep the victim's Cadillac and bankcard. Frazier said he still wanted his share of the murdered woman's property and money. So Fennie gave Frazier the diamond wedding ring he had taken from Shearin.

Although the ring was not what Frazier had wanted, he took it anyway. Frazier had wanted money for drugs. No one would take a ring for drugs. But the ring was still better than nothing. Frazier took it and gave it to his girlfriend.

Fennie tried unsuccessfully to use the automatic teller card at several banks.

Colbert paid to have the Cadillac washed inside and out in order to destroy any fingerprints that might connect the trio to what had happened to Mary Shearin. Expecting several days to pass before Shearin's body would be found, Fennie continued to drive the Cadillac around in the projects.

The next time Frazier saw Fennie, it was on a television newscast. Then, later, officers picked him up. But, Frazier said, "I didn't kill nobody, man. I ain't never had a violent crime."

Prior to the arrest of Alfred Fennie, detectives learned that Fennie managed to cash a forged check for $200 from Shearin's personal bank account.

Reconstructing the crime, lab technician Gary Kimble allowed himself to be locked in the trunk of Shearin's Cadillac while lab technician Ken Locke and other officers got inside the car and carried on a conversation. Kimble could clearly hear what officers were saying. This proved Shearin couldn't help but overhear her killers plot her murder while she was trapped in the trunk.

Kimble also used a crescent wrench to force a portion of the trunk open enough so that he could get three fingers out. When he got out of the trunk, Kimble and Locke pulled up the rubber gasket where Kimble had pried the trunk; they found a dent, exactly like another dent in the trunk. Crime lab investigators believed the original dent was made during Shearin's last efforts to save her own life.

The three suspects charged with murdering Shearin stood trial at different times during the months of October and November in 1992. Michael Frazier was first, then Pamela Colbert, and finally Alfred Fennie. They all had different court-appointed attorneys. Assistant State Attorneys Anthony Tatti and Bill Gross prosecuted the suspects before Judge Jack Springstead. Even though detectives said Fennie had been the person to actually fire the fatal bullet into the back of Shearin's head, prosecutors said the other two defendants were just as guilty of murder as if they had pulled the trigger themselves.

In closing statements, Tatti said of Frazier, "In the law, it doesn't matter if he pulled the trigger or not. What he told you he did makes him guilty."

The murder was premeditated on the parts of all three suspects, Tatti said. The murder was planned from the moment the cinder blocks were placed in the car; and all during the time the three defendants rode around in Shearin's Cadillac discussing and planning the grisly murder while the victim was in the trunk of her own car listening to their every word. They put her in the trunk and terrorized her for two or three hours," he said.

"He wanted his share," Tatti added, pointing at Frazier with his eyes and finger. "And after all that, he is still frustrated because he didn't get his share. He was the one who saw fingers. Michael Frazier told the people in that car about the fingers because he didn't want to get caught."

Tatti showed the jury a poster-size photo of Mary Shearin that revealed her bruised arms, thighs, and groin. When the woman was being raped, Tatti wondered out loud, "Did Michael Frazier walk away and smoke a cigarette, or did he hold her down for Fennie to rape her?"

By posing this question, Tatti was putting a question into the jurors' minds about Michael Frazier's account of what had happened. Frazier claimed he'd been out of the car at the time of the rape, yet Tatti believed the bruises on the victim's arm indicated that someone had used a lot of force in holding her down.

Prosecutor Tatti asked the jury to notice bite scars on Frazier's arm. "Two men were there, murder on their hearts," Tatti said.

"When that man reached in to pull her out, she bit him. The prints of Mary Shearin's teeth are on his hand and he cannot make them go away. The only doubt is whether he actually pulled the trigger. This man believed that getting his share was worth taking her life."

During Pamela Colbert's trial, Colbert did nothing to win sympathy from the jury. In fact, she appeared distant, cold and bored. She sucked on hard candy while the prosecution presented its case against her. Colbert's appointed attorney, Chip Harp, apologized for his client's behavior and told the jury that her apathy was generated by an asthma medication that caused drowsiness.

During Colbert's cross-examination, Prosecutor Tatti walked over to the witness stand. Then he turned and raked his hands through his hair, his eyes seeming to glare beyond the courtroom.

Colbert claimed she had not known the woman in the trunk was being kidnapped. But how could Colbert possibly think there was a woman locked in the trunk without knowing she was being kidnapped? Tatti asked, "Did she say, 'Hey, guys, lock me in the trunk. I like it in here'? Don't you agree she was being kidnapped?"

Colbert held her head up, chin out, and responded. "She was being detained, to my recollection."

Tatti pointed out that Frazier warned Colbert and Fennie that Shearin was working her way out. Frazier had said they should pull over before Shearin got the attention of an approaching car or before she managed to open the trunk and take her chances against the interstate traffic rather than face the people inside the automobile who were talking about killing her.

But Colbert's cool response to Tatti was, "That's hearsay."

If Chip Harp thought he could get Colbert off the murder charge, he surely had second thoughts as his defendant presented her testimony. And in his closing statements, Harp apologized for his client. "I admit my client did not do really well on the witness stand. Pam's a cold person. But you've got to go on the facts or the lack of facts," Harp told the jury. "Personalities should not ever play a part in these proceedings."

When it came time for Alfred Fennie's trial, Michael Frazier had decided it was in his best interest to take the witness stand and testify against Fennie. Frazier told basically the same story he had told detectives when he was arrested. He gave the same account that he had sworn to when he testified in his own defense.

During the penalty phase at Fennie's trial, Assistant State Attorney Bill Gross put a cartridge in the VCR to show the jury photos of Mary Shearin's body. Gross got down on his knees and put his hands to the temples of his head and softly said, "Ladies and gentlemen: Can you hear her voice begging for life, asking to go home to her children? Tears cannot be processed as a part of evidence. If they could process the tears in that car trunk with lumalite, that trunk would glow. If they could process fear, that trunk would glow. If they could process longing for her children, that trunk would glow." (A lumalite makes some body fluids glow when looked at through special eyewear.)

The juries that found Frazier and Colbert guilty of first-degree murder suggested the judge sentence those two defendants to life in prison. The jury that decided Fennie's fate, after he was found guilty of first-degree murder, urged that he be sentenced to death in the electric chair.

At Colbert and Frazier's sentencing on November 23, 1992, the victim's family members asked Judge Jack Springstead to sentence the convicted murderers to as much time as the law would allow. "We were a family and you took part of that away," relatives said to the killers. "I hope you get whatever God intends for you, here or after. I hope you get what you deserve."

Judge Springstead sentenced the two cousins, Michael Frazier and Pamela Colbert, to serve life sentences in prison for their roles in the killing and kidnapping. At the sentencing for Alfred Fennie, on December 1, 1992, Springstead said the only punishment for such a crime was death in the electric chair.

After Fennie was taken from the courthouse to the county jail to await his transport to death row, the victim's family hugged prosecutors and investigators. They had lost a part of their family—wife, mother, and daughter—but at least Mary Elaine Shearin's killers would pay for their crime.

STORY 17:

Mother And Daughters
Dumped In The Bay

The breeze over Tampa Bay on Sunday, June 4, 1989, proved to be an ill wind. And with reason. What pleasure boaters found floating in the bay that day would surely haunt them for years to come. About 18 miles out in the bay, southeast of the St. Petersburg Pier, three decomposing female floaters surfaced. The U.S. Coast Guard retrieved the bodies and could not believe what they saw. All three victims were bound hand and foot, duct tape strapped over their mouths, and stripped from the waist down. Ropes tied around their necks had apparently been anchored by concrete blocks. One victim had managed to get a hand free before she died.

Dr. Edward Corcoran, the associate medical examiner who performed all three autopsies, determined the victims died of asphyxiation, either by strangulation, or drowning, or both. For four days, police officials didn't have a clue as to the identity of the victims.

On Thursday, June 8th, motel employees at the Rocky Point Day's Inn on the Tampa end of the Courtney Campbell Parkway, connecting Tampa and St. Petersburg, called the Tampa Police Department. They reported that a room rented to Joan Rogers and her daughters Michelle and Christe on June 1 had not been slept in. A cursory check of the room revealed the presence of brushes, combs, and toothpaste. There were several articles of new clothing, including swimsuits still containing price tags from Mass Brothers department store. Also found were a high school class ring, ladies sandals, sneakers, and bikini panties with the price tags still on.

With wet towels and swimsuits lying on a vanity in the bathroom, it appeared the trio had been to the swimming pool.

"We haven't seen them since the first day they checked in," employees reported. "The last time anybody here saw the woman and her girls was at the motel restaurant about 5:30 in the evening."

On Saturday, June 10, Detectives Dan McLaughlin and Steve Corbet, of the St. Petersburg Police Department, were among St. Petersburg and Tampa Police officers who went to the causeway boat ramp, just off the Courtney Campbell Parkway, where a 1986 blue Oldsmobile Cutlass registered to 36-year-old Joan Rogers was found. Inside, officers found a note written on motel stationery and bearing directions from the motel to the ramp. The contents included the words "blue and white." This bit of information led detectives to believe the Rogers women, still missing from the motel, had been looking for a blue and white boat.

The car registration showed Joan Rogers lived in Ohio. In checking the registration, the police learned that on Tuesday, June 6th, a family member in Ohio notified Ohio and Florida Highway Patrols that Joan Rogers and her two daughters, 17-year-old Michelle and 14-year-old Christe, were missing. They had been due to return home June 5th but nobody had heard from them.

A check of dental records showed that the floaters were indeed Joan, Michelle and Christe Rogers. As hard as it was to imagine, somebody had bound the mother and daughters, stripped them from the waist down, put duct tape over their mouths, weighted them by the neck with concrete blocks, then tossed them over the side of the boat into the bay.

As news of the horrible homicide hit the bay area and spread, some witnesses began to surface. One couple came forward to report seeing an Oldsmobile at the causeway boat ramp about 2 p.m.

Thursday, June 1. That was just 90 minutes after Joan Rogers had checked into the motel.

Meanwhile, the investigation was expanded to include Ohio, where detectives interviewed friends and family of the mercilessly slain victims.

The kin said that Joan, Michelle and Christe had left Ohio for what they thought would be a fun and relaxing time in Florida. Equipped with a Nikon camera and five rolls of film, the trio drove from their dairy farm in Willshire, Ohio, and headed for Florida. That was on Friday, May 26. Once in Florida, they visited Walt Disney World, Silver Springs, and other Florida amusement attractions. They had one last stop to make, Bush Gardens in Tampa, before their vacation was complete. Then they would head for home.

The Rogers women arrived in Tampa June 1st and checked into the Rocky Point Days Inn Motel.

As news of the horrible slayings spread over the Tampa Bay area, phone calls poured in to the police from people who claimed they might have information that would lead to a suspect. In one instance, police learned that an individual who had been serving time on a rape charge had been released at 9:30 a.m. on June 1st. An inmate told a corrections officer that someone driving a dark-colored Bronco picked up the freed convict. Detectives set up night surveillance on the suspect.

On Friday, June 16th, St. Petersburg Detective Don Rivers went to Orlando, about 125 miles northeast of St. Petersburg to check places where Joan Rogers and her daughters had stayed. Perhaps somebody had been traveling with the girls and had decided to kill them. But Rivers soon established that the three women had been alone the whole time they were in Orlando.

As the investigation continued, more people who wanted to help detectives solve the case came forward. Numerous phone calls from people who thought they had leads, continued to flood the St. Petersburg and the Tampa police departments.

Detective Robert Schock, of the St. Petersburg PD's Major Crime Unit, sought out everyone who had stayed at the Rocky

Point Motel on June 1st to see if they knew anything or had seen anything unusual in connection with the victims; or if they had seen a blue and white boat parked at the motel.

Upon checking the guest register, Detective Schock found a local man who owned a boat, had signed into the motel using a false name. He was not really a suspect at this point, but Schock obtained his address and went to speak with him. During the first year, about 40 detectives spent more than 10,000 hours working on the case. It was even featured on the national television shows "Unsolved Mysteries" and "Hard Copy" again and again. They kept coming up empty.

Two hand-written notes were the only real evidence cops had to work with. Experts concluded Joan Rogers had written one. On motel stationery, she had noted directions from the motel to a boat ramp, about a mile west and on a side road that ran alongside the parkway (causeway).

But the second handwriting, which was found on a tourist brochure giving directions to the motel, was a mystery. Joan, Michelle nor Christe wrote it, handwriting experts determined.

Meanwhile, Tampa PD Detective Kevin Dunkin determined that the man, who had given a wrong name on the motel registration June 1st, could not possibly be a suspect. The man had used an alias name at the motel because he was having an extramarital affair. Upon checking his story, Detective Kevin Dunkin found his boat was being painted on June 1st.

Two years after the bodies were found, the investigation led back to the victims' home state. Investigators took a closer look at people who knew the victims, at family members, including an individual who had molested Michelle several times while she was growing up. The probes considered that the killer might be somebody who knew the three victims well.

On Sunday, January 27, 1991, St. Petersburg Police Detectives Cindra Cummings and John Geoghehan went to Van Wert County, Ohio, where they re-interviewed friends and family members. Officers also interviewed mental health counselors who had connections with the Rogers family. Altogether, 70 people were interviewed during the detectives' 10-day stay.

Leaving no stones unturned, detectives obtained videotape taken by a Fort Wayne, Indiana, television news crew at the victims' funeral. The tape was impounded and viewed numerous times by investigators, who carefully studied the faces of people who attended.

While carrying on their investigation in Ohio, Detectives Cummings and Geoghehan learned one family member went to the bank on June 6, 1989, and withdrew $6,000. He said he had withdrawn the money just in case he needed to travel to Florida to look for Joan and the girls.

In April 1991, Cummings and Geoghehan, along with St. Petersburg Sergeant Glen Moore, who had been placed in charge of the investigation, met with FBI specialists in Quantico, Virginia, to go over the available clues and to assist the FBI in its developing a profile of the triple killer.

An analysis done at the University of South Florida showed the victims died in the area near where their bodies were found. Authorities believed that whoever dumped the women had spent many hours on the bay. An inexperienced person would have found it difficult to maneuver a boat that far out at night.

The case continued to baffle Sergeant Moore and the other detectives. Moore repeatedly issued public alerts, through the television and newspapers, saying that police were looking for somebody who had a blue and white boat that had left the causeway June 1 with the woman and daughters aboard. During the investigation, 17 witnesses told police they had noticed a dark colored Bronco or Blazer truck and a blue-and-white boat parked behind the Rocky Point Day's Inn within the time frame of the killings.

By May 1991, Sergeant Moore dismissed any suspicions that any of the victim's kin might have been involved in the case. The probes looked at two suspects. One wintered in Florida, the second lived in the area the year around. Still, crime fighters had no evidence connecting either man to the Rogers slayings.

That same month, Sergeant Moore called a press conference and released the FBI profile of the killer to the media. The description was run over and over again on television, radio, and in the newspapers. The person being sought was believed to have the following characteristics: a man of social skills who could present a non-threatening manner; one neat and meticulous who exhibits compulsive-type behavior; people who know him would say he finds pleasure and satisfaction from controlling and dominating others, one who takes pleasure in another's suffering; he is white, possibly in his 30s, with above-average intelligence; he has a fantasy life and is interested in bondage. When the victim's bodies were found, the killer was edgy, tense and perhaps withdrawn while assessing the possibility of discovery. Afterward, he displayed an avid interest in the case, possibly clipping articles about it from newspapers.

"The police believe the man has killed before and will kill again," said Sergeant Moore. "Police believe he has probably killed since the bodies of Joan, Michelle and Christe were found.

"The killer charmed the woman and her daughters into an evening trip on his tidy boat," Sergeant Moore went on. "He remorselessly planned and carried out their killings. It is believed the killer raped and killed the women because he enjoyed the suffering of others.

"There are people out there who know something about this case. It just hasn't rung any bells yet," Moore continued.

"There are significant indications that anyone who knows the killer's identity is in danger because of their knowledge," Moore said. "Anybody with information should call the St. Petersburg police as soon as possible.

"This is a very heinous crime, particularly when you have family members probably seeing each other being violated sexually and then seeing the mother, sister or daughter thrown into the water to die a horrible death.

"I would say the honeymoon is over for this killer. We're going to hunt him down until we find him," Moore said.

After numerous phone tips and interviews, Moore obtained a better description of the vehicle that had been parked at the motel on June 1st. It was described as a dark-colored Bronco or Blazer with dark tinted windows and pulling an 18-to 24-foot blue-and-white boat.

Detective Ralph Pflieger was one of many detectives trying to solve the Rogers murder case. As he was reading a Florida Department of Law Enforcement flier, a rape case that had occurred off the shores of Madeira Beach, located just north of St. Pete Beach, caught his eye. The rape had occurred in June of 1989, just two weeks after the Rogers murders.

The victim, a Canadian tourist, said a stranger had noticed her taking pictures and started talking with her. He then invited her and her female traveling companion out on a sunset cruise on the Gulf of Mexico to take pictures. The tourist accepted the boat ride, but her friend refused to go, which seemed to disappoint the stranger, according to the police report. While out on the gulf, the man raped her in his boat. Afterwards, he ripped the film from her camera and threw it overboard. He then wiped her camera clean, as if trying to remove fingerprints from its surface.

When the Canadian tourist began to scream, the boat captain threatened to put duct tape over her mouth. "Don't scream. Is screaming worth losing your life over?" he demanded.

The woman later described her attacker's boat as being blue-and-white. Although the tourist was traumatized and upset, she was going to return to Canada without reporting the rape, but her traveling companion talked her into going to the police. As the Canadian tourist described her attacker, a police artist made a suspect composite.

The same person could have committed the rape and the murders, but who was he? Sergeant Moore and his team of detectives were frustrated. It was already 1992, and they had not arrested a single suspect in the Rogers slayings. So far, all during the investigation, whenever police asked for help from the public in putting information together, witnesses had come forth. Now, police had another idea. Detectives had one piece of physical evidence that might lead to the killer. They would use the brochure with the unidentified handwriting giving directions to the Rocky Point motel.

Sergeant Moore released pictures of the brochure to the press. Also, he posted the unidentified handwriting on billboards in the Tampa Bay area.

Then in May 1992, a Tampa woman called the police with a lead. She said that her former neighbor, Oba Chandler, might be the killer in the Rogers case. She had noticed that Chandler, an aluminum contractor she had hired to do some work at her house, signed their contract with the same type handwriting as that on the billboard. On top of that, she said, the composite of the rapist looked like Chandler. Police wasted no time visiting the woman.

Handwriting experts analyzed the writing on the contract and that on the travel brochure and determined the same person had written them.

Though Chandler no longer lived at the Tampa address near the woman caller's home, police learned he was an avid boater. Moreover, he had owned a blue-and-white boat until he sold it in August 1989. Upon investigating Chandler's record, detectives found he had a long history of criminal activity.

Detective Katherine Connor-Dubina flew to Canada to show a photo lineup to the Canadian rape victim. The victim instantly picked Oba Chandler's photo from it. Connor-Dubina was quoted in the *St. Petersburg Times* as saying, the rape victim's "face flushed like no tomorrow" when she got to the photograph of Chandler.

In September 1992, Special FDLE Agent John Halliday arrested Oba Chandler at his home in Port Orange, Florida, and charged him with the May 15, 1989, rape of the Canadian tourist. A search of Chandler's home turned up a mint green, short sleeve shirt with a mesh bottom half, like the one the woman told police her attacker had worn.

A description of a boat the woman was raped on matched the description of a boat that had been owned by Chandler. He had sold the watercraft in the fall of 1989. Investigators found the boat through the original for-sale advertisement Chandler had placed in a boating magazine. The boat was obtained and put in the sheriff's impound in Pinellas County to be used as evidence.

After Chandler's arrest on the rape charge, Sergeant Moore thought there was a strong possibility Chandler might be the person who had killed Joan Rogers and her daughters, Michelle and Christe, just two weeks before the rape. While the murder investigation continued, with detectives working to gather enough evidence to charge Chandler with the murders, Chandler was held in jail in lieu of a $1-million bond on the rape charge.

While he was in custody, authorities slapped another charge on Chandler for an unrelated $750,000 armed robbery, which had occurred Sept. 11, 1992, outside a motel in Pinellas Park, near St. Petersburg. Chandler had allegedly robbed, at gunpoint, two employees of a wholesale jewelry manufacturer with headquarters in California. Chandler then sold the stuff to friends and relatives in Ohio and Kentucky, according to Assistant State Attorney Bob Lewis.

By this time, St. Petersburg Chief of Police Terry Upman was ready to charge Oba Chandler with murdering Joan, Michelle, and Christe Rogers. They discovered many similarities between the rape and the slayings. In addition, police had now lifted Chandler's palm print from the tourist brochure found in Joan Rogers' car.

The local grand jury agreed Chandler should stand trial for the slayings. On Tuesday, November 10, 1992, he was indicted on three counts of first-degree murder.

At his murder trial the last week of September 1994, five years after the bodies surfaced in Tampa Bay, Chandler waived his rights to remain silent and testified in his own behalf. Executive Assistant State Attorney Doug Crow often asked him about the Madeira Beach rape for which he had been accused and which had similarities to the murders.

"I will answer no questions, sir, that relates to that case," Chandler said, citing the Fifth Amendment.

"Did you meet the Rogers women in Tampa?" Crow asked.

"I don't remember," Chandler answered, noting he drove 40,000 to 50,000 miles a year while working in the Tampa area and he could not recall everybody he met. Chandler later admitted he had given directions to the Rocky Point Day's Inn motel to Michelle Rogers when he stopped at a convenience store, just off Interstate 275, in Tampa. "Michelle pulled herself from the car window. I could see her pulling herself up over the roof of the car," he said, noting Michelle handed him a brochure and he wrote down directions to the motel.

When three female floaters appeared in the bay three days later, Chandler said he didn't realize they were the same people he had directed to the motel. He said he finally recognized Michelle Rogers' photograph in the newspaper when an article came out linking the Madeira Beach rape with the Rogers murders. Once he saw authorities were checking handwritings, "I panicked. It freaked me right out," he said.

Chandler said he had not remembered where he was on the evening of June 1st and morning of June 2nd, when the women were murdered, until he saw his own phone records where he had used his cellular phone to call home from his boat. He had been out fishing on Tampa Bay, he said, and his boat had broken down. So he ended up staying out all night. Chandler said there had been a leak in his gas line. He flagged down a Coast Guard boat, but the two men and one woman aboard did not respond to his call, he said. Later that morning, two men and a woman came by in a boat and helped him tape up his gas line so he could return to shore.

In November 1989, Chandler knew he was a suspect in the homicide. But his reason for fleeing the state was because of the Madeira Beach rape, he said.

When prosecutor Crow asked Chandler if it worried him that he was suspected of the Roger murders, he said, "Well, it worried me but I figured you people were smart enough to find out who did it."

"Perhaps we have, Mr. Chandler," Crow shot back.

Chandler said he went to Ohio to earn money to hire an attorney in case he got arrested for the beach rape case. He used pay phones to call his home in Florida to inquire if police had been to his house looking for him, in case his telephone was tapped. In June 1989, Chandler moved to California. He stayed out west less than a month because the cost of living was too high. He then moved to Armond Beach, a city on Florida's east coast, where he stayed for a year.

The day after Chandler testified, rebuttal witnesses for the state contradicted his testimony. Prosecutors obtained an expert boat mechanic, who had designed fuel systems for several type vessels, to go to the police impound and check Chandler's boat to see if there could be any truth to Chandler's alibi.

The expert said it would have been impossible for the gas tank to go dry, as Chandler had said. The boat had an anti-siphon valve, which has been standard equipment on boats for more than a decade, to prevent fuel from draining due to a leak in the line. Even if the fuel line were to rupture, the gas would not leak out because "the fuel line and all the connections are above the top of the tank." Gravity would prevent the fuel from running out of the tank.

Chandler's defense attorney asked the judge for permission to bring in its own boat expert from Tarpon Springs, since the prosecution had summoned a surprise witness after Chandler's testimony. Circuit Judge Susan Schaeffer allowed the request. But after talking with their expert, the defense decided not to call him as a witness.

Normally, under Florida Law, a surprise witness is not called to the stand. In this case, however, since the prosecutors didn't know what Chandler would say on the witness stand, they were allowed to bring in the boat expert.

After closing statements were presented, it took the jury less than two hours to return a guilty verdict. One juror was quoted as saying the guilty verdict had been determined 10 minutes after jurors went into deliberations, but they were emotional and needed time before returning to the courtroom. It took the same jury 30 minutes to recommend Oba Chandler die in Florida's electric chair.

Oba Chandler had a smirk on the face when he entered the courtroom for his pre-sentencing hearing October 8th. This day he was not dressed in the gray suit he had worn during the trial, but his attire was that of dark green jail garb. Judge Susan Schaeffer asked Chandler if there was anything he wanted to say to the court at that time. Chandler politely said no.

Chandler sat at the defense table, fingering his reading glasses, sometimes putting them on, sometimes just holding them in his hand, while his attorneys argued that the convicted murderer should live rather than be executed. While the lawyers talked, Chandler would cock is head first to one side, then to the other. He put on his glasses and seemed to be following along on a copy of cases his attorneys quoted from.

Then defense attorneys brought up Chandler's troubled childhood, of how his father had committed suicide while he was just a boy.

"The jury's verdict was reasonable," Crow said to the judge. A unanimous decision by a jury to impose the death penalty on a convicted killer is a "rarity."

Crow restated how horrifying the experience surely was for Joan and her daughters, Michelle and Christe. Chandler had charmed them onto his boat; then on the dark bay, where the females were helpless, he had gagged them with duct tape, stripped them nude from the waist and tied their hands and feet. He tied a "noose" around their necks and weighted them down with concrete blocks.

"We can only imagine how it was on that boat, while three people had nooses around their necks, duct tape on their mouths, bound, and weighted with concrete blocks, then a sibling, or mother. Or even worse for Joan Rogers to be in that state while she awaited the deaths of her daughters, tossed one-by-one over the boat into the bay."

Chandler showed no emotion.

Then Crow said, "This is an over whelming case for the death penalty."

Judge Schaeffer agreed. At Chandler's sentencing November 4th, 1994, Schaeffer said: "Oba Chandler, you have not only forfeited your right to live among us, but under the laws of the state of Florida, you have forfeited your right to live at all."

Judge Schaeffer ordered that Chandler, age 48 at the time of sentencing, be transported to the Department of Correction in northern Florida to be held on death-row while awaiting electrocution in Florida's electric chair.

COP LOG I

Mushrooms growing in cow pods

–to–

Nude man holds up market

On morning visits to Sergeant B's office, reading the cop log was often like reading comics. It was hard to imagine many of the things that actually happened during the 24 hours between each morning conference. While some incidents were painful to imagine, others were so ridiculous they were humorous. Time spent with Sergeant B and reporters from the five local newspapers and the newscaster from the Brooksville radio station, was always interesting–to say the least–and often unusual. On the other hand, listening to reporters adding commentary was a bit entertaining. Getting lost in reports was easy. Here are a few of the many incidents filed in the cop log:

Mushroom hunting a no-no here

Three teenagers were caught with possession of a hallucinogenic drug usually obtained from a fungus found in mushrooms that grow in cow pastures. According to Leroy Gould, professor of criminology at Florida State University, the mushrooms producing the drug are usually found growing in manure. These mushrooms are toxic and "can kill a person," Gould said. A small amount of the drug will generate hallucinations.

The teenagers had two plastic shopping bags of mushrooms they had picked from cow piles in a pasture in Brooksville. Deputies said there was a white cooler in the truck bed containing two plastic bags of mushrooms. Upon being asked their intentions, the teenagers said the mushrooms were to boil down to make tea, and that this drink would give them an "excellent high." Uses of drugs such as psilocybin, that causes hallucinations, are declining, said Gould. Such substances were used a lot in the 1970s; psilocybin has been used for generations by the American Indians. For people to have possession of mushrooms containing psilocybin is against the federal drug laws, except when used in ceremonies by the American Indians in the Native American Church.

Man finds place to stay in jail cell

A 25-year-old Brooksville man, who said he had just gotten out of jail in Tampa, found himself right back behind bars in Brooksville. It was reported that Jason Gray was seen climbing through a window to enter a house in Spring Hill. Arriving at the address, Deputy Kevin Morrison opened a latch on a window that had been broken and went into the dwelling. The man was hiding behind a closed door of a walk-in closet in the master bedroom. He said he had just gotten out of jail in Tampa after serving five months. He thought the house belonged to his mother who had died the previous year. He only planned to stay in the house until he could find a job and get financially on his feet. The general manager of a bank out of Ocala told authorities the house had been foreclosed on and the locks had been changed about three days prior to the incident. The man was jailed on the charge of burglary of an unoccupied dwelling.

Local man finds shopping isn't free

A Brooksville resident went shopping at the Winn Dixie Supermarket on Cortez Boulevard in Spring Hill. He loaded his cart with $150 worth of New York strip steaks, round steaks, roasts, ham, and pork loins. He even threw in a package of socks and two T-shirts.

He bagged the $150 worth of items himself and left the store without paying. Outside, when confronted by the store manager and two other store employees to return the items, the 37-year-old man dropped the bags. He rapidly pulled a knife and lunged it toward the store workmen. He then ran behind the Winn Dixie and headed west to Beall's Department Store. The suspect might not have been caught had he not sat down on a bench behind the store to rest. He was charged with aggravated assault and retail theft.

Road Rage: Unable to keep his cool

Unable to hold his temper, a Citrus County man jumped out of his automobile and slung a knife at a woman who turned in front of him to enter a Brooksville service station. The woman had just gotten out of her car to go inside the station when three men, all strangers to her, pulled alongside her car. The men jumped out and one started slinging a large knife, striking her in the forehead and knee. She fell to the ground, then the suspect got in his car and the three fled. The woman went to the hospital where she received numerous stitches in the forehead and knee. Witnesses obtained the license plate number from the suspect's car. An 18-year-old suspect from Crystal River was later arrested on battery charges.

More Road Rage: Driver has gun pointed at him

February was an aggravating time for some local motorists with so many people visiting the Sunshine State and making roads more traveled. A stranger with a gun threatened a young Brooksville couple riding along on Commercial Way. The young couple said a gray-haired man about 55 years old pulled up beside them driving a GMC pickup and pointed a black revolver. He said, "Pull over so I can blow your f—ing brains out!"

The incident occurred when the young man was driving south in the fast lane and attempted to pass another vehicle. He looked in the rear view mirror and saw a blue pickup rapidly approaching. The pickup almost struck his car in the rear; so he stepped on the gas peddle. After passing the vehicle, he pulled into the slow lane to get out of the way of the fast traveling pickup, which had stayed on his tail. That's when the driver pulled up beside him and yelled that he was going to shoot him. The young man stepped on the gas pedal again to get out of the way.

Then the man in the pickup caught him and again pointed the gun. "I said, pull over. I'm going to blow your f—ing brains out." The young man hit the brakes. He slowly drove until the pickup was out of sight.

300-pound motorcycle man robs motel guests

A 300-pound man wearing a black ski mask pulled a blue steel revolver on three people and took their money early on Saturday morning in a motel parking lot.

The masked bandit approached motel guests and pointed a .44 caliber revolver at them and told them to hand over their money. One man asked if he could give him his cash, and keep his credit card. The fat bandit said that would be just fine. After collecting their money, he told the trio to walk across the parking lot. A woman looked back and saw the robber going toward a rack of motorcycles.

He got his goose

Jeffery Goodson's goose is dead. On New Year's night, someone went into Goodson's duck and goose pen, which is in the yard at his residence in Masaryktown, and murdered the fowl.

When Goodson went to check his critters about 10:30 on New Year's morning, he found Gargamel's body. Someone had gone into the pen in the "dark of the night" and "cut his whole neck and head off." The intruder left the goose's body, but took the head with him.

Gargamel was his pet, his "baby," said the brokenhearted man.

This goose was as attentive as any dog, or any other animal, Goodson had ever owned. Every day Goodson would let the goose out to eat grass. Gargamel would stay right where he was supposed to stay. "You could talk to him and he would talk back."

Goodson blamed his 74-year-old neighbor with the slaying. "He's a crazy. Nobody else would do it. I'm accusing him."

The neighbor denied killing the goose. He claimed he saw Goodson's dog going into the pen on New Year's Day. "Anyway," he said, "I have arthritis, and I couldn't do that."

"A dog didn't do it," said Goodson, noting there were no marks on the goose's body. He said the neighbor would be able to kill a goose. "I've seen him cut oak trees down all by himself. Someone with arthritis couldn't cut down a tree and then haul it off all by himself."

Goodson said he and his neighbor have been at each other's throats since he moved to the area three years prior. But the renewed problems started on New Year's Eve night when he started burning trash in his pit.

"I was just burning what you're allowed to burn in the dry season. He called up and demanded I put the fire out." But Goodson didn't put the fire out, he said. "I'm not going to let him run my life. My fire pit has been in the same place for three years and I've never heard a word of complaint about it."

But the elderly neighbor claimed Goodson loads the pit with garbage and burns the fire about every two weeks, generating a nasty odor through the countryside.

Each man accused the other of cruelty to animals. The neighbor said Goodson once dragged a goat behind his automobile to teach it a lesson. Goodson denied this accusation, and said the older man often goes out at night and shoots gopher tortoises (which are protected by law in Florida).

Goodson said he was "definitely" accusing his neighbor of killing his beloved Gargamel, although he had not actually seen him. "If I'd seen him, he wouldn't be leaving on his own. He'd be going out on a stretcher," Goodson declared.

Holy Cow? Pregnant cow's apparent craving for citrus has her in trouble—again

Jimmy Dee's cow can't seem to stay out of trouble.

After going through a two-strand electric fence and devouring oranges on another man's property, Dee's cow was herded home yesterday; and Dee received a citation to appear in county court.

It seemed the cow has a craving for citrus. She got out this morning, breaking the post and stretching the wires out of proportion when she jumped the fence. Again, the cow intruded onto the neighbor's property, this time chewing up a bunch of tangelos.

The tangelos didn't quite satisfy her, though. She destroyed practically a whole row of sugar cane. The cow was picked up running loose on a nearby road by a livestock deputy and delivered to the Hernando County Animal Control.

Jim Varn, supervisor at the shelter, said Dee's cow is "just a big pet." Her sudden citrus craving could be due to her "going to calf real soon." Her wandering ways could also be attributed to her wanting to go for a ride, Varn said. When the truck came to take her home, she just loaded right up. "It's unusual for a cow to just climb aboard. Usually you have to rope them and guide them on," he commented.

The cow's stay at the shelter was brief. She was brought in at 10:30 in the morning and picked up about an hour later. Dee's cow's little excursion cost Dee $30 to bail her out of the shelter, which covered impound fees and board. On top of all this, Dee was issued two citations to answer in county court, not to mention the cost of damage to the neighbor's citrus trees. "Probably be better if the cow would acquire a taste for hay," Varn said.

Man charged after 'barffing' on sidewalk

Jacky "Cowboy" Johnson, age 37, threatened Brooksville Police officers, telling them he knew local Judge Jack Springstead and he would have their jobs. But officers charged him with disorderly intoxication and resisting arrest with violence, all the same. Cowboy, a house painter, was staggering along Cherry Street, then "barffed (vomited) on the sidewalk in an uncoordinated fashion," an officer reported.

Officers entered Johnson's name in the computer and found he had warrants pending. While waiting for confirmation on the warrants, Johnson became "very disruptive, loud, and began banging his hands on the hood of the patrol car" and yelling obscenities at officers. Regardless of warnings, Johnson wouldn't cooperate, officers said. After Johnson was placed in the patrol car, he kicked the rear left side window. Officers then placed shackles on his feet.

At the police station, the defendant threw a chair and ashtray. When an arresting officer attempted to cuff his hands behind his back, Johnson kicked him. During the scuffle, Johnson fell, scratching his forehead. Refusing medical treatment, Johnson was taken down the street to the county jail.

Man charged with letting a child drink eight beers

Sheriff's deputies were dispatched to a Spring Hill address upon receiving a call about a sick or injured child. Upon arriving at the location, paramedics from Fire and Rescue said the 11-year-old boy had been found unconscious lying on a bed in his house.

A woman told authorities the youth had passed out in her front yard. Knowing where he lived, she took him home where he then passed out before she could get him inside.

When the child came to, he told officers his friend, Bobby Teal, age 21, had told him to skip school. So when it was time for him to leave for school, he went next door where he got in Teal's van. Teal and two other people, a 14-year-old girl and another man, also got into the van. Teal told them to "duck down so the cops wouldn't see them." Teal drove to a convenient store and bought a case of beer, then drove to the end of the road. This was where they drank beer, the youth said.

Teal was arrested that evening in the convenient store parking lot where he had purchased the beer earlier. He was booked into jail and charged with false imprisonment of a child.

Hot times: Fry gets even with his folks

Danny "Boy" Fry wanted "revenge," he told sheriff's detectives, so he set fire to his folks home shortly before midnight, turning the cool February evening to a raging furnace. He was jailed on charges of second-degree arson.

According to a sheriff's report, deputies were dispatched to the Fry home after a phone call from Fry alleging a domestic disturbance. Once at the scene, officers found the home belonging to Herbert and Gloria Fry in flames with smoke flowing from the roof. The fire, which caused $150,000 estimated damage, was put out by the Spring Hill Fire Department.

When Fry reported the domestic disturbance, he claimed his parents were "tearing up the residence." Then the line went dead. The house was burning when deputies arrived. Deputies reported finding several things about the residence out of order. The screen garage doors were pulled off their tracks and left on the ground. The hood was up on a car in the garage. A front window was broken. A lamp and table were on the ground, and a china cabinet was overturned.

The Frys had been visiting with friends at the time of the incident. They said the house was in order when they left home. Fry had been away from the residence when officers arrived. Upon his return, he said, "I'm drunk. I was in the woods and I was scared. I did it for revenge," he said, on the way to the county jail.

That's 'nacho' chip!

A petty theft and criminal mischief complaint was filed against a woman who ate a nacho without paying at a convenient store in Brooksville. A sheriff's report noted the woman entered the store and started picking at the nacho chips. The clerk said the woman took a nacho and ate it. Then she pulled down her pants, told the clerk to kiss her ass, and made obscene threats. The clerk said when she tried to call the sheriff's office the woman yanked the telephone from her.

The accused woman told a sheriff's deputy she had eaten the nacho to see if it were fresh. She also admitted she had grabbed the receiver from the clerk when she was calling the cops to tell on her. She denied she pulled down her pants. No charges were filed.

Mayor of Massaryktown shoots himself in hand

Jack Slabic, the mayor of Massaryktown, shot himself in the left hand with a .39-caliber pistol while trying to move the gun from one place to another. Slabic's wife heard him screaming and ran into the house. He was standing over the kitchen sink bleeding. Thinking he was cut, she called authorities for help. The mayor was directed to use caution in the future when handling a gun.

Thief apparently 'shopped' earlier

A thief took patience in selecting just the right outfits when burglarizing a warehouse in Brooksville sometimes Wednesday night or early Thursday morning. The intruder took clothing only of a specific style and size, with a total value of $5,250. Deputies reported that it appeared the thief had entered the store by throwing a piece of concrete through a window.

The vendor said she suspected a woman who had been in the store a few days previously. The woman had tried to steal clothing then. The clothing taken during the burglary was the exact same clothing the woman had tried on that day. The woman returned to the store the day of the burglary and asked the owner for a business card and apologized for coughing on her the day she had tried on the expensive clothes.

Vandals spill 25,000 gallons of human waste

Kids playing around the waste treatment area are believed responsible for the creation of a real mess.

A complaint made to the sheriff's office stated that somebody overflowed 25,000 gallons of human waste on the ground inside a fenced-off area on property at the sewage plant sometime between Tuesday at 2 p.m. and Wednesday at 9:30 a.m. Once on the fenced-off property, the source went to the control valve used for the treatment of waste, opened the valve, ran waste into an empty tank and overflowed 25,000 gallons.

The waste was of no value, however, the great amount of sand and lime used to cover the refuse was quite expensive. There was no physical evidence as to who might have created the mess, since the area was covered with crap.

Man cuts buddy in death pledge

"For no apparent reason," Wally Rico, 42, held a knife to Jacky Golightly's throat and asked him if he wanted to meet his maker. The two men were sitting in Golightly's van outside the Silver Fox Lounge in Spring Hill. Rico said, "We are both going to die," and put a knife to Golightly's throat. Rico grabbed Golightly's left wrist and ran the six-inch blade across his forearm. Golightly said he tried to take the knife from Rico but he just wouldn't give it up.

Finally, Rico fell asleep and Golightly managed to get out of the van. He stopped a motorist and asked him to call the police.

When authorities arrived, Golightly was standing in the parking lot waiting for help. Rico was asleep in Golightly's van with the knife on his lap when medical service personnel arrived. Sheriff's deputies found the knife on the floor. Rico was charged with aggravated battery and booked in the county jail with bond set at $3,000.

Man arrested for firing a gun

A Brooksville man told authorities he fired a .22-caliber rifle to frighten people who were partying next door. He just did it to encourage them to quite down. Never the less, he found himself charged with aggravated assault with a deadly weapon.

Richard White, 71, said he was at home with his wife on July 4 and was disturbed about 2:30 p.m. by his neighbor's having a noisy party. White took his rifle from the bedroom. He told his wife he was going to "fire a few shots to get their attention." He went outside his house and fired twice in the air.

The neighbor, however, didn't take too kindly to the behavior. The shots created a "well-founded fear" to the neighbor, Buzzy Grey. Grey said White pointed the gun at him and said he'd shoot him and he wasn't just a whistling "Dixie." White didn't think he was violating the law by shooting his own gun on his own back porch, he said.

Snake bites man who aggravated it

Most people living in the Sunshine State know you shouldn't try to catch poisonous snakes. Maybe snakes aren't as aggressive in Texas.

J.T. Olsen, of Elmott, Texas, jumped into the Weeki Wachee River and tried to catch a water moccasin he believed had bitten him on the right hand about 3:40 p.m. Thursday. Fortunately for Olsen the snake got away. By the time Emergency Medical Service arrived, Olsen was sick and throwing up from the bite on the hand. He was taken to Oak Hill Hospital, in Spring Hill, where he was treated and later released.

Tidy intruder really made himself at home

It must be something about living in the south that makes a body feel at home, even if he breaks in. Owners of a quiet residence in the country found somebody made himself at home in their house while they were at their second home in Miami Lakes. Elizabeth Little said she had left Brooksville on January 1 and returned on September 2. But what she found when she got back was disturbing. Not only did an intruder take advantage of the couple's unintentional hospitality, he also burglarized the mobile home.

After drinking several beers and helping himself to the Scotch, the intruder made himself coffee and then cleaned up his mess. While inside the mobile home, the intruder obviously found the padlock key to the tool shed where Mr. Little kept his tools. Upon leaving, he took with him a Remington 20-gauge pump shotgun, a Panasonic 19-inch color television, a clock, assorted tools (mostly wrenches and sockets), and a 12-volt car battery. The thief had gotten the battery from the pickup truck parked on the property. Total value was about $750.

According to Mrs. Little, the mobile home had been locked and was still locked when she returned home. Possible entry was through a bedroom window, deputies said. However, if the intruder came through the window, he must have straightened the bed cover behind him, as it didn't look disturbed.

Man warned not to go outside nude

A 14-year-old female caught a man on her video camera outside his house nude. She showed the video to her father, who took the show to the sheriff's office. The father said he was afraid for his daughter's safety with a man running around outside nude.

Deputies went to talk with the 36-year-old laborer. He said he only went nude in his own home. Deputies showed him the video.

"Well, I might have walked out on the steps and looked down the road while nude," he said. The man was advised not to go outside nude. No arrest was made.

Hunger causes woes for teens

Eating tuna fish sandwiches and smoking cigarettes can get you in a whole heap of trouble, so a couple of hungry 15-year-old youths learned Thursday when they got slapped with a burglary charge.

The male juveniles went into a woman's home in the county without her permission, entering through the rear sliding glass doors. Once inside the boys ate a tuna fish sandwich they found in the refrigerator. They also smoked several of the lady's cigarettes before leaving the residence. Both juveniles were charged with burglary and released to the custody of their parents.

In a separate case, an 18-year-old Spring Hill man was arrested for "depriving the supermarket from selling a box of Instant Breakfast by opening the box and removing its contents."

Also, deputies were called to a convenient store in Spring Hill when a young man fixed himself a hotdog and went outside and ate it without paying.

Nude masked man robs store of lottery tickets

A man armed with a stick and nude except for a light blue ski mask over his head and tennis shoes on his feet robbed a convenient store on County Line Road early this morning.

Deputy James Pollock answered a call to assist Pasco County authorities shortly after 2 a.m. after the man left the store on foot and crossed the road into Hernando County.

Jon Powers, public information officer for the Pasco County Sheriff's Office, said the nude robber went into the Presto store about 2 a.m. armed with "a large stick" and demanded money from the female clerk. The intruder took a small amount of cash and then ripped the lottery dispenser from the wall. The dispenser contained 200 Cold Cash scratch-off tickets. The tickets are all numbered and the State Lottery Security was notified, Powers said.

The Pasco County K-9 unit tracked the man to a wooded area in Hernando County where evidence has led authorities to believe he jumped onto some type of bike and left the area. The man, with a body that appeared to be 25-to-30 years old, had light skin and a deep voice.

Coffee used as a weapon

Candy Grame, a 36-year-old Brooksville woman got in trouble when she called the law crying that she had been accosted. Grame was charged with aggravated battery with a deadly weapon for throwing hot coffee on a man she said had made sexual advances toward her in a motel room.

Grame claimed her boss Joseph Stewart, who operated a vending machine company out of Chicago, had asked her to meet him at a motel in Weeki Wachee. At the motel, Grame said she called Stewart's room and he asked her to come there, which she did. In his room, Grame said Stewart told her she was going to be fired from her job if she did not cooperate with his sexual plans for her.

She said Stewart got up from his chair, grabbed her by the shoulders and threw her down on the bed. He stuck his hands down her blouse and grabbed her breast. At this point, she threw hot coffee, which she had brought to the room, on Stewart and ran to call the cops.

Upon questioning Stewart in his room, deputies reported that Grame's statement did not fit evidence in the motel room. Deputies said Stewart had several burns on his chest and stomach. The room had two chairs facing each other, one having a wet stain in it, "as if some type of liquid had run down between someone's legs." There were also wet splatter patterns on the wall behind the chair. And the bed in the room was covered in notebooks.

Stewart said he had come to Florida to fire Grame. When he was going over the reasons for her dismissal, she got angry and threw the hot coffee on him. She then threw her set of keys to the company-owned van and ran from the room. Stewart called the New York office and told them what had happened. He was advised by his supervisors to change his clothes, check the van to see if anything was missing, and if it were, to call the police.

Stewart was changing from the wet shirt when officers arrived. When the knock came at the door, he thought it was Grame's husband. He checked through the peephole and saw police before opening the door.

After making her statement to authorities and repeating several times that it was true, Grame finally admitted she had lied.

She then said everything Stewart said was true.

Grame was charged with aggravated battery with a deadly weapon (the weapon being the hot coffee) and giving a false statement to law enforcement officers. She was booked into the county jail on a $5,500 bond.

Man shopping for marijuana beaten, robbed

Jeffery Draper, 39, went out to purchase some dope but instead found himself abandoned on a dusty road.

Draper, who lives "temporarily" at his mother's house, had been at a Spring Hill pub about 8 p.m. Monday when he met two men who claimed they could provide him with marijuana. So he left the pub with the men to purchase the illegal substance.

Draper said he was unaware there was a problem until the driver entered the Tooke Lake wooded area, at which time he questioned: "Where are you taking me?" and demanded they let him out.

"You're not going anywhere, we're going to rob you," one said. The car stopped and both men began hitting Draper. He managed to hit one of his assailants "square in the face."

He didn't remember how he got out of the car. Randy Jones, a local resident who was out driving on dirt roads in his four-wheeler pickup truck the next day about noon, found him. Draper was lying on the side of the dirt road and appeared to have severe injuries to his head and was bleeding from the nose and mouth. Jones went to notify authorities. While he was gone, Draper crawled into the edge of the woods and hid. He was later found by a team from the Emergency Medical Service, treated, and taken to Oak Hill Hospital where he was treated further and hospitalized.

Man hands over 'pot' when asked for his ID

Ever heard it pays to think before you act? Obviously Jake Sanders acted before he thought. The Spring Hill man, who had been sleeping on the roadside, found himself booked in jail pending a $500 bond after he handed a deputy a bag of marijuana rather than an identification card.

Deputy P.A. Johnson answered a call regarding a man running back and forth on the street screaming and shouting. Callers believed he was intoxicated. When Johnson arrived at the 1400 block of Greenview Avenue, the man was asleep on the roadside. The deputy woke him and asked for identification. But what the deputy received was an envelope containing about one-gram of "fresh, green marijuana leaf." The marijuana was field tested to determine its worth. It was the real thing, they noted.

Horse Play? Owner of top-rated Arabian horse worried after someone gave the animal a bottle of wine

Somebody, "during the dead of night," tried to intoxicate the number one Arabian horse in the country. So says the horse's owner, Josiane Flaherty.

Should the guilty party be located, however, she doesn't know whether she would go as far as to prosecute. The intruder was probably somebody who knows of Send-Out's craving for booze.

"Send-Out loves to drink. He would probably take their side," Flaherty said.

Each day after the 3-year-old trains, Send Out and Mr. Flaherty relax by "coming inside the house and drinking Budweiser," she said.

Though Send-Out is allowed to drink beer with the owners, his having drunk wine with strangers terrified the Flahertys. The Arabian just won the $40,000 American Jock Club cup in Delaware, she said. Mrs. Flaherty's sister, who lives next door, called to let the Flahertys know someone was out by the fence "messing" with Send-Out.

"I got so scared," Flaherty said. She grabbed a flashlight and ran out. When she flashed the light at the intruders, they jumped in their car and spun away. Flaherty hurried to her car and started chasing it down her long driveway. Before reaching the end, the driver of the get-away car slammed on his breaks. Then the thought entered her mind that the people in the car might have a gun. She memorized most of the license plate number before turning back.

Send-Out has been carefully watched for a week since the incident with the wine, Flaherty said. She is sending the animal to stay with his trainer where he will be less likely to get in trouble. After all, she said, "Send-Out does like to drink."

Woman steals funeral money

The Lovelace brothers found an evening of pleasure with a woman they had just met being more costly than they had figured. Kate Brown, 20, of Brooksville, was arrested for taking $3,500 from the men while they slept. After being interviewed by Sheriff's Detective Doug Campbell, Brown admitted she took the money. She returned the $1,640 she had left.

On March 7 the brothers, Jim and Greg Lovelace, were traveling through the area and stopped at the Weeki Wachee Holiday Inn for the night. Rather than going to bed, they went out drinking, starting at the Marker 50 in Brooksville. This is where they met the "lady." When they left the Marker 50, they all went back to the Holiday Inn bar and drank until the bar closed at 2 a.m. Brown agreed to go back to their room with them. When the brothers awoke, the woman was gone and so was their money.

A security guard had obtained the license plate number on Brown's car when he had seen one of the brothers behind the wheel doing "donuts" on the parking lot. The brothers told authorities they had been on their way up north to attend another brother's funeral and they had the cash to put toward funeral expenses.

Teen arrested for disturbing grave

Two 18-year-olds found themselves charged with disturbing the contents of a grave when they did a little digging at the Ft. Dade Cemetery in Brooksville early on Thursday morning. Brooksville residents Marc Brightstar and Chad Clemmens were released on a $2,000 bond each.

Deputy James Pollock was working night patrol when he saw a man, later identified at Marc Brightstar, at the cemetery. While trying to determine Brightstar's purpose for being in the cemetery at 1 a.m., Pollock located a grave with a hole knocked in the concrete tomb.

Brightstar said he did not create the hole, that he only had a stick and was poking inside in an attempt to see a body or bones. Brightstar said Clemmens, who had fled upon the deputy's arrival, had not been involved in disturbing the grave.

Never the less, Pollock arrested both men. Pollock alleged Clemmens used a hatchet to break a hole through the top of the vault in a grave in the center of the cemetery, which had been there since 1962.

Broken window incident ends in stabbing

Melanie Blake, a 31-year-old cosmetologist, found a different use for her manicure scissors than trimming cuticles. The Lake Panasoffkee woman was arrested at about 2:30 a.m. on charges of aggravated battery, with bond set at $7,500, after she allegedly stabbed Jason Booker, 27, twice outside Miss Kitty's Hilltop Lounge in Brooksville. Booker received wounds in his left side and in the abdomen.

Upon the arrival of police at the country music barroom, Blake made a "spontaneous" remark that she stabbed Booker twice because he broke a window out of her car. After the stabbing, Blake threw the scissors onto the rooftop of the lounge.

It's shepherd vs. cattlemen

It seems that a rancher and a shepherd are feuding over a fence in Brooksville. A 69-year-old cattlewoman complained to the sheriff's office because her neighbor, a sheepherder, refused to make repairs on her 25-year-old fence.

The shepherd's fence and the cattlewoman's fence are about six-feet apart. The officer noted that the shepherd's fence is in a "state of disrepair."

The cattlewoman claim the shepherd's broken down fence allows his sheep to leave his property. The sheep then cross under her cattle fence to eat grass from her pasture.

The cattlewoman told the sheriff's deputy that this is an ongoing problem. She said that when the sheep crawl under her barbed wire fence, wool from the sheep covers the barbs, making the fence useless in keeping her cattle in. The cattlewoman said she had tried to talk the shepherd into fixing the fence, but he just won't do it.

COP LOG II

Cops called to domestic melee

Domestic melee noted in cop reports show couples fighting like cats and dogs one day, splitting up, then getting back together and fighting again.

Of course, squabbles were not always between spouses. In some cases, a father and daughter were at odds, or a father and son, or two brothers. There were always more cop reports that involved domestic violence than any other violent acts committed by one person on another.

While I was the cop reporter for the *Daily Sun-Journal*, family violence was declared the number one health problem in the United States by the U.S. Surgeon's Office.

She asked for trouble and got it

A 37-year-old Spring Hill woman threw a glass at her husband, hitting him on the left ear and causing a laceration to go completely through the ear lobe. The husband said his wife had been throwing things all evening, and that she left the house and came back several times. She tried to provoke him into hitting her, and when he did not, she struck him with her hand. He called the cops and had her arrested for aggravated battery with a deadly weapon.

Couple's fighting ends in arrest

A partly clothed New Port Richey couple were shouting and screaming at each other, causing a disturbance on the parking lot of the Holiday Inn motel in Weeki Wachee Sunday night. The man went to their motel room and fell asleep. The woman remained on the parking lot and refused a deputy's request to restrain herself. The deputy then talked with the woman's husband who told the officer he could not control his wife.

Just do whatever you have to do, the husband advised.

The deputy arrested the 57-year-old woman at about 8:30 Sunday morning on charges of breaching the peace and booked her in the county jail pending a $250 bond.

The man, age 67, bailed his wife out of jail on Monday evening. Before the couple reached the car on the jail parking lot, the woman began shouting, scratching and hitting him—a battery believed to have resulted from the husband's having taken so long to obtain bail money. Officers arrested her again, this time on spouse battery charges, with bond set at $500. The husband didn't say if he would bail her out again.

Woman stabs spouse with knife

A 39-year-old Brooksville woman was arrested Monday morning after she stabbed her husband in the back with a kitchen knife after returning home from a drinking binge.

Cops noted that the husband ran from the apartment to "escape the attack" and called 911. After he hung up the phone, the dispatcher called the locked-in telephone number. The person answering the phone screamed, "Get the police here," and again hung up.

Upon arrival of the Brooksville Police, the woman standing inside the front door was instructed to drop the knife she held in her outstretched hand like a gun. She told officers she had walked into her apartment and was attacked by some unknown person. Deputies arrested her anyway and booked her in jail under a $1,000 bond.

Assault by vehicle investigated

A man, age 52, complained to the sheriff's office that his estranged wife, 46, ran into him with her car then later returned to the house and threw an acid cleaning solution on him.

The reporter said:

The woman came to the man's trailer while he was inside sleeping. She continued to blow the car horn until he went outside to see what she wanted. She yelled, "Come over here." But he wouldn't do it.

Then she drove her 1977 Dodge out onto the road, and then spun back into the yard and banged into his 1977 Chevrolet. She backed up and again started toward his car. He stepped out between the two cars. She proceeded forward and allowed the car bumper to strike him just below the knee. When he doubled up in pain, she threw the acid cleaning solution on him, he said.

Baby falls from car during spouse ruckus

During a fight between former spouses, a 2-month-old baby fell from an automobile and hit the pavement. Explaining what led up to the accident, both Bob and Suzy had different stories. Bob, 28, said his ex-wife, Suzy, 27, with whom he shared a residence, came to their home and commenced yelling. When he went outside, she started spinning the car tires and backing from the driveway. When she turned the wheels and stopped the car, the door flew open and the baby fell out. At that same time, he reached through the car window and turned the engine off, and then he disconnected the battery.

Suzy, on the other hand, alleged that Bob had called her to the residence. She went there and he raised the car hood. She started backing out and then stopped in the road. At this time, Bob opened the door and the baby fell out, she said.

The baby received an abrasion above the eye.

Man drops dead while fleeing from disturbance

After fleeing from his home during a family disturbance and asking neighbors to call the police, 60-year-old Phil Beck fell dead.

His son, Michael, was arrested after the incident on charges of aggravated assault. The son was accused of throwing a ceramic lamp at his younger brother, Philip.

According to neighbors and family members, heated arguments between the father and son were not uncommon. The neighbor said the father appeared at his home during the argument hyperventilating and saying, "Call the cops. He's a f—ing maniac. He's going crazy again." Then he dropped dead on his porch.

When deputies arrived at the man's residence they found broken pieces of lamp on the floor. Michael appeared intoxicated. He said, "Nothing's wrong. Me and my father just had a fight."

Philip said Michael had come home drunk and started arguing with his father. When the father left the house, Michael threw the lamp at him.

The mother, 63, was found hiding in the closet. She appeared as if she were about to have a heart attack.

Michael was booked in the county jail under a $15,000 bond.

Man charged with 'whipping' teen

A Brooksville man arrested Monday for striking a juvenile on her legs with a stick until they were bruised and bleeding told authorities he had the right to do it because he was an adult and she wasn't.

Johnny Joe Green, a 33-year-old construction worker, was charged with aggravated battery with a deadly weapon and resisting arrest without violence and was booked in the county jail under bonds totaling $5,500.

This is how officers said the incident occurred: The 17-year-old girl, Betsy, was playing with her "little cousin" at the edge of the woods when her uncle approached them and started yelling, accusing them of exposing their bodies to boys in the neighborhood. Betsy denied any such thing and told Green she and her cousin had been playing alone. Green refused to believe them. He then told the "little cousin" to go into the house for her whipping, which she did. He ordered Betsy to leave. Betsy explained that her mother told her to stay there until she got home from work. In anger, Green pulled a tree limb down and started striking her on the thigh and calf repeatedly, which resulted in swollen, bleeding welts. Betsy ran home and told her mother what had happened. Her mother called the sheriff's office. Officers said Green "snatched" his hands away from the deputy while he was being handcuffed, but officers tired again, finally snapping the cuffs in place. He was taken to jail.

Fearing for husband, woman shoots her son

During a confrontation between her husband and a son, a Hill 'n Dale woman shot her son. She was charged with aggravated battery with a deadly weapon for the incident. Authorities said the woman shot her son in the chest with a .22-caliber revolver on Saturday night. The State Attorney's Office reported the matter was being investigated further. In the meantime, Dorothy Whitened was released from jail on a $5,500 bond.

Whitened, 44, told deputies she shot her son because she was afraid he would do harm to her husband, John Whitened, 50, who had recently gotten out of the hospital and was still having difficulty walking.

The Emergency Medical Service went to Hill 'n Dale and transported Jimmy, the woman's son, to the subdivision entrance where the Bayflite helicopter ambulance had arrived to fly him to

Bayfront Medical Center in St. Petersburg. The young Whitened
underwent a five-hour surgery to remove two bullets lodged near
his vertebrae. "It is believed three bullets went into the young
Whitehead's chest," said Sergeant Frank Bierwiler,
spokesman for the sheriff's office. On Monday, Whitened
was listed in serious condition and paralyzed from the neck
down.

Upon deputies' arrival at the Whitened residence (occupied
by John and Dorothy Whitened, Jimmy Whitened, Jimmy's girl
friend, Debby Drake, 18, and the couple's 20-month-old son)
John Whitened was standing in the doorway holding the weapon.
Deputy Tommy Harris asked that Whitened put the gun down,
which he did.

Inside the house, Deputy Harris saw Jimmy lying near a bloody
area, his face down on the kitchen floor. He began asking Harris to
please help him get up.

The shooting occurred after the 22-year-old son came home
drunk and got into an argument with the rest of the family, John
Whitened said. He pushed his father and girlfriend down on the
floor. During this time the mother, who had been in the bedroom,
came to the kitchen to see what was happening and found the
residence "torn" apart.

She then went back to the bedroom, got the gun from a dresser
drawer, returned to the kitchen where she stood in the hallway
four or five feet from the disturbance and said, "Move out of the
way, John." Once her husband stepped aside, she fired two or
three shots at her son.

Sergeant Bierwiler said Jimmy had asked his father for money.
The father gave him what he had, which was $29. When Jimmy
started to leave and tried to take his baby son with him, the tragic
incident occurred.

Previous arrest records show Jimmy was out of jail on bond for
charges of assault on his girlfriend. He had allegedly threatened to
kill her while holding a knife to her throat.

Brothers' quarrel ends in shooting

A family quarrel that started at a wrestling match on Friday night at the Tampa Sun Dome ended back home in Spring Hill with one brother shooting the other. The injured brother was taken for medical attention and the other was arrested for aggravated battery with a deadly weapon.

James Jocker, 35, fired a shotgun and at Donald Jocker, 33, and a pellet struck the younger Jocker in the eye.

According to the sheriff's report, the brothers had gotten in a fight at the wrestling match over seating arrangements. James said Donald punched him in the nose a couple of times. James said he didn't do anything about the punches at the time, but warned Donald, saying: "Buddy, you did it this time. It will never happen again."

James gathered up his children and left the Sun Dome. On his way home, he stopped only to pick up a six-pack of beer.

Later that evening, when he heard his mother and brother arrive home in a cab, he took a recently purchased shotgun and loaded it with .410-shot. As Donald got out of the cab and walked toward the house, James aimed the gun at him and pulled the trigger. Then he put the shotgun down and walked toward Donald.

Donald said, "My God, you shot me."

And James replied, "Bullshit. I didn't shoot you."

James told authorities he didn't mean to hurt anyone, and that he had "just wanted to scare his brother."

Teenager arrested after shooting at his father

A son greeted a father by shooting at him when he arrived at his home yesterday. The 17-year-old Brooksville youth was arrested on an attempted murder charge and was transported by sheriff's deputies to a juvenile detention center in Ocala.

Sheriff's Deputy Tom Polletta reported the father's statement as follows:

The father pulled into the driveway of his home. The son stepped out in the back yard with a rifle in his hands. The son then started yelling at the father and fired three rounds of shot from the .31 Winchester lever action rifle.

The father "crouched" in the seat of his 1973 pickup truck to avoid being hit. One bullet did puncture the left rear truck tire.

Being in fear of his life, the father backed from the driveway and fled north on the road. The son got into a 1985 automobile and chased after him. Reaching the end of the road, the father jumped from the truck and ran into the woods. The son then turned the car around and drove south.

The father said that earlier Tuesday evening after he came home from work his son was acting strangely, staring at him and gritting his teeth. After a while, the son left in his car.

Being concerned over these actions, the father went to talk with his son's girlfriend but was unable to converse due to her being upset and crying. The father went back to his residence. That is when the shooting occurred.

At about 8:30 p.m., while Deputy Polletta was at the residence with the father, the son called home on the telephone and said he was at the adult education center and that he and his mother were leaving for Michigan right away.

The juvenile was arrested Wednesday evening about 8 p.m. when he was spotted leaving his father's house. A couple weeks prior, deputies were called to the same residence when the father accused the son of punching him in the face.

Three family feuds end in violence and arrests

Fighting between parents and their children seems to be on the rise during the past few days, according to cop reports.

In separate incidents, a fight between a mother and daughter sent the pregnant mother into labor; a father shot his son; and another father threatened to shoot his daughter.

An argument between a 14-year-old girl and her pregnant mother escalated to a fight which resulted in the mother receiving a laceration to her forehead, going into labor, and the daughter being arrested.

The Spring Hill Rescue arrived at the home and treated the mother and then transported her to the hospital with labor pains. A short while later, she gave birth.

The daughter was taken to the hospital for "medical clearance" and then arrested and released to the Health and Rehabilitation Services.

In the second incident, a father who did not like the way his daughter was living her life threatened to shoot her with a handgun. James Edwards, 61, of Weeki Wachee was arrested for aggravated assault with a deadly weapon after he threatened his daughter and his granddaughter in his daughter's home.

The daughter said her father tried to hit her with a wrench shortly after midnight on Monday morning when he came to her home in Weeki Wachee Woods. His friend got him to leave, but he returned about 30 minutes later and told the daughter he was going to kill her.

The 16-year-old granddaughter told Deputy David Dougherty she had been sleeping when her grandfather came inside the house. She could hear him "banging and breaking glass." She was frightened so she stayed in bed.

"He was breaking glass to get in and so when he finally got inside he started screaming and yelling and cussing," the granddaughter said. "He was yelling, 'I'm going to kill you. Both of you.'" The granddaughter said she started crying. "He came in with a wrench in his hand. He was yelling at mom, threatening to kill mom."

Edwards left but returned 30-minutes later with a gun and shot at the ground, the granddaughter said. She started screaming, then he came to her, kissing her and telling her he wasn't going to have mom's shit going on and that he would go to jail if he had to.

And lastly, in the father and son shooting incident. Eddie Cramer, 56, of Brooksville, shot his son in the side with a .22-caliber revolver after the son armed himself with a "large bottle" and made threats.

The sheriff's report notes that the father returned home after a prior incident and tried to calm down his son, Eddie Cramer Jr., 26. However, the situation escalated and the son armed himself with the bottle and threatened the father. The father grabbed the revolver and shot once in the ground as a warning to his son, but he continued making threats. Cramer shot again and the bullet hit his son in the side. No arrest was made in this incident.

Teenager reports his father tied him to dishwasher

A 15-year-old Hernando County youth was placed at the Rap House, a "safe place" for run-always in neighboring Pasco County, after he told sheriff's officials that his father chained him to the dishwasher.

The youth said his father got him out of bed Thursday morning and tied a rope around his left ankle, sealed it with a metal bracket, then tied the opposite end through a hole in the dishwasher and sealed that with glue and electrical tape. The youth said the dishwasher was located in the hallway, giving him access to the kitchen and bathroom. He said his father had planned to leave him tied up from the early morning until he returned home in the afternoon.

The youth said his mother got out of bed, got ready for work, and then left the house without bothering to release him. The youth contacted a friend who brought two other friends to the youth's house. The three used a wrench to remove the metal bracket.

The deputy reported that he observed rope burns on the youth's left ankle.

The mother denied her son had been chained. Never the less, the youth was placed in the Rap House.

COP LOG III

Rapes and rumors of rapes

Woman confronted again

Daisy Mays, who recently reported that a man came into her home and ordered her to perform oral sex on him, has been confronted by the same man again, the 29-year-old told sheriff's deputies.

On her way home from work on Wednesday about 1:30 p.m., Mays stopped at a convenience store at the corner of U.S. 98 and State Road 50. She got out of her car and went into the store. After making a purchase, she got in her car and started to drive home. Turning on Spring Hill Drive, Mays reached to the radio and started changing the station. At that time, a man raised himself up from the back seat and asked, "Why did you change the station? I liked that song."

He pressed some type of object to her neck and made a slit into her skin, then pulled her hair and ripped open her blouse. He said he could kill her at anytime he wanted to. He demanded she turn from Spring Hill Drive onto Brad Circle, which she did. He ordered her to stop the car. She did. But she surprised him with a dose of mace in the face. The man laughed and grabbed the mace and sprayed it on her. Mays managed to get out of the car and run toward Spring Hill Drive where telephone company employees were working. They called the sheriff's office.

According to Mays' statement, the man who popped up in the back seat of the car is the same man who went into her residence the previous Thursday through the garage door, ripped the telephones from the wall, and tried to make her perform oral sex on him. She got away that time and ran to a neighbor's house and called authorities.

Statements the stranger made to Mays indicated that he knew her and had been following her for a long time, she said.

Child raped on school ground

A 7-year-old girl was reportedly raped at an elementary school in Brooksville after she was snatched from the school playground during recess. About 40 children and adults were on the playground at the time the child was pulled into the bushes and the rape occurred, noted Police Lt. Terry Chapman.

The child didn't tell anybody about the incident, but then a teacher noticed she was bleeding and sent her to the school nurse. Later, the child told her parents she had fallen. A doctor said she had been raped.

Police put out a sketch of the suspect according to the "brief description" they obtained from the child. They believe the assailant was a male about 5-feet 2-inches tall, thin with brown hair and freckles. Authorities believe the suspect might have come from the area of the high school.

Dropped wallet leads to arrest of rape suspect

A man, 23, who had grabbed an 18-year-old woman and raped her repeatedly in a field along U.S. 19 in Spring Hill Saturday night, was arrested Sunday.

According to the sheriff's office, the woman escaped from the man when he discovered he had lost his wallet. She ran into the busy highway in order to get a car to stop.

Hernando County sheriff's detectives went to Alachua County with a warrant for Herbert Glasco's arrest after finding his wallet at the crime scene, said sheriff's Lt. Michael Hensley. Glasco was charged with sex battery, kidnapping, aggravated battery and battery.

Lt. Hensley said the young woman was walking south from the Weeki Wachee Spring attraction, where she worked as a mermaid, to a nearby Burger King to meet friends when she noticed automobile lights moving slowly behind her. The attacker, later determined to have been traveling south from Gainesville to Clearwater, pulled into the grassy highway medium, jumped out of the car and tackled the woman, choking her and striking her several times with his fist.

During the struggle, the victim tried to alert passing motorists, none of whom stopped. Glasco held the woman and conducted sexual acts on her for more than an hour, cops said.

The attacker led her to believe he was going to take her with him when he finished with her there. The fact that he lost his wallet probably saved her life, cops said.

When Glasco discovered he had lost his wallet, he became frantic in searching for it and the woman was able to get away. Officers found the wallet containing a Florida Driver's License at the crime scene. Detectives obtained a warrant and went to Alachua County where they arrested Glasco at his girlfriend's house. Glasco was brought back to Hernando County and booked into the county jail under a $74,000 bond. The victim was taken to Oak Hill Hospital where rape tests were performed.

(Glasco was later found guilty by a jury and sentenced by Judge Jack Springstead to serve 25 years in prison.)

Woman assaulted in sheriff's substation

A 71-year-old woman who worked for a sheriff's substation reported to officials she was sexually battered. The woman, who worked four hours a week, was preparing to close the office for the day when she was forced into a back room and assaulted. The man she said battered her was the president of an area crime watch. He was arrested on charges of sexual battery and booked into the county jail pending a $5,000 bond.

Rape attempt probed

Waking up in a wee hour of the morning with a stranger in the bed was quite disturbing for a 51-year-old Hill 'n Dale woman. When Maude awoke a man was lying on top of her and fondling her, she said.

"Just lay still. Just lay still," the man demanded.

Maude refused and jumped from the bed. She turned on the light and the man ran from the house. Maude said she had checked all the locks and deadbolts before going to bed. After the incident, she found her front door and front door screen standing open.

Deputy Mearl Letts and K-9 Alf were unable to pick up the trail from the footprints left on the dew nor from bicycle tracks heading west from the property.

Sergeant Frank Bierwiler said sheriff's officials do not believe the attack is related to other reports of rape said to have occurred recently in the Hill 'n Dale area. In 1987, three reports of rapes were reported. Two women, ages 22 and 23, and a 12-year-old girl said they were attacked in their bedrooms. The rapist in those incidents was not found.

Man arrested for sexual battery on his stepdaughter

A 30-year-old Brooksville man was arrested yesterday and charged with committing sexual battery on his 6-year-old stepdaughter. The man allegedly battered the child "repeatedly" between October of 1988 and July of 1989. He is being held without bond in the county jail on charges of eight counts of sexual battery.

Under Florida Law, sexual battery on a child age 12 or younger by a person age 18 or older can be sentenced to life in prison, which would require the defendant serve a sentence of 25 years, said Sergeant Bierwiler.

Teen held against her will

Two Brooksville men were arrested on Thursday night for allegedly committing sexual battery and kidnapping a 13-year-old West Hernando County girl.

Bradley Johnson, 21, and Lewis Greensleve, 20, both of whom had prior arrests, were charged with kidnapping and sexual battery. They were jailed on a $15,000 bond each.

The girl said she was abducted by the two men in a red pickup truck about 6:45 p.m. and was driven around the western part of the county and that both men had sexually molested her. They let her go at about 8:45 p.m. at a business place on Shoal Line Boulevard in Hernando Beach. While crying uncontrollably, she told a person there what had happened and that person called the sheriff's office.

Six deputies responded immediately, Hensley said. Both men were apprehended a short time later at the intersection of Shoal Line and Osowaw boulevards. They were driving a red, 1987 Nissan pickup truck. The girl was taken to Oak Hill Hospital and then to Lykes Memorial Hospital where she was treated and released to her parents.

Woman lets man into her home, then gets raped

Another woman in Hill 'n Dale reported she was raped in her home. But this rape is different than rapes that occurred during November and May.

The woman said a well-dressed salesman driving a blue van came to her house with a briefcase. Her big dog was on its chain and the salesman asked if it could get loose. She told him she didn't have any money to buy anything. Then he asked if he could use her restroom. When he came out of the bathroom he grabbed her by her hair, forced her into the bathroom, and attacked her, she said.

The woman picked the suspect's photograph from a group of other photographs. Deputies spotted the blue van at the River Country estates and arrested 29-year-old Blake Larson there. He was later charged with sexual battery for the alleged incident.

The photograph of the suspect is different than the composite of the man believed to have committed the previous rapes in Hill 'n Dale. And in those incidents, the victims were in their beds sleeping when the rapes occurred.

Woman throws hot water on man she says raped her

A Brooksville woman told sheriff's officials she was sexually battered, but the accused said the woman had agreed to have sex with him. Sammy Simpson, 29, was charged with sexual battery on Thursday morning after he was treated for burns he suffered when the woman he allegedly raped poured hot water on his back.

The woman said she was lying on the living room sofa when Simpson came into her house through the back door and said he was going to get her, that he was going to kill her, and that he was going to give her something good to go to the police with. She said he dragged her by her hair to the bedroom where he hit her on her face and stomach. Then he dragged her to the living room, forced her to kneel and perform oral sex on him, and then forced her to the sofa and raped her.

After Simpson raped her, he continued lying on the sofa. She left the living room and went to the kitchen where she had hot water boiling on the stove, took the hot water back to the living room and poured it on Simpson's naked body.

She was afraid he would get her so she ran from the house and down the street. She caught a ride to a location where she was able to call the sheriff's office. She was then transported to Lykes Memorial Hospital and treated.

Simpson was located at the woman's house and also taken to the hospital for treatment. He claims that he knocked on the woman's door and she allowed him to enter. He said she was wearing only under garments when she answered the door and that she agreed to have sex with him. But she might have been in fear, he said.

Simpson said he fell asleep while the two of them were relaxing on the sofa and was awakened when the "hot substance" was pored on his back.

Man Claims to be Satan

He told the girls he was Satan and they were his children, according to a sheriff's report. Stephen Cole, 24, is being held in the county jail under a $10,000 bond for sexual acts he is believed to have committed since the first week of July.

Cole, a security guard, allegedly French kissed and tried to fondle the 13-year-old girl on the breast and kissed and fondled the 14-year-old girl. Cole admitted fondling the girls on three occasions "in the woods behind the house," and that he was aware of their ages, deputies said. Cole said he was "just kidding" when he told the girls he was Satan, but that he had "dabbled in devil worship back in Indiana."

Football players get house arrest for having sex with 13-year-old

Three Hernando High School football players who had sex with a 13-year-old girl pleaded no-contest in circuit court yesterday after the state prosecutors and the attorneys for the defendants reached a plea bargain agreement.

Judge Jack Springstead sentenced the three 19-year-old football players to serve two years community control, also known as house arrest, and 200 community service hours for the incident. The service hours, however, will be waived for each of the young men who stay in school. The men, who have been enrolled in night classes since being dismissed from school after the January incident, are expected to remain in high school and later enter college football programs.

According to reports released from the sheriff's office at the time of the incident, the three football players and the 13-year-old girl had all been to a beer party in South Brooksville. The trio offered to take two girls home. After one girl was dropped off at her Spring Hill home, the young men had sex with the 13-year-old in the back seat of a borrowed car. All three defendants were charged with one count of sexual battery with a child under 16 years old.

Grandfather sentenced for child molesting

A man sentenced to 7 to 10 years in prison for molesting his grandchildren told the judge: "I though I was teaching them something."

At the time, the 60-year-old grandfather thought he was doing wrong only "from a religious standpoint." So he prayed about it. He said he would like to get a program going where he could help other men with sex problems, even if he could stop "just three men" from committing sex acts upon children.

Upon passing sentence, Circuit Court Judge Richard Tombrink informed the man he would have some time on his hands while in jail and he could use it to write to the legislature and try to get a program started that might help other men who prey on children for sexual pleasures.

The man's attorney, Jimmy Brown, asked the court not to send his client to prison, noting that two of the man's daughters and their children had forgiven him. The third daughter and her children refused to forgive "grandpa" and asked that he pay for what he did. The grandfather was arrested October 23 on charges of indecent assault upon a child under 12 years old. He later admitted fondling another of the children as well, court records show.

The grandpa and grandma walked out of the courtroom with their arms around each other's waists. He agreed to turn himself in to the Hernando County Jail September 21 at 9 a.m.

EPILOGUE

Reminiscing recently on the patio at his home, Ken said that, in upholding the death penalty, the state should make a public display of executions. What is the use in having a convicted murderer in a room alone and strapped in "Old Sparky," the state's electric chair. "If it's gonna be, let it be at high-noon. Do it in the court square."

Ken, however, has always expressed his opposition to capital punishment because it is possible that an innocent person be put to death. "There are prosecutors who would convict people just so their side would win," he asserted.

Most of the swampland murderers still waiting on Death Row will probably not die in the electric chair. The state has since put into legislation that a death-row inmate have the right to choose whether to die by lethal injection or the electric chair. The first inmate to die after the ruling chose the needle. He died February 25, 2000.